Within, Against, and
Beyond Liberalism

Global Dialogues: Non Eurocentric Visions of the Global

Series Editors:

John M. Hobson, Professor of Politics and International Relations, University of Sheffield

Bryony Vince, Doctoral Researcher, University of Sheffield

This series adopts a dialogical perspective on global politics, which focuses on the interactions and reciprocities between West and non-West, across Global North and Global South. Not only do these shape and reshape each other but they have also shaped, made, and remade our international system/global economy for the last 500 years. Acknowledging that these reciprocities may be asymmetrical due to disparities in power and resources, this series also seeks to register how "Eastern" agency, in tandem with counterparts in the West, has made world politics and the world political economy into what it is. While this series certainly welcomes purely theoretically based books, its primary focus centers on empirical rethinking about the development of the world political system and the global economy along non-Eurocentric lines.

Titles in the Series

Islam and International Relations: Exploring Community and the Limits of Universalism
Faiz Sheikh

Historical Sociology and World History: Uneven and Combined Development over the Longue Durée
Edited by Alexander Anievas and Kamran Matin

Re-Writing International Relations: History and Theory Beyond Eurocentrism in Turkey
Zeynep Gulsah Capan

Interrogating Illiberal Peace in Eurasia
Edited by Catherine Owen, Shairbek Juraev, David Lewis, Nick Megoran, and John Heathershaw

Modern Japanese Political Thought and International Relations
Edited by Felix Rösch and Atsuko Watanabe

Sufism: A Theoretical Intervention in Global International Relations
Edited by Deepshikha Shahi

Within, Against, and Beyond Liberalism: A Critique of Liberal IPE and Global Capitalism
David Blaney and Naeem Inayatullah

Within, Against, and Beyond Liberalism

A Critique of Liberal IPE and Global Capitalism

David Blaney and Naeem Inayatullah

ROWMAN & LITTLEFIELD
Lanham • Boulder • New York • London

Published by Rowman & Littlefield
An imprint of The Rowman & Littlefield Publishing Group, Inc.
4501 Forbes Boulevard, Suite 200, Lanham, Maryland 20706
www.rowman.com

Copyright © 2021 by The Rowman & Littlefield Publishing Group, Inc.

British Library Cataloguing in Publication Information Available

Library of Congress Cataloging-in-Publication Data

ISBN: 978-1-5381-5516-5 (cloth)
ISBN: 978-1-5381-5517-2 (electronic)

Contents

Preface

We did not set out to write a book on liberal international political economy (IPE). As in the case of *International Relations and the Problem of Difference*, we found ourselves with a set of interconnected essays demanding a larger frame. Recently, we have been preoccupied with economics, liberal political economy, and by extension liberal IPE. Perhaps more accurately, from the beginning, our joint and separate work has centered on critically reading the liberal tradition and, more often, its early modern precursors. We read liberal political economy because of its importance in defining the meaning of modernity and reflecting modernity's strengths and weaknesses. We see its strengths in its grasp of capitalist markets as systematic, dynamic, and geared toward producing wealth and human moral progress, particularly in realizing individuality, equality, and freedom. Of course, taking liberal economists' accounts seriously also exposes limits: in particular, its methodological or ontological individualism that serves to rationalize serious inequality and human suffering. Our critical engagements with liberal political economy draw on elements of the socialist tradition. We have often drawn on Polanyi, as we do here, but also Marx, though our relationship with Marx is sometimes uneasy. We are exploring our relationship to Marx in a book in progress that will serve as a companion to this one.

Many individuals contributed to this book through their encouragement and/or careful reading of various chapters. We want to thank Beate Jahn, Rose Shinko, Ron Krebs, Nick Onuf, Patrick Jackson, Taylor Long, Joan Tronto, Emma Kast, Justin Rosenberg, Kaela Bamberger, Paulo Chamon, Austin Doullaird, Duncan Fuller, Xavier Guillaume, Inanna Hamati-Ataya, John Hobson, David Johnson, Anna Leander, Alina Sajed, and various anonymous referees. Versions of chapter 4 were presented at the Centre for Feminist Research and the Graduate Program in Political Science at York University;

the fortieth anniversary of *Millennium* at the London School of Economics; and the Department of Political Science and International Relations at the University of Geneva. We wish to thank seminar participants for their comments. We also want to thank participants in the Minnesota International Relations Colloquium, where versions of chapters 1 and 3 were presented. David would like to thank Maggie Poulos, Xian Lu, Lan Yaqing, and Luo Zhantao for research assistance and Paul Gabriel Cosme, Milosz Fernandez-Kepka, Amanda Peterson, and Emma Van Emmerik for editorial assistance.

Naeem would like to thank Kenesha Chatman, Ben Hobgen, and Sarah Shank for their logistical vital support and good cheer. Naeem is grateful to his family—Sorayya, Kamal, and Shahid—for providing such rich sustenance. David still can't understand why Sherry insists that he make time for his scholarly work, but he is very grateful.

Earlier versions of many of these chapters appeared elsewhere, although all have been revised for this book. We are grateful for permission to publish this material here. The earlier version of chapter 1 originally appeared as "Liberal Fundamentals: Invisible, Invasive, Artful, and Bloody Hands," *Journal of International Relations and Development* 15:2 (2012): 290–315. The earlier version of chapter 2 appeared as "Global Capitalism, (In)Equality, and Poverty" in Toni Erskine and Ken Booth, eds., *International Relations Theory Today*, 2nd edn. (London: Polity Press, 2016), 161–74. Chapter 3 was written originally as "Liberal IPE as Colonial Science" for *The Sage Handbook of the History, Philosophy, and Sociology of International Relations*, edited by Andreas Gofas, Inanna Hamati-Ataya, and Nicholas G. Onuf (New York: Sage, 2018), 60–74. An earlier and much shorter version of chapter 4 appeared as "A Problem with Levels: How to Engage a Diverse IPE," *Contexto Internacional* 17:3 (2015): 889–911. The original version of chapter 5 appeared as "Units, Markets, Relations, and Flow: From Bargaining Units to Unfolding Wholes" in James Caporaso, ed., *Oxford Research Encyclopedia of Politics* (2018), 1–22.

Introduction

Doubts haunt the liberal world order. Even the most avid apologists (see Ikenberry 2018, 2015) worry that liberal international institutions are falling on hard times. Socialists sense an opportunity that the nativist, proto-fascists have already seized. We should not be surprised. Aristotle (1995) warned that growing inequality favors the rise of demagogues that are a threat to the republic. Polanyi (2001) more recently argued that the economistic fallacy leads liberals to overplay their hands. Preaching the naturalness of market exchange, they recognize no limits, acting as if there is nothing that is not appropriately commodified and marketized. The destructive consequences for human beings and nature lead to reactions, both those we might embrace and those quite worrisome for the fate of freedom itself. It may be premature to suggest that the Owl of Minerva has spread its wings for liberal thought and liberal orders; nonetheless, it is looking a bit like dusk. But hasn't it looked like twilight for liberalism from the outset? Liberalism comes intertwined with a set of critiques about its limits and failings (Jahn 2019, 229–30). As we suggest in chapter 1, liberalism is a symbolic field defined both by an idealized vision of itself and the doubts that these idealizations hope to deflect. Later chapters suggest that the liberal imagination requires a refusal to acknowledge the structures of domination and subordination that accompany its implementation as colonial capitalism. Liberalism defends itself against doubts by declaring its premises proper science: its commitment to ontological individualist assumptions erases the structured systems of oppressive social relations as possible objects of inquiry. While liberals often operate as if what is ruled out by assumption cannot weigh on our idealizations of a liberal world order, their doubts and concerns always reenter through a side door. Now, in an era where social dislocation and inequality have become acute and increasingly politically salient, liberal idealizations

1

have lost their capacity to convince. Instead, liberal doubts win the day. These essays are written within, against, and beyond this backdrop.

READING LIBERALISM

Beate Jahn (2013) provides an appealing account of liberal internationalism. She brings what she sees as the "disjointed pieces" of liberal thought (the political, economic, and cultural elements) together into a "broadly consistent picture" (6) or a "comprehensive conception" (9). Assembling this conception allows Jahn to isolate "the core dynamics of liberalism" from closely related "concepts like capitalism and modernity" and subject liberalism to "immanent critique" (10–11). Locke is the key figure. Rereading Locke, she conceives of liberalism as a "political project" that rests on private property as a means to individual freedom. Yet extending private property (and thereby freedom) occurs only via progressive "expropriation of the commons." And expropriation requires the exercise and maintenance of "unequal power relations (by economic, political, ideological, and military means)." Freedom as private property entails its seeming opposite: coercion and subjugation. In concluding reflections on Locke, she finds that this systematic inequality is "justified through a philosophy of history that attributes to different actors different levels of development corresponding to different rights and obligations" (71). Liberalism can work, she argues, only when attached to theories of progress and the identification of civilizational hierarchies. What strikes us as particularly notable is Jahn's attention not only to conceptualizing liberalism but also to what it justifies.

We are inspired by this account. We liken her work to our own on how Enlightenment notions of progress justify the costs of market economics (Blaney and Inayatullah 2010). In this book, we continue to highlight how liberal thinking justifies forms of inequality and human suffering. At the end of the initial chapter on "Liberal Fundamentals," where we return to the Scottish Enlightenment, we wonder "how a valorization of market society's wealth production allows us to abide its incivility, its disorder, and its bloodletting." Subsequent chapters explore more fully how liberal thought works to justify or deflect criticisms of what we call variously market society or capitalism. In this respect, we see continuity with Jahn's project.

But we distinguish our work from Jahn's in other respects. We do not aim to provide a "consistent" or "comprehensive" conception of liberalism. First, this is because we doubt such an account is possible, as Jahn (2013, 10–11) also recognizes at points. We begin this book in chapter 1 by returning to a different set of proto-liberals—the Scottish Enlightenment figures Hume, Smith, Millar, Steuart, and Ferguson—to indicate the complicated and contested terrain of liberalism. These liberals don't simply justify liberalism; they also subject it to damning critique. They don't simply embrace its extension; they also suggest means of limiting and correcting it, for some almost to the point of abandoning a commitment to liberal civilization altogether. It is this very lack of homogeneity and full coherence that intrigues us. We see the tensions in the texts of liberal thinkers as "lenses through which they struggled to make sense of the world" (Inayatullah and Blaney 2017, 25). Also, the world they try to describe is far from a set of fully coherent and homogenous practices. Still, thought and practice intertwines and we start with a now uncontroversial assumption that liberal thought at once reflects, justifies, and partly constitutes the existing world order. *How* it reflects, partly constitutes, and, especially, justifies the existing world order is part of the work of this book. The book also considers how liberal thought pushes us to think beyond and against itself and how the world liberalism constitutes extends beyond the boundaries it sets for itself, an idea we develop more fully below.

Second, our engagement with liberalism might be considered narrower and, perhaps, more focused. As the title hints, we enter debates on liberalism as global political economists. We construct our object of inquiry a bit differently than Jahn. We focus on liberal international political economy (IPE) both in a narrow sense as neoliberal institutionalism and in a broader sense since liberal thought always comes with a political economy and a theory of the international. We also treat liberalism as a political-economic doctrine that is intimately intertwined with the theory and practice of capitalism. This may be simply our comparative advantage—the limits and strengths of our specialized training as political economists. But we worry that limiting international theory by emphasizing the "political language" of liberalism (Bell 2016) underplays key features of liberalism and capitalism (see Blaney 2017, 2020). Liberal political economy clings to the idea of equality of opportunity and hinges itself on the value of meritocracy in order to counter what otherwise might to the popular mind appear simply as the random results of the market or the result of a systematically uneven playing field. Of course, markets have a kind of distribution rule—to each according to what their property supplies for others. But this motto loosens the tie of work with desert and effort with reward and thereby threatens a collapse of popular support for market-based social life, a worry that preoccupied Friedrich Hayek (see chapter 2). We can't sustain the idea that merit is readily measured by property ownership as an ethical claim unless we assume a fair competition and equality of opportunity. But equality of opportunity remains tied to hierarchy—albeit the dynamic social hierarchy of capitalist society as opposed to the relatively fixed natural hierarchies of various styles of caste systems. Despite its commitment to freedom and equality, liberal thought justifies extreme social inequality in the name of efficiency and incentives for economic activity. Liberals tend to tolerate or even embrace coercion, including colonial relationships, as a necessary evil since coercion produces a social good of expanded wealth and a positive impetus to reform for the backward and indolent. Yet liberals obscure attention to forms of social domination, hiding it from view, by their obsessive methodological individualism and unit-level strategies of explanation (see chapters 3 and 4). We provide a consistent counterpoise by emphasizing structural diagnoses of poverty, by locating social ills in processes of domination in which some people are sacrificed. We emphasize system, the connectedness of outcomes and actors' positions, not the efforts or traits of ontologically isolated units. We call this counterpoise *social* understanding or explanation—an explanatory strategy that emphasizes what we call "social determination" in chapter 4. We don't mean by this that social life is predictable or predetermined, though some degree of predictability is necessary for actors to know how to go on in the language games that make up social life, as Wittgenstein emphasized. But we do mean to suggest that our role as social scientists is to see how actors' behavior makes sense within the confines of the systems of social relations in which they are embedded.

Third, while our critique engages liberalism immanently, highlighting tensions within liberal conceptions, we also find inspiration from places seemingly beyond liberalism. Liberal political economy emerges from the modern experience and is often taken as the definitive conception of modernity. Yet liberal modernity always shares the intellectual universe with opposing critical traditions. Any list of opposing traditions would include Marxist political economy and other critical scholars inspired by Marx and the socialist tradition more broadly, and those counter-modernists, such as Arturo Escobar, who we discuss in chapter 6. Both liberalism and many critical scholars, including Marx, recognize modernity's achievements, such as wealth production, the emergence of greater individual autonomy out of group life, the attainment of individual rank and worth as an achieved status, the celebration of equality as a popular sentiment, and the commitment to freedom. But we highlight key differences. Liberals tend to celebrate the achievements of modernity while making the attendant costs and limits of modernity, especially poverty and inequality, either disappear from sight or appear as necessary to modernity's achievement. Our ability to recognize and address these costs and limits requires drawing on the counter-critical insights. While liberals consider these achievements as an arrival into a permanent condition, as the end of development and perhaps as the end of history and theory, Marx and the Marxist tradition historicize these achievements and thereby regard them also as limits that further progress will overcome. For those who draw inspiration from indigenous social movements, such as Escobar, the history of liberalism cannot be told as a story of failed promises. Rather, liberal modernity has been a nightmare of dispossession, cultural destruction, and genocide. If there is a time after liberalism, a *post*development, these scholars associate this time with recovering or rebinding people to relations with each other and the land existing before liberalism as colonial capitalism warped the world. Here, the times before, during, and after modern capitalism blend into each other. Perhaps, this blending is necessary. We suggest in chapter 6 that the socialist vision and the postdevelopment vision are closer than usually understood since they share a space that both opposes and depends on the consequences of modern capitalism.

WITHIN, AGAINST, AND BEYOND LIBERALISM

In these essays, we often linger on the differences between liberalism and critical traditions of political economy. We have emphasized many of the differences in this introduction thus far, though we have noted connections and overlaps as well. We think of our work as located within the space of liberalism, but we think of the space of liberalism as including both the reactions against liberalism and the way the world liberalism constitutes spills beyond the boundaries liberalism draws for itself. Building on what we have said above, we can think of liberalism as occupying logical, temporal, and geographically bounded spaces. Each of these intertwined spaces defines and circumscribes the scope of liberalism. But liberalism also points beyond these spaces. Thinking with liberalism is always also to think beyond it.

We can trace the meaning of liberal modernity to a particular approach to understanding social life. We can see this as the logical space constructed by liberal thought or the symbolic field it occupies, but also always as a temporal and geographical notion. Liberal political economy commits to the individual as the basic building block, both methodologically and ontologically. Its narrative begins with individuals in a state of nature or, what are equivalent conceptions, an original position in which the basic rules of society have yet to be worked out, as in Rawls (1971), or the timeless and nearly featureless space of "the market" as imagined by economists. In the liberal political economy story, the pursuit of interests by free and equal individuals creates public goods for the society as a whole, notably in the expansion of wealth via market production and exchange. Circumscribed by individual freedom and market outcomes, the state's role is necessarily minimal. Indeed, liberal theory treats the state as the extension of individual rights: a social contract binds society together and constitutes the minimal state. The presence of these conditions indicates for many liberals that humans finally have arrived at the pinnacle of history where freedom and prosperity are finally realized.

This pinnacle is reached by some before others and liberals deploy stories of progress or evolution that allow us to grade humans according to their stage of development—an unevenly developed spatial terrain. But a space in which liberalism is only partly achieved suggests the end of history has not yet arrived. Capitalist modernity is imagined as an ideal without geographical limits. Though the full social contract may extend only as far as the boundaries of the state, the practices emphasized by liberal political economy necessarily extend beyond boundaries: market production and exchange are transnationalized features of a world economy of individuals, firms, and states. Confident of the inevitability of the march toward liberal governance and economics, liberals often counsel patience. Such patience depends on the inexorable workings of history where reason will win out in the end. But our patience is often tested. The impulses that drive humans to liberal market capitalism may be universal, but obstacles have been set in the road of human progress. The rights that make liberal equality possible often are systematically denied: governments rule without apparent consent and restrictions on freedom limit the extent of the market, and consequently the expansion of wealth fostered by capitalist economic activity. These obstacles move liberals to call for an increase in the intensity and extension of the liberal project. Arguments defending limiting the sway of liberal practices are rarely persuasive to liberals to whom such "illiberal" differences are simply beyond the pale. By overriding any considerations that validate nonliberal ways of life or individual practices, liberals are able to justify the coercion often necessary to extending liberalism to nonliberal societies. The paradox of forcing others to be free—the coloniality of modernity and capitalism—continues to plague liberalism. But liberal political economy finds it too easy to erase the stories of violence, oppression, and slavery when, *in principle*, all relations are free contracts among autonomous units. The symbolic field of liberalism and its traveling companions, modernity, and capitalism are always already global and temporally extended into a future without end. Yet liberalism's confident universalism carries the mark of the violence imposed on those who somehow remain beyond the extent of its symbolic field.

Liberalism as a symbolic field also remains uneasy about social inequality, both within liberal societies and across countries. Liberalism is aptly named since individual "liberty" is usually treated as primary and social equality, secondary. Where individuals are granted the (equal) rights necessary to make their own decisions and establish their own status, we cannot expect an equal result: some individuals will achieve more success and be more highly rewarded simply through the unrestricted workings of exchange (Boghosian 2019) intensified by asymmetries of wealth or power. And the more liberty is emphasized, the more the inequalities of a free competition will be treated as legitimate. Though a commitment to equality remains central for modern thinkers, liberalism also provides a powerful account of *acceptable* inequality. But the pursuit of individual interests in a competitive world can create something akin to a new caste system of differentially valuable persons produced by differential access to wealth. In a liberal world, some are at liberty to become enormously wealthy while others become destitute, and those with greater opportunity and means are more able to express their liberty and individuality. If states or international society do more than assure the fairness of the competitive processes, doing nothing to place a ceiling or floor on the accumulation of wealth, then capitalist modernity produces not only wealth but also socially structured (or competitively structured) and ranked domestic and global spaces. The liberal symbolic field may displace the dominance of God-given or tradition-given social rankings, but only to take us toward the idea of a competitively produced ranked society. Given modern aspirations, such a society may seem all too similar to older notions of caste to allow liberals to rest easily.

This tension between formal equality and achieved inequality produces competing impulses within liberal societies that underlie much of contemporary political debate. On the one side, the dangers of inequality move society toward securing limited social and economic rights that restore the relative equality of citizens or sustain pressure to subordinate the market to social purposes requiring elements of socialist planning. Without some state action to promote equality, liberty means little for less advantaged individuals. On the other side, the fear remains that moves toward greater equality threaten the liberty of individuals generally. Creating equality produces sameness or a leveling defeats liberty and frustrates the expression of individual differences. Liberalism is then caught between two poles. It cannot abandon its commitment to equality altogether, since unfettered liberty risks recreating a rank-ordered society, but moving toward the pole of equality generates fears of undercutting liberty. Far from outgrowing these problems, liberals continue to face the necessity of negotiating truces between competing impulses that respond to but never resolve the tensions. It seems doubtful that final resolutions can be found within liberal thought and practice alone. The political play around questions of inequality and freedom denied always requires engagement with other traditions of thinking and practice.

We can locate the space of critical political economy, including Marxism and various socialist impulses, and the postdevelopment tradition as both overlapping with and pushing us beyond liberalism. Marxism and other socialist imaginaries emerge more directly from liberalism but also have liberalism as their major target. Postdevelopment thinking emerges within and more fully against liberal modernity. In these responses, we find different approaches to social understanding, prompted by but repressed within liberalism's logical, temporal, and geographical field. Marx and the critical political economy that follows his lead begin not with autonomous units but with social systems that emerge within the dynamics of history. Postdevelopment thinkers begin with the relations of person/community and place. For a liberal political economy that begins with isolated individuals, exchange and markets must always be historically existent in some form, but, of course, never fully realized in modernity's present, and their global and logical ubiquity thereby constitutes a liberal utopia. For Marx, the Marxist tradition, and Karl Polanyi, around whom we center chapter 6, the extension of capitalist markets to the world produces a global capitalist system as a "stark utopia" (Polanyi 2001, 3) of dispossession, massive inequality, poverty, and alienation. For these critical counters to liberalism, capitalism emerges historically, simultaneously destroying other human pathways and prompting imagining histories beyond liberalism. While the values of equality and freedom have won their current historical form in the arrival of a liberal order, their fuller or different content remains an aspiration in which equality means not an equal opportunity but a universal capacity to realize individual and collective projects, or, in the case of Escobar's postdevelopment, to realize alternative worlds. Greater equality and freedom for individuals and groups await us in a symbolic order against and beyond the logical and temporal space of liberalism.

Liberalism can't fully reach these geographical, logical, and temporal spaces offered by its critics. For liberalism, there is no "after" or "beyond" its symbolic order, since it is simultaneously claimed as always already universal and as the necessary and final point of arrival. There is no logical, temporal, or geographical "beyond"—no alternative worlds. The liberal ontological field fixes its units as autonomous individuals, rendering social life as nothing more than the aggregate of individual behavior, and thereby excluding attention to the *structuring* of domestic or global social relations by capitalist modernity. Where history has either ended or the history of the emergence of particular systems of social relations largely erased from view, we can expect the liberal symbolic field to rule out any unfolding of social life toward new forms or the "recovery" of alternative worlds. Yet reflections within and against liberal spaces prompt us to see the historicity of capitalism, the weight of structures, and understandings of freedom and equality beyond a liberal symbolic field.

THE MENU OF CHAPTERS

We speak of a menu of chapters because they are not strictly sequential, though we believe the ordering adopted here provides a sense of flow. Yet certain themes run through some chapters, then drop away, only to return later. We find this statement true particularly of questions of ethics, especially distributive and commutative justice, which are central to chapters 2, 6, and the Epilogue, though never far from the surface in any chapter. Chapters 1 through 4 carefully dissect the mechanisms in liberal thought that justify inequality and suffering, exposing their intellectual inadequacies and the bad faith sometimes involved. The role of unit-level methodological strategies to resist making domination central to our account of social life is given pride of place in chapters 3 and 4. Chapters 1, 3, and 5 stress the relationship of liberal thought and colonialism/empire, practices tasked with imposing market relations and justified as the right or privilege of the more developed. Chapters 4, 5, and the Epilogue explore the importance of forms of *social* explanation that shed light on processes of social domination and the responsibility of actors for their position in social hierarchies. Though these key themes cut across chapters, we think each chapter also stands alone as an investigation of liberalism and liberal IPE from within and beyond.

Chapter 1, "Liberal Fundamentals," explores the relative capacity of important Scottish Enlightenment thinkers, all early liberals in our view, to both deny and face the costs of emerging market societies. They trade in hands, at once "invisible," as in David Hume's and Adam Smith's general embrace of self-regulating systems, but also involving "invasive" hands of reform (John Millar) and "artful" hands of economic management (James Steuart). Most starkly, Adam Ferguson suggests that market societies fall into corruption and conquest, offering us only "bloody" hands and points us beyond a liberal vision. We conclude that this array of thinkers suggests that liberal theory and practice, what we call here a liberal symbolic order, can be described by the tension between an assertion of smoothing natural harmonies and doubts created by the high costs of market society.

We investigate this tension in liberal thought through a careful examination of the ethical issues surrounding the extreme inequality characterizing capitalism as a global system in chapter 2, "Global Capitalism, Inequality, and Poverty." We trace Thomas Pogge's thinking as he confidently asserts an inalienable right to a share of global resources, only to fall back to weaker positions based on either a commutative principle of payments for damages or simple prudence on the part of the advantaged. We believe he makes the strongest case for the idea that the poverty of many is intimately connected with the wealth of others. We also trace out the liberal/libertarian defense of inequality and expose its vulnerability to the claim that rewards are the result of unfair practices, recognized by none other than noted libertarian, Robert Nozick. However, other libertarians, like Friedrich Hayek, counsel against redistribution even in the case of damages since it obstructs the workings of markets, though he recognizes somewhat begrudgingly that market society depends on a mistaken belief in the idea of merit. We again end with the idea that liberal understandings of equality leave us with what appear to be insurmountable tensions. This chapter makes clear the challenges we face in overturning justifications for inequality. That is the work of the remaining chapters of the book.

In chapter 3, "Liberal IPE as Colonial Science," we trace what John Hobson calls the "sublimated Eurocentrism" of liberal IPE to its roots in neoclassical economics on which it depends for its basic assumptions and claim to scientific status. We develop a parallel between an early neoclassical economist, Alfred Marshall, and Robert Keohane's liberal IPE. Both mix a static scheme in which behavior is understood as a choice given constraints with social evolutionary thinking, including a telos of human development in which the West plays the central, pioneering role. The Eurocentric bias is explicit in Marshall, who adopts cultural/racial arguments to explain the dominance of the West and the necessity of empire. Liberal IPE appears to construct the need for dominance (i.e., hegemony) as simply a logical implication of their theoretical system: the need for a predominant power to ensure cooperation among independent states. They seem to ignore that England was an empire, not simply one among many states, and that the United States plays a similar imperial role in the liberal order. Eurocentrism remains just below the surface and liberal IPE appears as a colonial science.

Chapter 4, "Levels, Eurocentrism, and Positive Science," locates Eurocentrism in international relations (IR) deep in its intellectual architecture—in the levels of analysis scheme itself. Eurocentrism appears, then, not as a matter of ignorance or oversight, but as constitutive of IR itself as a form of "exiogophobia"—an allergy to social explanation and a fixation on unit-level explanation as the epitome of proper science. Our inquiry unfolds in three major steps. First, we follow Ghassan Hage's story of the pushback to his efforts to explain suicide bombers in a way that reclaimed their humanity so that they appear as "ordinary human beings" in particular circumstances. We link resistance to social explanation to a "condemnation imperative" that insists on understanding individual behavior as a function of unit-level traits. Second, we show how the levels scheme organizes IR and its practitioners into a Eurocentric practice that obscures social explanation in social life and supports justifications of inequality that emphasize the lacks and cultural or racial inferiority of those who are subject to domination. Third, texts by Walter Rodney and Francis Jennings are typical of efforts that built on dependency theory and world-systems analysis to provide a social explanation and humanization of African and Native North Americans that were marginalized by IR as it made unit-level explanation the standard for scientific practice. Rodney and Jennings foreshadow the kinds of scholarship on social processes as relatively integrated wholes that we explore in the next chapter.

We juxtapose liberal IPE's axiomatic bargaining units with heterodox global political economy's (GPE) commitment to Schumpeter's notion of the "social process" as an "indivisible whole" in chapter 5, "Units, Markets, Relations, and Flow." Reminiscent of chapter 3, we describe liberal IPE orthodoxy's reliance on neoclassical economics and its timeless and institution-less theory of choice and constraint. Though it partly distinguishes itself from neoclassical economics, liberal IPE remains limited by static and asocial formulations that systematically underplay the role of social domination. We explore the possibilities offered by three heterodox global political economists inspired by dependency theory and world-systems theory (WST): K. N. Chaudhuri's *Asia Before Europe* (1990), Eric Wolf's *Europe and the People without History* (1982), and L. S. Stavrianos's *Global Rift* (1981). They carefully document the broad historical trajectories of development and underdevelopment, always attuned to global processes and structures of interconnection. While emphasizing the indivisibility of the social process, these thinkers don't ignore the role of the units. Or, perhaps better, they do not ignore the role of parts in comprising and being structured by complex wholes. We end by suggesting that an analysis and appreciation of these three books start with the herculean theoretical and historical effort to overcome both a "dualism" and "duality" of structure and arrive instead at dynamic interaction, or "flow." We end this chapter with a provocation from Anna Tsing's *Friction* (2005). She challenges those of us that trade in universals like "capitalism" to consider that capitalism only evidences itself as it travels as imaginary or dream to localities where it confronts the friction of the specificities of time and place. What then could it mean to speak of the responsibility associated with interconnection or global social processes, as we did in chapters 2 and 5? Chapter 6 considers a version of this question.

Chapter 6, "Complex Societies and Alternative Worlds," counterpoises two readings of Karl Polanyi's critique of the "stark utopia" of liberal political economy. One, a GPE reading, draws directly on *The Great Transformation* to discuss the damage to human livelihood wrought by the progressive liberalization of global markets for labor and finance. Following Polanyi, this GPE reading imagines *global* institutions of "democratic provisionism" that limit the scope of the market by securing the livelihood of people as a right to a share of global social wealth. The GPE vision of democratic provisioning turns on the idea that global capitalism has made the world a global society in which real freedom can be realized. A second, "postdevelopment" reading of Polanyi has been elaborated by Arturo Escobar. Escobar takes Polanyi's idea of the "economistic fallacy" as inspiration for diversifying our understanding of the human experience and seemingly resists the notion of a global society. He points not simply to the varying modes of human social life but also to the differing ontological presuppositions that foster the making of different worlds. Escobar contrasts the destruction wrought by modern industrial capitalism's colonial conquest of the human/natural world with the communal binding of people and place that allows both resistance to extractive capitalism and the creation of sustainable worlds. Though Escobar doesn't put it this way, his vision of communal worlds appears to depend on recognition and implementation of a right to make a world within a world of worlds. Freedom appears as the right to make worlds separate from the global society brought by colonial capitalism. We end by working to reduce the distance between these two readings. The idea of democratic provisioning should have space for enacting different worlds and Escobar's vision requires recognition from national and global institutions for its realization.

In the Epilogue, after very briefly summarizing the main lines of argument we pursue in these essays, we once more think through the implications of the idea of "social determination" for the responsibility to redress extreme inequality in the form of absolute poverty or work to secure livelihood with a right to a share of social wealth. We get to that point via an important digression that considers recent claims about "Eastern agency" in the creation of capitalism and the responsibility of the West for the violence and oppression integral to colonial capitalism. While the West may not be solely responsible for the rise of capitalism, the emergence of colonial capitalism as a system of social relations of domination and subordination structures social powers and links global wealth to the poverty and suffering of many.

Chapter 1

Liberal Fundamentals

Liberal fundamentals often become fundamentalism. For liberals, God's place in a "theological-political order" is replaced by "History," where history produces an "Absolute Good" that knows no borders. These "neo-fundamentalists," in Todorov's terms, have the mindset of "activists": "the world needs to be made over, its problems must be resolved once and for all, if necessary by armed force" (Todorov 2005, 15–17). Today's liberals, including believers in market miracles and various social reformers who doubt the virtues of unregulated capitalism, call upon states and various international organizations to help secure their progressive vision of the world; coercion is justified by liberal ends (see Latham 1997; Barkawi and Laffey 2005; Jahn 2005). Though only a few (mostly economists) explicitly embrace David Hume's and Adam Smith's notion that harmony naturally unfolds across global space like an *invisible hand*, they are more likely to share Smith's student John Millar's more anxious, *invasive hand* of reformism—his desire to quell an anxiety about the limits and failures of liberalism by means of imperial crusading. Too few pay heed to James Steuart's warning that statesmen must apply an *artful hand* in shaping government action consistent with economic forces and the home country's particular conditions. None, however, fully face the darker, *bloody hands* of liberal institutions and practices that Adam Ferguson highlights.

Smith and his Scottish Enlightenment peers explicitly embraced a universal history (Onuf and Onuf 2006). The Scots portrayed the diversity of human cultural and historical experience as fitting into four stages of human progress—from the savage age of hunting and gathering via ages of herding and settled agriculture to an age of commerce (Meek 1976; Wokler 1995). These ascending stages of modes of subsistence are accompanied by corresponding changes or advances in institutions, laws, and manners. With the

13

rise of a commercial era in particular, human society loses its rude qualities: violence is replaced by more refined and pacific manners. A new spirit of liberty emerges that recognizes individual freedom, property rights, and legal equality and the state adapts and minimizes its role in relation to the growing importance of markets and individual freedom (Berry 1997, chaps. 3 and 6; Skinner 1965). Together these propositions produce something like today's idea of a liberal peace.

The Scots imagined this civil or civilized society in relation to other, backward forms of life, including ancient peoples, Europe's own past, and contemporaneous but temporally superseded peoples inside and beyond Europe. On one side, the "savage" is exemplary of an early and poor, rude, or barbarous state of humankind. On the other side, the Scots characterize modern civil society as precisely what savage or barbarous societies are not, so that the commercial era serves as a "utopian projection" or "didactic" project envisioned in terms of peace, liberty, property, and equality (Trouillot 1991, 18, 26–9). We argue that this projection and project partly account for liberalism's idealist motivation and fundamentalist energy.

Civil society cannot simply and stably serve as a "utopian projection," however. As we shall see, the Scots were well aware of the deficiencies and possible dangers of a commercial era: poverty lurks unchecked or appears as a consequence of market society; inequality threatens liberty; the specialization of the division of labor alienates individuals from responsible social and political life; and commercial interests fuel imperial adventures instead of checking them. The gaps between the "utopian projection" and the realities of civil society create doubts and anxieties that are themselves sources of motivation and energy. Where the other of rudeness and incivility comes to pollute civil society itself, the defense of the boundary between the savage and the civilized must be rigorously policed. Here, we find a key source of the fundamentalist response: these problems cannot be accepted as internal to liberalism itself; instead, they are to be overcome by liberalism's complete realization. As the liberalism of markets or peaceful norms spreads across space and as it is practiced more intensively, it will erase the residual presence of barbarism. The inability to face the limits of liberalism leads liberals to a purifying, fundamentalist response.

We define liberalism, then, as a symbolic field that asserts an idealized vision of itself against the doubts generated by its assertions of progress and exertions of reform. Though the Scottish Enlightenment figures we survey were all aware of the limits and deficiencies of a liberal order, none abandons secular progress outright; nor do they reject markets and market society. These endorsements appear as articles of faith without which they might sink into a philosophical abyss or the chaos of historical backwardness and disorder. Internal backwardness and disorder, then, serve as the "real"—as an "antagonism" that "prevents closure" of liberalism as a "social field" (Edkins 1999, 113) or that prompts necessary but impossible gestures of natural harmony on which liberalism depends (Kordela 2007, 17). Put bluntly, liberalism depends on a boundary between itself and barbarous others that it must draw but can never fully secure.

Our intuition is that we might usefully turn to Smith and his Scottish interlocutors to understand the ambiguities of the contemporary "liberal moment" (Gleditsch 2008; Latham 1997). The goal is not simply to champion a critical rejection of liberalism, nor do we dismiss that side of liberalism that promises greater wealth, minimizes scarcity, and expands human liberty, equality, and peace. What interests us is retrieval. By recovering the fuller heritage of liberalism, we might locate the resources for resisting fundamentalism within liberalism itself; its capacity to confront rather than avoid the impossible difficulties of commercial society (see also Inayatullah and Blaney 2004; Blaney and Inayatullah 2010).

But are these Scottish Enlightenment figures liberal at all? We are aware of the venerable work that places the Scots prior to the articulation of a self-conscious liberal tradition (Skinner 1998), locating them as heirs of civic humanism or republicanism (Pocock 1975), or more precisely as Whigs (Burrow 1998). Consensus is elusive, however, since others place them more clearly as proto-liberals (Haakonssen 2005; Meek 1965; Teichgraeber 1986). Though important for other contexts, this debate need not divert us. Regardless of the manner in which we date or delineate liberalism, current conceptions of liberal thought treat the Scots, particularly Smith, as precursors. Warren Montag (2006, 7) argues that, in a world of neoliberal market orthodoxy, Smith's "words shape our dreams and destinies." Many textbooks in GPE treat Adam Smith as a key marker for a "liberal tradition" of IR (Isaak 2000, 4; Gilpin 1987, 26–31, 44, 81; Crane and Amawi 1997, 6–8; Frieden 1995, 70; O'Brien 2004, 5, 18–21). Smith and Hume recently have been trotted out as early advocates of liberal peace claims (Wyatt-Walter 1996, 5–28; Manzer 1996, 369–82) and others note the place of Steuart in that tradition (Hirschman 1977, 113–28). For contemporary IR theory, at least, we can say that the Scots serve as figures in the creation story of liberal IR.

A powerful challenge to the idea of the Scots as liberals comes from Daniel Deudney (2007). He argues that the current divide between liberals and realists is created by gathering selectively from republican thought and splitting it into two: liberals get free markets and security communities and realists get the balance of power. Though we haven't done justice to his argument, we would give a different interpretation of Deudney's claims. We believe he underestimates the work done by this splitting of the republican tradition; it reduces complexity by purifying schools of thought into more parsimonious sets of propositions, and it gives competing intellectual temperaments a chance to play out their idealizations undisturbed by other temperaments. On the one side, we get tragedy without progress; on the other progress without tragedy. Scottish Enlightenment figures exemplify this tension: they embrace the liberalism of progress, but they can't quite shake the shadow of tragedy. We will return to this issue in the conclusion.

We begin our account with Hume. Because he displays few doubts about the achievements of commercial society, he serves as a baseline against which we read the other thinkers. In the second section, we discuss Smith's vision of history as a harmonious machine that produces desirable social outcomes out of less than desirable motivations but which recognizes the various failings of commercial society that often require a visible hand. For John Millar, who we take up next, doubts and anxieties cannot be smoothed by the invisible hand alone. Unlike Smith, he endorses aggressive reform and correction, including extending market society to the globe, in order to secure the utopian results promised by liberalism. We argue in the fourth section that James Steuart faces these doubts more directly. By contrast with Smith and Millar, he accepts the need for the continuous and artful management by the state of economic processes that never automatically produce harmony. Finally, and in marked contrast to his peers, Adam Ferguson gives full expression to these doubts and anxieties, warning that commercial interests may combine with the venality of leaders and the apathy of citizens to produce not harmony and peace, but bloody imperial conquest that also bankrupts and corrupts domestic society. He points us beyond the customs and manners of liberalism as a possible way to resolve the problems of liberal societies. We build on Ferguson's suggestion in the conclusion as a way to negotiate the dangers of liberal fundamentalism. We suggest that we cannot expect to resolve tensions within liberal societies as long as we narrowly restrict our thinking to liberal truths thereby eliminating the possibility of drawing on plural ontologies that offer multiple versions of virtue and progress.

HUME AND THE UNDOUBTED
BENEFITS OF COMMERCE

David Hume displays a "singular optimism" about the emerging commercial order (Boyd 2008, 65, 89). In his *Essays*, Hume (1985) works to deflect challenges posed to a market society without nostalgia for lost virtues. By extolling the new virtues of commerce, Hume helps us formulate an idealized image of market society against which doubts may be articulated—a baseline against which we can map the Scottish Enlightenment's liberal anxieties.

We begin with Hume's position in the so-called "rich-country-poor-country debate"—a debate in which international trade's orderliness and the prospects of acquiring and sustaining wealth were hotly contested (Hont 1983, 271–315). Hume argues that natural mechanisms disperse wealth across countries. Reducing imports through state intervention (to defend the position of the rich country) or artificially stimulating economic progress (to augment the position of the poor country) is thereby unnecessary and undesirable. On the one side, poor countries are not permanently disadvantaged because "the advantages initially gained" by some "are compensated . . . by the low price of labor." "Manufactures" will "gradually shift their places, leaving these countries and provinces which they have already enriched, and flying to others." The key equilibrating mechanism involves the flow of species into the successful trading nation that, by "a maxim almost self-evident," raises the prices of commodities and shifts trade in another state's direction (Hume 1985, 283–4, 290). On the other side, Hume insists that rich countries will not suffer substantially. As in later theories of product life-cycles or of a new international division of labor (Vernon 1966, 190–207; Froebel et al. 1980), "the finest arts" will remain in the centers of production, with "coarser" arts alone moving to "remote countries" (Hume in Hont 1983, 276). Further, the process of species outflow, which signals some industries to move, will also shift resources to domestic production or toward upgrading exports (Duke 1979, 572–87). Hume (1985, 312) associates this harmonizing mechanism with "the course of nature": "All water, wherever it communicates, remains always at a level. Ask naturalists the reason: they tell you, that, were it to be raised in one place, the superior gravity of that part not being balanced, must depress it, till it meets a counterpoise."

We may doubt Hume's answer, but he brooks no doubts and his ideas on historical progress are similarly buoyant. Progress is a product of human nature itself, whose "regular springs" operate in all social and climatic contexts (Berry 1997, 68–70). But market society alone brings human advance to its highest state: "*industry, knowledge*, and *humanity*, are linked together by an indissoluble chain, and are found from experience as well as reason, to be peculiar to the most polished, and what are commonly denominated, the more luxurious age." Commerce brings "laws, order, police, discipline" to a new "degree of perfection" and "begets mildness and moderation." By comparison with "times of barbarity and ignorance," with their infestations of "superstition, which throws government off its bias," "factions are then less inveterate, revolutions less tragical, authority less severe, and seditions less frequent" (Hume 1985, 271–4, 312).

A parallel civilizing of external affairs follows: "Even foreign wars abate of their cruelty." But if wars must be fought, Hume assures us that this loss of "ferocity" will not be accompanied by a decline in citizens' "marital spirit" or the willingness to be "vigorous in defense of their country" (Hume 1985, 312). Hume's *History of England* (1807) suggests that the flourishing of trade, the polishing of arts, and the better organization of central government reduce the excesses of individual royal or noble ambition. These developments also create more effective use of military force, as in the extension of rule and trade via the creation of colonies (Buchan 2006, 177–8). And, he adds, with advances in modern military technology, even these foreign adventures of civilized states appear less dangerous:

> Though [artillery] seems contrived for the destruction of mankind, and the overthrow of empires, has in the issue rendered battles less bloody, and has given greater stability to civil societies. Nations by its means have been brought more to a level: Conquests have become less frequent and rapid: Success in war has been reduced nearly to a matter of calculation: And any nation overmatched by its enemies, either yields to their demands or secures itself by alliances against their violence and invasion. (Hume 1807, 432; quoted in Buchan 2006, 178)

Hume apparently means that competing empires can more readily calculate the balance of power and are less likely to engage in damaging warfare, not that the uncivilized will check the spread of civilization by force. Such a balance of power curbs military adventures across the sovereign spaces of modern civilization but not across temporal or civilizational differences. The spread of civilization and the progressive pacification of international affairs are guaranteed.

THE VISIBLE INVISIBLE HAND: ADAM SMITH

Of course, it is Smith, not Hume, who speaks of the "invisible hand." He uses the term to capture how "the good may be educed from ill" (Smith 1976a, 36; see also Griswold 1999, 319) and, more specifically, how the uninterrupted operations of the market transform self-interested individual actions into the public good. Human action spontaneously produces progress while progressive history necessarily realizes a harmonious and orderly end (Skinner 1965, 22). In *Theory of Moral Sentiments* (1976b), Smith's optimism is informed by his reading of the Stoics, who saw the "world [as] governed by the all-ruling providence of a wise, powerful, and good God." Where "every single event ought to be regarded, as making a necessary part of the plan of the universe, and as tending to promote the general order and happiness of the whole," even "the vices and follies of mankind" are part of the "prosperity and perfection of the great system of nature" (Smith 1976, 36; see Merikoski 2002, 60–5, on Smith's Providentialism). Smith sees "human society" similarly as an "immense machine, whose regular and harmonious movements produce a thousand agreeable effects" (Smith 1976a, 316).

Despite this confidence in Providence, Smith's optimism is "haunted" by the "moral shortcomings in commercial society" (Teichgraeber 1986, 128), which he enumerates. As haunted as he might be, Smith promotes the salutary historical narrative after every notably critical discussion. He goes to great lengths to establish the superiority of a commercial society though he leaves more space for a critical treatment of modern capitalism than he himself admits.

Smith remains particularly anxious about two issues: the ill effects of specialization and the problem of poverty. These concerns also threaten to overturn his progressive theory of history. Foremost in Smith's mind are the problems associated with specialization. Turning the common laborer into a narrow specialist has a number of negative consequences; having "no occasion to exert his understanding," a man "whose life is spent in performing a few simple operations . . . generally becomes as stupid and ignorant as it is possible for a human creature to become." This is no small matter. The detailed laborer becomes "incapable of relishing or bearing a part of any rational conversation," unable to "conceive any generous, noble, or tender sentiment," and therefore inept at "forming any just judgment concerning many even of the ordinary duties of private life." He becomes unqualified to ascertain the "interests of his country," and powerless in "defending his country in war." In direct contrast, the absence of a division of labor in savage societies means that each individual performs "varied occupations"; inventiveness is "kept alive"; "every man is a warrior"; every man is a "statesman"; and each is able to "form a tolerable judgment concerning the interest of society." While specialization provides a material plenty unavailable to the savage, this advantage is "acquired at the expense of [the laborer's] intellectual, social, and martial virtues." The sober consequence is that "in every improved and civilized society this is the state into which the laboring poor, that is, the great body of the people, must necessarily fall" (Smith 1976b, 302–4).

From these passages, it is difficult to tell if Smith actually believes, as he commonly asserts, that the working classes are better off than savages. So worried is Smith that he abandons the invisible hand, calling upon the very visible hand of the state to provide public education. If the state does not provide such counter-measures to the division of labor, "all the nobler parts of the human character may be, in a great measure, obliterated and extinguished in the great body of the people" (Smith 1976b, 303). In stark contrast to his quietist sensibilities, and more consistent with Millar as we shall see, Smith advocates government intervention lest commercial society destroy the very thing it is meant to advance—ennobling and civilizing wealth (Winch 1996, 119).

But Smith is no romantic about savage society. He quickly reasserts the fundamentals of liberalism: a more limited division of labor is not an alternative for us in the present. Though useful as a foil, savage institutions and manners are superseded once and for all. He reassures us that a reformed commercial society combines wealth creation with a process of the refinement of character that extends to most citizens of civilized societies (Smith 1976b, 204–11).

Smith's treatment of poverty suggests a still more radical turn. He repeatedly asserts in *Wealth of Nations* that a commercial society produces greater material well-being for common people than do previous forms of society. Indeed, this is the key criterion by which to assess contemporary society: "No society," Smith (1976b, 88) boldly asserts, "can surely be flourishing and happy, of which the far greater part of the members are poor or miserable." Earlier in the text, he promises that in a "well-governed society," the "universal opulence extends itself to the lowest ranks of the people" (Smith 1976b, 15). In his discussion of returns to labor, Smith (1976b, 72–97) explains that wages will rarely fall below the level of subsistence and should rise above subsistence with vibrant growth. It is worth noting that the automatic mechanism Smith describes includes higher infant mortality rates among the poor that reduce the oversupply of laborers (see Montag 2006, 12–14; Blaney and Inayatullah 2010, chap. 2). But such comparisons are not always entirely favorable to a commercial society, because, as Smith warns us, we find "great inequality" in a commercial society, where "the affluence of the few supposes the indigence of the many" (Smith 1976b, 232).

Consistent with his overarching stoicism, Smith quickly turns inequality from a serious problem of political and moral corruption into an actual advantage of a commercial society. He links the relative well-being of the "ordinary day-laborer" to the rule of law that also maintains "the rich in the possession of their wealth against the violence and rapacity of the poor." Indeed, law preserves "that useful inequality in the fortunes of mankind which naturally and necessarily arises from the various degrees of capacity, industry, and diligence in the different individuals" (Smith 1982, 338). Similarly, in his parable of the "unfeeling landlord," Smith explains that the wealthy landlord spends only on his selfish desires but thereby employs vast numbers of people, spreading subsistence to many. Thus the "vain and insatiable desires" of the rich lead them, as if "by an invisible hand," to "divide with the poor the produce of all their improvements" and "without intending it, without knowing it, advance the interest of the society" (Smith 1976a, 184–5). Inequality, even where opulence and indigence stand in striking opposition, proves not the stark weakness that Smith seemed to indicate.

Nevertheless, Smith's own writing mostly challenges this sanguine conclusion. Though he argues that markets keep laborers above some "absolute" standard of subsistence, Smith recognizes the social stigma and damage to character accompanying relative poverty. "The poor man," he confesses, "is ashamed of his poverty." This is hardly surprising since indigence produces a kind of social invisibility: "The poor man goes out and comes in unheeded, and when in the midst of a crowd is in the same obscurity as if shut up in his own hovel" (Smith 1976a, 51). Even assuming Smith's most optimistic assumptions about commercial wealth, we cannot deny the harm created by the coexistence of "affluence" and "indigence." Nor can we sustain the claim that poverty is a condition distinct to savage or barbarous societies. Following Marshall Sahlins (1972), we might argue that market society expands needs thereby putting affluence beyond the means of many; poverty is strikingly associated with, perhaps even tied to, the emergence of modern society. Sahlins would add that since "primitive" societies produce affluence by keeping needs to a minimum, poverty cannot be assumed as an original condition for which commercial society is the antidote. Poverty and market society go hand in hand.

Despite such admissions, Smith's dominant mode of relating to poverty (and other realities of commercial society) is nevertheless to project them into the past or to dilute their potency by pointing to the relative advantages of the age of commerce. He reduces his anxiety by projecting market society's ills onto those who occupy past cultural forms and superseded time. But other elements in Smith's account indicate that poverty and the moral corruption due to specialization are intrinsically linked to a wealthy commercial society. These elements serve as an internal but repressed other against which a commercial society is defined. Poverty and moral corruption appear then as a "constitutive outside": that which modern society "depends on, even as it refuses to recognize . . . forces that escape its control" (Mitchell 2000, 4–5, 12–13).

THE INVASIVE HAND: JOHN MILLAR

John Millar, Smith's most famous student, is also haunted by liberal anxiety but cannot summon Smith's fuller stoic faith. Millar begins with Smith's "four-stages theory," translating the complexity of human differences into a "remarkable unity"—a set of soothing and uniform patterns of human development (Millar 1979b, 175–6). In accordance with Smith's pattern, he closely examines commercial society's failings (including the corrupting influences of inequality and the division of labor) only to quickly deflect such concerns. He soothes his anxiety and *mostly* vindicates the claim that humanity reaches its pinnacle with modern society.

But Millar deviates from Smith in a crucial way. Lacking Smith's depth of faith in the smoothing machine, he more emphatically embraces the visible hand of the state. While he continues to defend a "spirit of liberty" and "natural rights" necessitating minimal government (Millar 1979a, 326), Millar's more energetic state vigorously redresses social ills and extends the logic of a liberal commercial society across social space. Like Smith, Millar works to turn inequality and the economic dependence of the common laborers into an advantage by outlining a set of distinctly liberal/libertarian justifications for inequality: the independence brought by wage-labor; the incentive to individual effort; and the spur to commercial advance (Millar 1979a, 331–2, 326, 336; Millar 1979b, 318–19; see the next chapter). Though some government measures may be taken to mitigate the worst poverty and ignorance, the state is charged largely with managing and correcting those in the under-class who might pose a threat to themselves and the social order. Civil society's commercial logic guides the reform by which the lower classes become objects of governance (Burchell 1991, 21). State intervention is at once embraced, given content, and circumscribed.

Though Millar largely vindicates the doctrine of progress by reference to the achievements of European societies, he recognizes that commerce does not spread universally or evenly across space. Inequality appears not only within nations but also across them (Chandler 1998, 128–32). Though uneven development generates some anxiety for a proponent of commercial society, Millar seems confident that this unevenness is less a permanent condition and more a product of historical circumstance. Where the capacity for progress seems blocked, Millar recommends pedagogical correctives via imperial interventions. A universal theory of progress thus generates a modern (liberal) imperialism that both vindicates the theory and justifies interventions on its behalf.

Smith is instructive as a comparison. Smith discusses the limited benefits of colonies and, as a corollary, the substantial benefits of free commerce (Smith 1976b, book IV, chaps. iii and vii; Onuf and Onuf 2006, 188). He says little about the native populations of the empires; after all, Smith thinks of colonies in classical terms—as settlements hived off from the home country. He comments on the varying efficiency in slave labor management in West Indian colonies (Smith 1976b, 98–99), but it is the settlers who comprise the relevant population that is advancing or not in these "new" lands.

Smith stops at one point to assess the world-historical importance of the "discovery" of the Americas. He cannot help but claim that the European voyages of exploration are "the most important events recorded in the history of mankind." A unified world encourages worldwide industry with goods traveling from every direction of the globe in order to meet humankind's needs and wants (Smith 1976b, 141). "To the natives, however," to whom Smith finally turns, "all the commercial benefits which can have resulted from these events have been sunk and lost in the dreadful misfortunes which they have occasioned." Despite this judgment, Smith moves quickly to reassure us that these "misfortunes" are not part of the logic of commerce, but arise "from accident"; in this case, the imbalance of military forces created by uneven development tempts Europeans to conquest and allows them "to commit with impunity every sort of injustice in those remote countries" (Smith 1976b, 141). Fortunately, history may lead us forward from the ills of colonization to an even more desirable location:

> Hereafter, perhaps, the natives of those countries may grow stronger, or those of Europe may grow weaker, and the inhabitants of all the different quarters of the world may arrive at that equality of courage and force which, by inspiring mutual fear, can alone overawe the injustice of independent nations into some sort of respect for the rights of another. But nothing seems more likely to establish the equality of forces than that mutual communication of knowledge and of all sorts of improvements which an extensive commerce from all countries naturally, or rather necessarily, carries along with it. (Smith 1976b, 141)

The operation of history as a harmonious machine seems to secure the relatively salutary vision of international affairs.

Here, the balance of power operates only as a subordinate aspect of a wider historical process—the expansion of commerce. The plight of native populations is ultimately resolved by the operation of commerce itself. The global (im)balance of power favors civilized Europe. Rather than a peaceful coexistence of different social forms, the natives are incorporated, whether voluntarily or not, into a modern world of commercial interdependence. Colonies occur naturally and necessarily; the degradation of native populations is merely a morally unfortunate side-effect of the unfolding of the natural order. Commerce provides an automatic antidote to the abuses associated with colonization—a pacification of IR—that appears inevitable, not something for which we must struggle.

Millar has, as we have said, less confidence in the natural and necessary workings of history and therefore more urgency to spread the laws and manners of civil society. Millar's impulse to humanitarian intervention is evident in his extended account of Ireland's history in *An Historical View of the English Government* (1787). When compared with Hume's view of the Irish as exceptionally barbaric, little above cannibals, Millar's account is perhaps paradigmatic of a more liberal view of cross-national relations (Smith, Paul 1996, 2227–48). His more liberal attitude does not preclude an imperial stance toward the Irish, however: liberal ideals support his defense of Ireland's colonization.

Millar concedes that the Irish have been a barbaric people by any reasonable standard, though it is "difficult to find any real foundation" for the claim that the Irish are especially barbaric, except perhaps in the "partiality and prejudices of English historians" (Millar 1997, 7–8). Rather, the Irish "exhibit that striking resemblance of lines and features, which may be remarked in the inhabitants of every country before the advancement of arts and civilization" (Millar 1997, 8–9). The problem with the Irish is not blood, but the level of development and historical circumstances, particularly the brutality of the early English conquest. Millar minces no words in describing the "rapacity of private adventurers"—"a band of robbers, who had stripped the natives of a part of their property" (Millar 1997, 1–3). Millar refuses English lawyers' appeal to a "right to conquest." In a liberal world, no such right exists (Millar 1997, 54–5).

Millar does not condemn colonization of Ireland in principle, however. The venal motives of settlers meant that early colonies did "very little, either to ascertain and extend the conquest, or to civilize the inhabitants, and reduce them into a regular government" (Millar 1997, 2). Early English intrusions instituted instead a landed oligarchy that mismanaged estates while inhibiting improvements by other inhabitants. In this situation, the settlers simply degenerated to the same low level of civilization (Millar 1997, 20–1). Where Smith accepts conquest as part of the impersonal operation of the natural order, for Millar, absent a consciously executed progressive mission, colonialism loses its historical purpose and attendant moral justification.

Millar's tone changes when he turns to a later period of more benevolent, deliberate, and reforming colonialism. Free of such external influences, Ireland was a clan-based society, evidencing high levels of violence, little sense of property rights, low levels of improvement in the arts and manufactures, and no settled government—the epitome of an illiberal culture without a functioning modern state (Millar 1997, 9–17). With later English efforts extending rule of law to Ireland, we find a corresponding if small stimulus to improvements, including an emerging spirit of freedom and independence (Millar 1997, 21–31). Things turn with the more complete pacification of Ireland at the end of Elizabeth's rule and the fuller extension of "the advantages of regular government and civilized manners to that hitherto uncultivated and intractable" domain (Millar 1997, 32–3). Establishing rule of law and property rights begins to protect the "people of the lower ranks" from the "numerous exactions, which their superiors had imposed upon them"; they began, as Millar seems to exclaim, "to taste, in some measure, the blessings of fecundity and freedom." Initial resistance merely signals the success of the colonial mission, which can be turned to consensual subordination if a colonizer stays the course and imposes liberal legal norms and governance practices. What follows are "considerable advances" in agriculture and industry (Millar 1997, 34–8). Colonialism thereby regains its developmental purpose.

For Millar, imperialism can transmit the modern spirit of liberty to the backward. Because progress in Ireland was blocked by religion and internal divisiveness, English governance can produce a growing spirit of liberty that leads finally to greater Irish independence. Contemporary Irish-English relations have evolved, he argues, toward Irish consent to the Union. Thus, beneficial consequences can transform conquest into consensual subordination (Millar 1997, 49–69) and we find ourselves in the pious calculus of the liberal imperialist where conquest fosters progress through the imposition of liberal sensibilities.

Tzvetan Todorov might allow us to treat Millar's stance as a form of the "neo-fundamentalism" we described at the outset. Where the world resists, where the symbolic order of liberalism appears incomplete or reinforces problems it claims to resolve, the universality of a liberal vision must be secured by relentless reform and liberal conquest.

THE ARTFUL HAND: JAMES STEUART

Political economist James Steuart, Smith's and Millar's contemporary, is more comfortable with doubts about market societies. This lapse led to his banishment by scholars from the liberal fold, a condition from which he is only gradually recovering (see Redman 1996; Urquhart 1996). Steuart demonstrates less confidence in the great and harmonious machine than either Hume or Smith: no natural balance reconciles the interests of nations as they develop commercially. Rather, commerce produces a developmentally fractured space, in which states at different stages of industry pursue industrial policies adapted to their distinct developmental and cultural conditions. As countries' relative economic prospects rise and fall, neither the free market nor continued development can mend this fractured space. Further, unregulated markets fail to reconcile economic development with a secure livelihood for the masses. Providence does not intervene; only persistently artful economic management can keep the disorder in check. We might say that Steuart's political economy focuses our attention directly on the "real"—the intrusions of economic disorder that persist in a civil society despite promises of natural harmony. This relative comfort with the disorder may be explained by his attunement to difference—a world of multiple and varied political economies (Urquhart 1996). Nevertheless, state intervention does not replace fixed economic laws. Steuart recommends shaping industrial policy to fit national differences, but only within a science that assumes the uniformity of self-interested economic motives and economic regularities—a position marking Steuart as a liberal economist.

The contrasts with Smith are striking. Though Smith also gestures toward modifying policy according to the situation and free trade principles may be modified for national defense or for additional national revenue, his chapters on trade policy (Smith 1976b, IV.ii) indicate that the operation of universal economic laws cannot be modified by public action. Similarly, in "Digression on the Corn Trade," Smith admits that government may have to respect the irrational belief of citizens that access to subsistence goods should be secure. Still, he believes that good (free market) policies and the force of history will gradually erase such irrationality.

For Steuart, political economy's task is always attuned to particular national circumstances. He stresses the active cultivation of the "spirit of a people." Given the "variety of forms of government, laws, climate, and manners, one may conclude, that the political economy in each must necessarily be different and that principles, however universally true, may become quite ineffectual in practice, without a sufficient preparation of the spirit of a people" (Steuart 1966, 17). Political economy appears, then, as a "great art" that adapts to circumstances, although often also aiming "to be able to introduce a set of new and more useful institutions" (Steuart 1966, 48–9, 52). For Steuart, policies are neither simply dictated by economic laws nor mere reflections of the national spirit. Changes in national spirit, rather than reflecting inexorable forces of nature, require public discussion; popular knowledge of political economy must deepen and new institutions must be popularly legitimated in a free nation. Starkly put, the political economy works best *not* when it goes on, like an invisible hand, behind the backs of people; "while people remain blind they are always distrustful" (Steuart 1966, 17–18). The political economy appears here less as a mechanical force and more as knowledgeable practice and political decision (Urquhart 1996, 385).

Like the other Scots, Steuart makes his argument in the civic humanist language concerned not only with processes of growth but also of corruption and decay (Doujon 1994, 495–518). For Smith, disarray is overcome mostly by the regularities of the natural order, which only the political economist who posits such order as the basis of his science can identify, and only if the statesman will allow the natural order to operate unencumbered (Poovey 1998, 247). Millar embraces this vision of natural order but lacks the faith to allow it to unfold without human intervention. He requires a state that erases doubts and subdues the inequality and poverty that pollute civil society. Steuart, like Ferguson as we shall see, places the contingencies and uncertainties of *Fortuna* at the center of civil society; domestic and international markets alike may bring gain or destruction to individuals and polities. Though Steuart calls upon the statesman to manage this flux, he accepts it as a persistent feature of a commercial era. The potential disorder may be managed, but it cannot be erased (Pocock 1975, chap. XIV; Milbank 1990, 34–6).

Steuart illustrates his economic realism by asking the reader to think of the economy as a watch—not the product of the divine maker who exemplifies perfect craftsmanship, but a humanly constructed watch (Steuart 1966, 217). If human social life is more like the watch of human creation, then a political economy that emphasizes self-regulation and automatic harmony trades in illusions. We require a state not as a night watchman, as in Smith, but as an artful repairman. Worse, the *laissez-faire* imaginary rationalizes the dominance of early-developers like England. Late-developers, like Scotland, are deprived of the very economic strategies required for economic growth and political independence (Davie 1967, 291, 295–6, 299; for contemporary parallels, see Helleiner 2002, 307–29).

Steuart does not reject economic logic, however. The successful states-man depends on the predictability of self-interested behavior to calculate the effects of his actions. He consistently reiterates that "the principle of self-interest" is the "ruling principle" of economics; it serves as the "main spring, the only motive which a statesman should make use of, to engage a free people to concur in the plans which he lays down" (Steuart 1966, 142). Thus, a leader is "never to flatter himself that his people will be brought to act in general and in matters which purely regard the public, from any principle than private interest" (Steuart 1966, 143).

Steuart (1966, 203) introduces an image of the statesman as ship captain to fix his meaning:

> The abilities of a statesman are discovered, in directing and conducting what I call the delicacy of national competition. We shall then observe him imitating the mariners, who do not take in their sails when the wind falls calm, but keep them trimmed and ready to profit of the least breath of a favourable gale. Let me follow my comparison: the trading nations of Europe represent a fleet of ships, every one striving who shall get first to a certain port. The statesman of each is the master. The same wind blows upon all; and this wind is the principle of self-interest, which engages every consumer to seek the cheapest and the best market. No trade wind can be more general, or more constant than this; the natural advantage of each country represent this degree of goodness of each vessel; but the master who sails with the greatest dexterity, and he who can lay his rivals under the lee of this sails, will, caeteris paribus, undoubtedly get before them, and maintain his advantage.

An able mariner can achieve much as long as he can read nature's signs; macroeconomic management depends on an accurate reading of the economic forces at play.

If the pivotal guidance of the statesman makes Steuart's political economy quite un-Smithian, his vision nonetheless includes a liberal constitution and minimal government; he opposes arbitrary power perhaps more than Smith. Nor is his industrial policy a precursor of central planning; he recommends rulers act with "the gentlest hand" (Steuart 1966, 210, 278–9). The statesman exercises what Steuart calls "an artful hand," as if in contrast with the idea of the "invisible hand" (Steuart 1966, 201). Economic management is consistent with the spirit of a liberal age: statesmen are constrained to act within and through the laws of self-interest operating in the economy—"the most effective bridle ever was invented against the folly of despotism" (Steuart 1966, 278–9). Further, common causes can garner support among the population if presented openly and clearly by an able statesman. Even restrictions on freedom will be little resisted if the population can see the good ends that result. As Steuart (1996, I.i) notes, the growing role of government in everyday social life comes to be accepted as normal and as consistent with liberty.

Steuart's specific policy advice is consistent with the imperative to respect economic laws. Modifying consumer or business behavior transpires by manipulating the money supply, managing interest rates, subsidizing or taxing activities, not through absolute prohibitions or moral exhortations. Taxation must minimize impediments to industry (Steuart 1966, V.iv), the same recommendation that Smith (1976b, IV.ii) gives. Finally, one of the statesman's key imperatives involves creating the infrastructure and sustaining policies that maintain confidence in the system of banking and credit (Steuart 1966, IV, introduction).

These policy tools aim at a public cause: guaranteeing livelihood for the large class of workers. Steuart (1966, 187) attends especially to the dangers of excessive competition among buyers when subsistence is in short supply. Competition among "free hands," as he calls them, also may reduce their wages to starvation levels: "From this, results the principal cause of decay in modern states: it results from liberty, and is inseparably connected with it." Though clearly a problem of economic imbalances, Steuart uses the language of the civil humanist—"decay." It is "upon the proper employment of the free hands" that "the prosperity of every state must depend" and the statesman should assure that the mutual dependence of civil society is maintained. No individual should be allowed to become so vulnerable that they fall into the kind of subordination that is characteristic of earlier societies, prior to an era of liberty (Steuart 1966, 76–7, 228–30). And no class should be allowed to exercise dominance over another (Steuart 1966, 273).

In perhaps Keynesian fashion (Sen 1996, 50), Steuart believes that the statesman must act when demand collapses to redress mass unemployment of workers, "by making soldiers of them; by employing them in public works; or by sending them out of the country to become useful in its colonies" (Steuart 1966, 202–3). One especially powerful tool is monitoring and adjusting the money supply so as to avoid stagnation (Steuart 1966, II.xxiii). Steuart suggests promoting the development of new industries to replace those on the decline and increasing skilled labor via training programs or immigration. The statesman might temporarily subsidize exports that are losing out to foreign competition or subsidize basic goods that affect the production of export goods. He does warn that all this must be done gently in order to avoid the "jealousy" of "rival nations"; he is attentive to possible reprisals and trade wars (Steuart 1966, 202–5, 232–4, 251–2, 257–8). In all of this, the key is to stop self-perpetuating decline; he has none of Hume's faith that international mechanisms will restore balances without substantial human loss. Here Steuart's vision of the statesman involves an active intervention to correct for market failures (Meek 1967, 16).

Steuart's more judicious assessment (compared to Smith's) of the strengths and weakness of domestic and international markets is not, then, a frontal challenge to the market logic of society. He not only insists on managing the flux that markets produce but also takes market society for granted. A more radical response, one that Steuart is unwilling to chart, challenges the primacy of the laws of economic behavior themselves.

LIBERALISM'S BLOODY HANDS: FERGUSON

Adam Ferguson's Highland origins infuse his work with a palpable ambivalence about progress and development (Forbes 1967, 41; Oz-Salzberger 1995, 99; Kettler 1965). His claim that a commercial age may undercut the very virtues on which social life itself depends sets him somewhat apart from his Scottish peers. His analysis of the eruption of modern barbarism—the interconnected perils of extensive imperial adventures and internal political corruption—subverts the neat temporal division of past and present. In Ferguson's vision, past societies may provide the resources to heal the excesses of liberalism.

Distinguishing Ferguson should not belie how closely he aligns himself with his fellow Scots. He explains historical advance as they do, with an account of the human being as "susceptible of improvement," having "in himself a principle of improvement" (Ferguson 1995, 7). Thus, "progress" is central to human existence, as the development of the species recapitulates the development of individuals: "from infancy to manhood" and "from rudeness to civilization" (Ferguson 1995, 7). Like Smith, Ferguson locates a smooth and beneficial congruence between basic human motivations and historical progress. Indeed, his discussion of the law of unintended consequences is often taken as definitive of the Scottish view (Berry 1997, 40–8):

> Mankind, in following the present sense of their minds, in striving to remove inconveniences, or to gain apparent and contiguous advantages, arrive at ends which even their imagination could not anticipate . . .
>
> Every step and every movement of the multitude, even in what are termed enlightened ages, are made with equal blindness to the future; and nations stumble upon establishments, which are indeed the result of human action, but not the execution of any human design. (Ferguson 1995, 119)

Spontaneous order and development, the workings of Smith's harmonious machine, appear crucial for Ferguson as well (Kettler 1965, 122–5; Hill 1997), though not all unintended consequences are positive.

Indeed, Ferguson's diagnosis of the ills of market society places him among the most acute critics of capitalism. This diagnostic perceptiveness turns on his treatment of the past as ethically relevant and his deployment of "savage" or "barbarous" values as a critical resource. His Highland side tells him that modern institutions cannot rest on self-interest and legal justice alone: a necessary civic sensibility is undercut by the competitive imperatives of commerce (Ferguson 1995, 23–4). Individuals consequently fail to give due weight to community concerns or courageously defend the community's interests (Ferguson 1995, 174–80). He points approvingly to the "system of virtues, which all simple nations perhaps equally possess; a contempt of riches, love of their country, patience of hardship, danger, and fatigue" (Ferguson 1995, 78). Past illiberal virtues appear not as outmoded, but as necessary for the survival of a commercial society. His solution to this wound in civil society involves, then, reviving public-spiritedness: the cultivation of "vigorous, public-spirited, and resolute men," who take on the character of the "statesman and warrior," instead of the "clerk and accountant" (Ferguson 1995, 213–14; see Dickey 1987, 183–97).

Ferguson's juxtaposition of social solidarity or community against a vision of abstract individuals in markets is useful. Like Karl Polanyi (who we discuss in chapter 6; see also Inayatullah and Blaney 2004, chap. 5), he uses the past as an ethical resource to critique the pretensions of modernity; in both thinkers, the triumphal story of modern progress is left in tatters. Yet something important divides them. Polanyi emphasizes how humans achieve wider social and political purposes by embedding the economy in a variety of institutions. Ferguson gives such creative institutional responses scant attention, however, proscribing any major alterations to the operation of the unregulated market (Ferguson 1995, 138–9, 225). He deploys, instead, the earlier ethic of the warrior-statesman in order to defeat the clerk and accountant of his own time. His response hardly seems adequate. Given Ferguson's insistence that the operation of market competition produces calamitous civic decline, it seems unlikely that the individual cultivation of past virtues can alter this social logic. The sociability of the warrior-statesmen finds little place in market society and Ferguson overlooks how reviving the ethos of the community would require substantial institutional change.

For Ferguson, market society is intolerable but also inevitable and inviolable. Given the incisiveness of his critique, it is difficult to understand his thin response. It may be that he left himself little recourse but to moralize (Brown 2001, chaps. 1 and 2). That part of the self-identifying with the modern cannot be denied, but it provides him little solace. Instead, he escapes into the past—the intimate other that motivates his critique. Ferguson offers us a golden age of civic virtue, but he does not arm this part of himself with the critical bite that would alter the modern other. He holds onto both images and we are left with a standoff: a golden age of manly virtues perpetually poised against the inviolable logic of the market. Ferguson's recourse to civic virtue offers us little beyond the contemporary (liberal) communitarian's perpetual and often ineffectual counterpoising of market liberalism and civic life.

In Ferguson's account, the threat to domestic liberty is intimately connected to international affairs. This connection turns largely on the consequences of the modern division of labor. Though an extension of the division of labor continues to promote the "commercial and lucrative arts," it severs work from ingenuity and community (Ferguson 1995, 206–7). More strongly, individuals are at risk of losing "the sense of every connection, but that of kindred or neighborhood; and have not common affairs to transact, but those of trade" (Ferguson 1995, 298). In this situation, Ferguson (1995, 210) observes that people may find their property secure, but their political lives impoverished: "the constitution may indeed be free, but its members may likewise become unworthy of the freedom they possess, and unfit to preserve it."

These dangers are compounded in military affairs. A sound military force requires a body of (male) citizens "inured to equality; and where the meanest citizen may consider himself on occasion, as destined to command as well as obey" (Ferguson 1995, 87). Thus, and far beyond Smith and Millar, the level of inequality in society concerns Ferguson: "he who has forgotten that men were originally equal, easily degenerates into a slave; or in the capacity of a master, is not to be trusted with the rights of his fellow-creatures" (Ferguson 1995, 87, 153).

But the division of labor between civilian and military affairs more directly threatens political liberty. The division of labor divides society into "classes," the most important distinguishes "the warrior and the pacific habitant." Ferguson (1995, 145) passionately describes the dangers of this separation:

> It was certainly never foreseen by mankind, that in the pursuit of refinement, they were to . . . place the government, and the military force of nations, in different hands. But is it equally unforeseen, that the former order may again take place? and that the pacific citizen, however distinguished by privilege and rank, must one day bow to the person with whom he has entrusted his sword. If such revolutions should actually follow, will this new master revive in his own order the spirit of the noble and the free? Will he restore to his country the civil and military virtues? I am afraid to reply.

Despite his fear, Ferguson does reply. He argues that standing armies may become the enemy that a people must resist to secure their independence (Ferguson 1995, 145).

If his descriptions of military affairs seem a precursor to accounts of the national security state, then his discussion of the dangers of empire might forewarn us of the integration of military and commercial interests central to modern forms of imperialism. Ferguson (1995, 148) notes that foreign expansion emerged from growing European commercial interests, but the greater danger is that empire becomes an end in itself:

> It is vain to affirm, that the genius of any nation is adverse to conquest. Its real interests indeed most commonly are so; but every state which is prepared to defend itself, and to obtain victories, is likewise in hazard of being tempted to conquer.
>
> In Europe, where mercenary and disciplined armies are every where formed, and ready to traverse the earth, where like a flood pent up by slender banks, they are only restrained by political forms, or a temporary balance of power; if the sluices should break, what inundations may we not expect to behold.

The separation of the citizen and statesman impairs not only the capacities of the citizen but also the judgment of leaders—"self-interested functionaries and men of narrow vision"—seduced by glory or gain disconnected from the good of the country (Benton 1990, 114). And the turn to the empire may be gradual and almost imperceptible, emerging by "slow degrees" only to be rapidly extended (Ferguson 1995, 128). Ferguson (1995, 201) thus forces us to behold the dangers of a world of European civil societies let loose on the other, producing a world "wading in blood."

There are also internal dangers. In arguments made many times since, Feguson notes that, as empires expand, they drain national resources and states turn to "credit" in order "to disguise the hazards they ran." The cost is left for "future ages to answer" (Ferguson 1995, 222). In addition to long-term financial decline, the empire breeds resistance, requiring persistent "subjection by military force." This need for eternal military vigilance also undermines the liberties of the country's citizens. Dictatorial powers turn inward; leaders begin to associate internal opposition with an enemy threat. And where the population has been bred to a happy and affluent servility, they may readily acquiesce to a "usurpation: of their freedoms" (Ferguson 1995, 258–9; see Broadie 2001, 88–91).

Once established, this external/internal empire is difficult to overturn. Fragmented by commercial life, the political community is incapable of acting as a "free people." Those who feel the weight of oppression find their protests mostly unheard, "for his fellow subject is comforted, that the hand of oppression has not seized on himself: he studies his interest, or snatches his pleasure, under that degree of safety which obscurity and concealment bestow" (Ferguson 1995, 262–3). Ferguson (1995, 264) ends by warning all who take refuge in the promises of a law of historical progress (or some religiously inflected claim of destiny): "The institutions of men, if not calculated for the preservation of virtue, are indeed, likely to have an end as well as a beginning."

Lest the realities of an uncivil world of civil societies overwhelm us, Ferguson quickly adds that the actual situation is "mixed"—that commercial society benefits from that mixture of good and evil sentiments "instinctive" to humans. Despite "frequent neglect of virtue as a political object," modern citizens, as Smith also stresses, will exhibit in some measure "a love of integrity and candour," "an esteem for what is honourable and praise-worthy," "a zeal for their own community, and courage to maintain its rights" (Ferguson 1995, 156). But Ferguson is not willing to leave the natural order alone. That risks the dangers of instability and decline; his doubts *cannot* be laid to rest with the incantation of the invisible hand. In modern liberal society, we cannot reject commercial society, nor can we ignore its wounds. The deficiencies of a commercial society "inhere in" the very process of human progress (Hill 1997, 683). Thus, progress has a complex temporal structure for Ferguson; he refuses to build a temporal wall between the past and the present.

This is a key insight, even as we remain unimpressed by his claim that individually cultivating virtues exemplary of earlier stages of society will redress the internal decay of a market society or avoid the kinds of imperial projects that lead its citizens to financial, moral, and political ruin. Ferguson provides lessons for those who continue to live in militarized liberal democracies: he suggests that the ills of the "empire of civil society," as Rosenberg (1994) terms it, will not be easily cured. He forces us to recognize that our anxious impulse to fix the defects of liberal empire by extending liberal empire is both massively destructive and self-defeating. And he inadvertently reveals that pious calls to virtue do not constitute an alternative vision of social life.

CONCLUSION

A return to liberalism's Scottish precursors suggests that the liberal symbolic order might best be described by the tension between its assertions and its doubts—between the claimed smoothing natural harmonies and their anxieties about the social ills attendant on commerce, perhaps laid to rest only by aggressive projects of reform and correction. These anxieties do not lead our figures to abandon market society or jettison a commitment to the inevitability or inexorability of modern progress. Their doubts lead them instead to a series of strategies that continue to characterize liberalism's efforts to purify progress of the taint of tragedy. We continue to justify apparent weaknesses as necessary to the natural order, perhaps turning them into advantages in a Providentialist fashion. We preserve our faith by aggressively reforming and correcting those others who resist the inevitabilities we have embraced. We accept the disorders and instabilities inherent in a modern market society but replace our hope in the automaticity of adjustment with a belief in the capacity of the state or some form of international governance to resolve tensions in some higher-order liberalism. We call for a moral revival to restore values that our contemporary liberal institutions cannot possibly sustain. Maintaining liberalism's idealized vision of itself in the face of these necessary limits and unplanned and ill consequences seems to call forth the purificatory zeal of the fundamentalist.

Though we have highlighted the necessary evasions and frantic efforts aimed at redressing liberalism's cracks and instabilities as a fundamentalist impulse, we also may recover moments in which our Scottish thinkers face the tragedies of their project and resist a purificatory impulse. Though Smith and Millar worry about the problems of poverty and inequality in a commercial society, it is only Steuart who clearly identifies these as perpetual concerns that withstand a final solution. Instead of fundamentalist longings for closure by the reform and extension of liberalism, he calls for artful, by which he means diverse, adaptive, and continuous policy responses to manage as well as possible what can never be fully managed. Ferguson is certainly anxious about the failings of commercial society, and his picture of alienation and conquest is the darkest the Scots offer. But in contrast to Smith and Millar, his response involves reaching beyond commercial values to check the bloody hands of liberalism. Though we doubt the efficacy of his formulation, we embrace his impulse: not to purify the world of the illiberal, relegating them to a superseded past, but to locate in other times and places resources that may help us construct meaningful and workable, if not ideal, modes of life (Nandy 1987, 9–13; Inayatullah and Blaney 2004).

Thus, when asked which "hand" we should choose (as we were at the ABRI-ISA Conference in 2009), we respond that such a question misstates the problem. The different strategies exemplified by the Scots come bound together within the symbolic field of liberalism and it is only an impulse to purify liberalism of its faults and secure its universal appeal that leads us to hide or ignore some elements of liberalism: claims of the natural and smoothing harmony of free markets hide and come paired with industrial policy, active demand management, and a social welfare state (as we might find in Polanyi's idea of embeddedness) and liberal peace has liberal conquest as its bloody twin. They cannot be unbound. Though these warnings and reforms may help us mitigate the worst of the bloody hands of liberalism, we sense that a deeper issue is at stake. What we can glean from these thinkers is how a valorization of market society's wealth production allows us to abide by its incivility, its disorder, and its bloodletting. If we wish to move past a response that offers us more liberalism and more blood as a solution to the problems of liberalism, we need something that is both within and beyond liberal fundamentals: a liberalism that accepts truths beyond itself; that looks to multiple ontologies for political and ethical resources; and that accepts plural and multiple versions of virtue and progress negotiated between liberalism's fundamentals and varying local ideals and conditions.

Chapter 2

Global Capitalism, Inequality, and Poverty

Some believe that equality entails a right to livelihood. In a capitalist global division of labor, such a notion might mean provisioning social, economic, and cultural needs necessary to live a full life (Gould 2007). We might institutionalize the guarantee of livelihood as a right to income (Levine 1988) or basic income (Standing 2017), though Gould, like Levine (1998, 64–6), would stress that wants and needs and the capacity to live a life of freedom are connected not only to a minimum level of income but also to securing various features of forms of social life so that people may thrive. Connecting a right to income or seeing securing livelihood as part of global justice often entails, as Carmody, Garcia, and Linarelli (2012, 7) suggest, embracing the idea that humans deserve all this "simply because they are human beings." Thomas Pogge's relatively modest proposals for global redistribution, investigated in detail below, rely on such language of "basic human rights" to spur academic and public opinion.[1] The language of rights regards the poor not as "shrunken wretches begging for our help, but as persons with dignity who are claiming what is theirs by right," including a "human right to basic necessities" (Pogge 2007, 4).

Yet what appears self-evident to Pogge and others seems largely beyond the horizons of professional economists, policy advisers, most people enmeshed in market competition, and, apparently, much of IR theory. Despite the proliferation of IR scholarship on human rights, questions of a right to livelihood rarely appear in work by specialists on human rights (see, e.g., Risse, Ropp, and Sikkink 1999; Donnelly 2013), or in IR textbooks that place topics of human rights in one chapter and poverty and inequality into a separate chapter (Lamy, Masker, Baylis, Smith, and Owens 2019), or include a selection from Amartya Sen on poverty/rights instead of an IR scholar (Mingst, Snyder, and McKibben 2019). Though the work of Richard Falk (2000) proves exceptional, much scholarship on rights and global institutions fixates on a "democratic deficit," usually ignoring deficits of "economic justice," as Gould (2004, 201–2) puts it.

Following Samuel Fleischacker, we might attribute this neglect to the relatively recent arrival of the claim to a right to livelihood, emerging only in the latter parts of the eighteenth century and only ambivalently in the work of Adam Smith. Prior to Smith, most of the canonical European thinkers regarded the poor or poverty as part of God's plan or, in increasingly secularized terms, as a feature of the natural order. Smith first introduced the idea that the poor deserve what today we might think of as the provisioning of basic needs by placing the distribution of property under the heading of *distributive justice*. We might read Smith, then, as an unexpected source of a cosmopolitan defense of egalitarianism where human dignity and liberty require an amelioration of inequality. But Smith leaves us with a fundamental tension since his work is a key source for an alternative cosmopolitanism associated with liberal/libertarian political economy. Here, liberty and inequality are necessarily intertwined and liberty and equality irreconcilable. Indeed, humanity's flourishing depends on economic growth that requires abiding severe inequality, as we suggest in our reading of Smith in the previous chapter. How do we navigate the ambivalence bequeathed by Smith?

In the second and third sections, we show how these tensions play out in contemporary debates between egalitarians and liberals/libertarians. Global egalitarians, in this case, Pogge, provide seemingly compelling arguments about a global right to livelihood and our duties toward the poor. However compelling his account to the egalitarian faithful, Pogge inadequately confronts the most powerful counter-arguments presented by liberal champions of market society. Pogge fails to consider claims that redistribution may effectively disrupt capitalist production; that inequality—including extreme poverty—is acceptable to many if it is the product of a legitimate process; and that, even if it can be shown that the current distribution of wealth results from a fraudulent and violent history, better to side-step such issues since redistributive schemes violate liberty, threaten class war, and damage the social good of wealth production. Pogge recognizes that political forces are arrayed against his view and shifts step-by-step away from a distributive argument about economic rights toward *commutative* claims about historical injuries done to the Global South and prudential concerns that might motivate the affluent. Interestingly, it is the commutative claims of historical injury with which libertarians struggle most.

Liberal political-economic thought, in this case, Jan Naverson's global libertarianism and Friedrich Hayek's seminal defense of market order, highlight these objections, but they fail to address the powerful desires that Hayek admits drive egalitarian projects. Hayek and Naverson emphasize liberty over equality but work to reduce the tension between the two by limiting equality to equal treatment under the law. They acknowledge that legal equality necessarily produces radical differences in wealth and income since markets differentially value people's differences.[2] Hayek recognizes that most people in market society accept inequality only because they wrongly believe that differences in wealth reflect differences in merit. He worries that the legitimacy of capitalist society depends on this false belief. He thereby embraces cultivating a noble lie that must, in our view, suppress knowledge of the violent appropriations and injuries that Pogge introduces to support his arguments about redistribution. We see this suppression as key to understanding elite and popular resistance to redistributive policies.

In conclusion, we draw these strands together suggesting that the scandal of radical inequality proves remarkably resistant to challenge. Radical inequality serves as the site of a secularized theodicy in which liberal political economists preserve the goodness of capitalism by assigning responsibility for poverty to the poor and by alluding to the invisible hand behind the global division of labor. Liberal IR theory seems resigned to this scandal. It largely accepts competitively achieved hierarchy, and works, at least implicitly, to preserving a tight relationship between work and reward, preserve and dessert.

ADAM SMITH AND THE PARADOX OF JUSTICE

It is a peculiarly modern claim that everyone merits a "life free from need." So argues Samuel Fleischacker (2004, 2), though others have pointed in this direction (Himmelfarb 1984; Geremek 1994; Jones 2004). The belief, he says, dates no earlier than the 1750s and finds a potent source in Adam Smith's work, though we have suggested elsewhere, following Polanyi, that security of livelihood might be protected better in pre- or non-capitalist social forms (Inayatullah and Blaney 2004, chap. 5; Blaney and Inayatullah 2010).

Fleischacker (2004, 2) argues that, prior to Adam Smith, the more common view was that "certain kinds of people ought to live in need" because "they would not work otherwise," or because "their poverty" was deemed "part of a divine order." Getting to an egalitarian position requires accepting that individuals have rights because each is or has a "good" that "deserves respect" and each is due to a material share of products to protect the realization or flourishing of that good. It further requires believing that the distributive project is achievable (and not somehow self-contradictory) and that the responsibility of securing distribution falls to the state, not private organizations (Fleischacker 2004, 7). Though we might stop to ponder the presumed individualism and statism of this argument, the crux of it, Fleischacker points out, is the claim that everyone deserves a share.

The idea that everyone deserves a share remains subject to challenge in terms that Fleischacker (2004, 9–10) identifies as anti-modern or non-modern, though as we note below, they persist into the present: that poverty is given by nature and beyond redress by human efforts; that poverty is "punishment for a sin" that bars the poor from equality; that "material things" are irrelevant to living a good life and therefore the rich and poor can live equally well; that poverty is a "blessing" that garners a life superior to the rich; and that the poor are comfortable and well-situated in their poverty. We label these commitments, respectively, *naturalization, punishment, antimaterialism, romanticism*, and *fixed differences*. Though not properly modern in Fleischacker's account, we can find these commitments echoed in the Eurocentric biases (perhaps racism) of contemporary IR theory (see Hobson 2012; see also chapters 3 and 4 in this volume).

Other commitments—more properly modern and cosmopolitan, though often combined with the anti- or non-modern (see Connolly 2008)—block the full implementation of egalitarian projects. People will not commit to securing a share for everyone if they believe that poverty spurs work among the poor; that the poor's ability to live a good life depends less on offering the security of income and more on providing a pedagogy of manners and morals; and that, while in theory the poor might have a right to material goods, the importance of other values, such as liberty, overrides the recognition of such rights (Fleischacker 2004, 9–10). We may name these, respectively, *incentive provision, colonial pedagogy, and libertarianism*. The first two remain features of many efforts to help the poor.[3] Though often joined to defeat contemporary egalitarian projects, we believe the liberal political-economic commitments that privilege liberty are decisive for most thinkers.

We can sharpen our account of this ambivalence by looking closely at Smith. Smith makes the shift to egalitarianism possible by refusing to treat claims to property *simply* as "matters of commutative justice": the duty to do no injury to others or compensate those proportionately for the damages done to their property. No earlier thinker in the usual canon—"not Aristotle, not Aquinas, not Grotius, not Pufendorf, not Hutcheson, not William Blackstone or David Hume—put the justification of property rights under the heading of distributive justice" (Fleischacker 2004, 27). By joining property and distributive justice Smith justifiably renders the judgment that it is absurd and immoral that, in Fleischacker's words, some should live in luxury while "hard working people make do with virtually nothing" (2004, 39).[4] More strikingly, as we saw in chapter 1, Smith makes the condition of the poorest the gauge for measuring society's success. His policy prescriptions aim at producing steady growth that keeps workmen's wages above subsistence, allowing them luxuries that make life more convenient and bestow social respectability. In addition, he repudiates the idea that poverty serves as an incentive. Indeed, he turns the tables by arguing that well-paid workers are more energetic and effective (Smith 1976b, 77–83, 88, 91). If the problem of poverty meant enduring the presence of the lower classes, Smith generated a constructivist vision that society should, and could, eliminate poverty altogether (Fleischacker 2004, 64).

Smith begins by rejecting the naturalness of the existing distribution of goods. Fleischacker (2004, 65) quotes the *Wealth of Nations* to demonstrate how Smith "pricks the vanity" of those who condescend to the poor: "The differences in natural talents in different men is, in reality, much less than we are aware of" (Smith 1976b, 19). But his point is stronger than Fleischacker suggests; Smith locates the very origins of those differences in social institutions. In the very next line, Smith (1976b, 19, emphasis added) suggests that both differences and similarities—such as those between the porter and the philosopher—have their source in the division of labor: "and the very different genius which appears to distinguish men of different professions . . . is not upon many occasions so much the cause, as *the effect of the division of labor*." In ignoring this line, Fleischacker misses Smith's location of inequality *within* a social structure. Smith undercuts the belief that either the affluent or the poor deserve their position and his implicit structural analysis paves the way for Hegel's and Marx's more thorough social determinacy and the analysts of global capitalism we survey in chapters 4 and 5. This structural diagnosis of poverty leads Smith to recommend the public provision of education and entertainment so as to undo the social degradation of workers. Smith (1976b, 318) makes necessary the visible hand of the state to provide education in order to ameliorate social ills (see Blaney and Inayatullah 2010, 46–57; and chapter 1 here). After all, Smith's conception of what the poor deserves "helped bring about the peculiarly modern view that it is a duty, not an act of grace, for the state to alleviate or abolish poverty" (Fleischacker 2004, 68).

From chapter 1, we know that these themes do not dominate Smith's analysis. He was wary of the state's visible hand and he privileged liberty before other (however legitimate) ethical concerns. Fleischacker himself shows how this tension continues to bedevil our approach to the poor. In ways similar to Hayek as we shall see, Fleischacker (2004, 39) notes that Smith justifies inequalities of property by arguing that a "system of strict property rights . . . protects the liberty of everyone in society" and provides for the poor better than "under an egalitarian distribution of goods." Smith's competing impulses here provide an appreciation of the difficulties facing global egalitarian projects. More precisely, Fleischacker (2004, 39–40) locates a "paradox of justice" at the heart of Smith's market society. Smith stoically accepts that the poor must suffer while the social order protects the property of the wealthy. And, yet, he also makes the "suffering of the poor *the* problem of the justification of society."[5]

POGGE'S (AMBIVALENT) RIGHT TO A SHARE

Thomas Pogge's work exemplifies a relatively strong claim for global redistribution (Gauri and Sonderholm 2012). Not unlike Smith, Pogge (2002,
196–7) pleads for attention to vast global and national inequalities, especially
the conditions of those living in "extreme" or "severe poverty." But, unlike
Smith, he embraces strong public action, proposing a global resource dividend (GRD)—a tax on states' use or sale of resources—dedicated to assuring
that "all human beings can meet their own basic needs with dignity." For
Pogge, the GRD is the least we can do, given that the "global poor own an
inalienable stake in all limited natural resources." This stake does not give the
poor a vote in how states use resources; it serves only to guarantee a "share
of the economic value of the resource in question" to everyone (Pogge 2002,
196–7).

Pogge (2002, 2, 205) envisions a one percent tax on aggregate global
income, producing enough to "eradicate severe poverty worldwide" at an
insignificant cost. Notably, Pogge (2002, 198) sees ending extreme poverty
as but the most minimal notion of what it would mean to address global
inequalities, which in addition would include attention to the relative
deprivation that pervades all aspects of social and cultural life and leaves
many perpetually at the bottom of society (see Selwyn 2017, chapter 2, on
this point). But we must begin somewhere. Pogge proposes starting with a
surcharge of $2 per barrel of crude oil extracted worldwide, increasing the
cost of gas to consumers by only five cents per gallon. Envisioned this way,
the GRD infringes minimally on the sovereignty of states and consumers.
States may continue to do as they will with their resources, but not all revenue generated from the state's resources belongs to the state or the private
actors authorized to exploit them. Some would be treated as global common
property and go to what in effect is a world authority. It is possible, then, "to
eradicate world hunger within a few years" and "without major changes to
our global economic order" (Pogge 2002, 205–6). The idea that even minor
changes in the global economic order are politically feasible is itself quite
contentious, as our arguments in later chapters suggest and Pogge himself
acknowledges as we see below.

It is important for Pogge (2002, 207) that his scheme *not* be tied to gen-
erosity or aid (i.e., charity) which, in our view, he correctly ties to donor
arrogance, the fickleness or narrowness of donor's interests, the stigma
of handouts, and receiver dependence. Rather, the GRD dividend must be
claimed as a right. Two questions emerge immediately: what is the basis of
this right? And, given Pogge's compelling argument, what one sympathetic
critic (Gould 2007, 381) calls a "masterful" presentation, why are we not
already there?

Pogge addresses the first directly and the second implicitly in three steps. First, his tax on resources assumes that the world's population shares a single resource base from which the affluent have benefited and from which the poor have been excluded. We are sympathetic to this claim. However, this asymmetric benefit and exclusion need not be seen as a violation of rights, since it results from the distribution of property rights, as Smith understood. Indeed, it need not be seen as a problem at all, as we find below in libertarians Naverson and Hayek. Pogge asserts nonetheless that, though defenders of "capitalist institutions" support "unilateral appropriation of disproportionate shares of resources," they nevertheless accept that "all inhabitants of the earth ultimately have equal claims to its resources" (Pogge 2002, 202). We are unaware of any acceptance of this principle by defenders of capitalist institutions. Nor are we sure that such an acceptance constitutes a viable theoretical basis for a right to the revenue stream generated by the GRD.

This creates a harder case: Pogge must show that defenders of capitalism ignore or deny others' right to access planetary resources. But Pogge (2002, 202, emphasis added) admits that "billions are born into a world where all accessible resources are *already owned* by others." Because he does not directly question these rules of ownership, Pogge is caught. He wants a minimal and politically practicable proposal so he doesn't challenge unduly the rules of the global economy. But he laments that, under the current rules, the distribution of assets and educational and employment opportunities for these billions shaped by existing property rights will not move them beyond poverty, certainly relatively but also absolutely. Hence his sense of urgency.

Thus, and second, Pogge must challenge the legitimacy of the existing distribution of ownership in order to justify the GRD as a dividend. He claims that the unilateral appropriation of the affluent and the disproportionate immiseration of the poor result from a singular process—a violent common history:

> The present circumstances of the global poor are significantly shaped by a dramatic period of conquest and colonization, with severe oppression, enslavement, even genocide, through which the native institutions and cultures of four continents were destroyed or severely traumatized. (Pogge 2002, 203)

Despite this statement, Pogge neither affirms nor denies a "special restitutive responsibility" born by affluent descendants toward descendants of victims of such crimes under commutative justice. He excludes reparations because he aims for something more modest and less politically controversial—a reduction in or elimination of extreme inequality. We "must not," he says, "uphold extreme inequality" after a historical process in which "moral principles" and legal rules were "massively violated" (Pogge 2002, 203; 2007, 31).

Despite his aversion to a deeper critical engagement, we admire his thoughtfulness and polemical sweep. Most political theorists ply their trade while ignoring such a shared violent history (Bell 2019; Mills 2019). Even when this history of conquest, colonization, and enslavement is considered, thinkers argue (or assume) it has worked to benefit non-Western others. From Locke, Mill, and Kant (Jahn 2005, 2013) to Hegel and Marx (see Blaney and Inayatullah 2010, chapters 5 and 6) and to more recent IR theory (Hobson 2012; chapters 3 and 4 in this volume), thinkers presume that contact with Europeans makes Africans, Asians, and Amerindians better off—irrespective of its intensity and barbarity. Western governments and populations have been unwilling to accept current responsibility for this history of violent appropriation, asserting instead that continuing relations of structural domination remain beneficial to the poorest in the global population.

Pogge remains in a tight spot. If those who make and sustain the rules affirmed a right to equal planetary resources for all or recognized a "common and violent" history, proposing the GRD scheme would seem insufficient and probably unnecessary. Inversely, it is precise because the affluent and their theorists refuse such an admission that Pogge buffers his argument with how much can be done (eliminate extreme income poverty) with so little (an increase of pennies on the dollar for a few resources). Despite falling back to this apparently weaker demand, Pogge seems unable to address the key question: why should even these pennies be deployed to combat radical inequality?

Pogge's third argument aims for great political resonance. The affluent and the poor, he points out, shares common social institutions. Using terms we prefer, we might say that global markets, the global division of labor, and the inter-state system connect us all, as World Systems analysts and Dependency theorists have long argued. Indeed, our previous work (Inayatullah 1997; Inayatullah and Blaney 1995) and chapters 4 and 5 here rely on this theoretical lineage. Despite largely ignoring the political economy, Pogge (2002, 199) points out:

> The presence and relevance of shared institutions is shown by how dramatically we affect the circumstances of the global poor thorough investments, loans, trade, bribes, military aid, sex tourism, cultural exports, and much else.

He is aware that under capitalism "[the global poor's] very survival depends on our consumption choices, which may determine the price of their foodstuffs and their opportunities to find work." For Pogge (2002, 199), such connections mean "we are causally deeply involved in their misery."

This argumentative strategy seems plausible because, in the Western academy and popular thought, notions of "interdependence" and "globalization" are pervasive (Kamola 2019). Our connection to others and their life chances would seem hard to deny. The more difficult question is what this connection means. Answering it seems easy for Pogge: international interactions are premised on rules controlled by the "developed countries." These countries must take responsibility for their "foreseeable effects" (Pogge 2002, 200). He understands this requires the "good will" of the "rich and the mighty"—the EU and the United States in particular—though he stresses that the obligation is not to "help the needy," but rather to perform the commutative "duty to protect victims of any injustice to which we contribute" (Pogge 2002, 211).

There are at least three reasons to find such an argument wanting. First, we see Pogge once again backing away from a stronger claim, searching for a weaker appeal that might find more political traction.[6] Here he seems to abandon a right to distributive justice—the right to a share for which modern egalitarianism established the basis—in favor of a commutative claim that points to an injury done by the wealthy and dominant groups that they have a duty to ameliorate. But even this weaker position doesn't address two additional objections that might be derived from Smith. So, and second, the liberals/libertarians who claim Smith as a key ancestor argue to great political effect that outcomes produced by markets are the result of millions of human decisions, but of no one's design. Though we share common institutions, the most central of them, the global market, is *not* in any party's control. The spontaneous and impersonal operations of the market replace the capricious will of God, and nothing can be done about either. As long as we describe outcomes as produced by market competition, no injury can be claimed and there is no duty to respond.

Finally, those that make the rules feel no obligation to change the rules of markets for the benefit of the poor (see Hulme 2012; Bull 2012). Nor should they, economists following Adam Smith might say. While Pogge (2002, 201) notes that affluent countries have followed their interests in rigging the rules and "thereby have deprived the poorest populations of a fair share of global economic growth," he overlooks that following one's interest is capitalism's distinctive feature and therefore perfectly legitimate. Changing the rules of the game so that the poor are assured benefits from capitalism's competitive process is like pouring sand into the gas tank of an automobile—destructive of the engine regardless of the quantity of sand. Nor does it follow that, because some, namely, the affluent, have been able to take advantage of existing rules, they have thereby deprived others of their fair share—whatever that might mean. Rather, they produce an abundance that benefits many others. In this case, the commutative standard would suggest an appropriate reward to the affluent for the benefits they provide to the less well-off, however unintended, as Smith and Hume suggest in invisible hand imagery (see chapter 1).

Pogge senses such resistance, so he augments (or shifts once again) his appeal from distributive or commutative duty to "prudence"—what we might call long-term or enlightened self-interest. The interdependence may compel apart from any moral considerations: we "share" environmental problems; concerns over biological, chemical, and nuclear weapons; the impacts of flows like immigration, epidemics, terrorism, and the drug trade; and disruptions emerging from innovations in technology and culture. Thus, poverty may be expensive for the rich if it leads to environmental devastation, disruptive flows of people, religious and ideological fanaticism, and violent opposition movements (Pogge 2002, 213). Under such conditions, a market society requires intervention by the state (or some global authority like that attached to the GRD), in part because competing parties cannot trust each other or themselves to act in their long-term self-interest. The state creates a kind of temporal stretching toward the future so that a more benign alternative comes into being (see Fuller 2008, 456–7). Market failure necessitates the redress of poverty, though not because the poor have any right to a share.[7]

Pogge thus tries to conjure global redistributive institutions. But while his performance is alluring in some respects, we also note his sleight of hand. He avoids direct encounters with the strongest counter-arguments, while simultaneously falling back into positions that implicitly give up the egalitarian basis for redistribution as a way of accommodating the very objections he doesn't directly face. If you fail to convince with the claim of a right, shift to an injury. If you can't produce redistribution as a remediation of injury, you call on the self-interest of the affluent. Though Pogge means to intensify concern for the livelihood of the poor that Smith made available to modern political economists, he reproduces Smith's ambivalence.

NAVERSON, HAYEK, AND THE IMPERATIVES OF MARKET OUTCOMES

Jan Naverson (2003) provides a global libertarian counterpoint to Pogge's global egalitarianism. He suggests that our responsibilities to others— regardless of their distance from us and no matter how needy—are only negative; we mustn't obstruct others' opportunities but we have no further responsibility to them. Naverson (2003, 426–7) allows benevolent and prudential motives for aiding the needy, but these are voluntary acts, never to be coerced. Coercion is ruled out because, as Naverson (2004b, 309–12) argues, liberty outweighs other moral concerns. These un-coerced and therefore unguaranteed acts appear morally worthy but retain their status as a charity (Gauri and Sonderholm 2012, 200), precisely the target of Pogge's case. The only coercion allowed in Naversen's world involves action to defend commutative justice; we must avoid damage to others (Naversen 2003, 421), and, therefore, the only legitimate claims to transfers of property involve restitution for injuries committed.

We look to Friedrich Hayek's work to make clear what is at stake in such libertarian arguments. Though Hayek, like Naverson, allows no talk of a right to livelihood or a right to some level of income, both embrace a cosmopolitan vision of equality under the law—where laws apply to all regardless of rank.[8] The results of law-governed free interactions must be accepted whatever the consequences for the distribution of property and income. Hayek (1978, 85) makes crystal clear the privileging of liberty implied by this limited but universal notion of equality:

> Equality of the general rules of law and conduct . . . is the only kind of equality conducive to liberty and the only equality which we can secure without destroying liberty. Not only has liberty nothing to do with any other sort of equality, but it is even bound to produce inequality in many respects.

Indeed, as Hayek (1978, 85) continues, some "living more successfully than others" indicates the proper workings of liberty.

Hayek ties some "living more successfully" to bold claims about inequality: "it just is not true that all men are born equal." This "hallowed phrase" might be allowed "to express the idea that legally and morally all men ought to be treated alike," but only if "we free ourselves from the belief in *factual equality*" (Hayek 1978, 87, emphasis added). To think of "equality" as "factual equality" would, in Hayek's view, reduce everyone to sameness and make equality absurd. Naverson (2004b, 309–11) notes, similarly, that the diversity of human dispositions is irreducible, except by coercion. Who could embrace a world where everyone is coerced to be the same?

Treating everyone alike before the law requires us to accept that as individuals go on with their lives their differences will produce different levels of income and status: "Equality before the law and material equality are therefore not only different but are in conflict with each other; and we can achieve either the one or the other but not both at once." Redistributive schemes, Hayek fears, are forms of "discriminatory coercion" (injuries in commutative terms) imposed by the state to make people alike (Hayek 1978, 87). Such coercion violates the foundations of a free society. Pogge's GRD would appear as just such an injury to libertarians like Hayek and Naverson (2004b, 336–7).

Injury results because libertarians tightly link difference with factual inequality and, then, factual equality with sameness. That is, human differences lead to factual inequality so that the elimination of factual inequality also eliminates differences thus creating sameness in humans. Indeed, these equations constitute Hayek's persuasiveness (Miller 1976, 149). He turns our fears of coerced sameness into an unequivocal acceptance of the naturalness of some "living more successfully than others," even in the presence of extreme poverty.

But these equations and their anxieties seem too tightly fused, as Adam Smith noted, and it is dangerous to leave them unquestioned. As Miller (1976, 149) argues:

> The principle of equality does not demand that each person receive the same physical treatment, rather that each person should be treated in such a way that he achieves the same level of well-being as every other. Because people have varied needs and wants physical resources such as food, medicine, and education should not be assigned in equal quantities to each man, but in different proportions to different people, according to their peculiar characteristics. No serious egalitarian has thought otherwise.

If Miller is correct, then creating conditions that allow each person to achieve similar levels of well-being need not produce sameness. Rather, the blossoming of differences that accompanies liberty depends on a level of material well-being that affords such flourishing (Gould 2007; see also our discussion of Polanyi in chapter 6).

Destabilizing libertarian equations doesn't quite end the disagreement. Hayek assumes that most people accept factual inequality as normal and natural in a free society. We have seen how this assumption (at least in the case of the world's wealthiest citizens) often thwarts Pogge's even minimally egalitarian proposals. But Hayek harbors some doubts about the steadiness of popular views. He believes modern citizens can accept factual inequalities; what they cannot accept is inequality that results from reward not being tightly connected to merit. This disconnection violates the common but powerful myth that a free and just society produces a direct and positive relationship between merit and reward (Hayek 1978, 93; Simon 1974). Even Robert Nozick (1974, 151, 158), a libertarian committed to formal equality alone, points out that "People want their society to be and look just" and articulates a set of criteria for fairness: initial holdings of property must be acquired justly and any transfers of property must be conducted justly.[9] In this common moral intuition and with a commitment to these rules, we find support for Pogge's argument that a connected, violent history would justify the GRD and more, since violence severs the assumed connection of merit and outcomes. The inequality that results from coercion cannot be considered just.

Hayek (1978, 94) recognizes the power of merit as a claim that might lead to redistribution of resources and devotes great effort to counteract this sentiment. He assaults this idea directly, finding the desire for proportionality between merit and reward not only "indefensible" but a great danger to a free society. If people believe that merit and reward ought to be related, and then realize how actual life fails to match the ideal, they will be tempted to violate liberty by taking the property of some and giving it to others, as in Pogge's GRD. Hayek is right to be concerned. Habermas (1970, 122) suggests that the legitimacy of a depoliticized society, governed by a technocratic market rationality, is threatened by the inability "to link status assignment in an even subjectively convincing manner to the mechanism for the evaluation of individual achievement." And Pogge is perhaps right to appeal to this moral intuition of citizens to mobilize support for global redistributive efforts in response to a common history of fraud and violence.

But Hayek (1978, 94) remains bold in the face of his fellow citizens' moral intuitions about merit:

> in a free system it is neither desirable nor practicable that material rewards should be made generally to correspond to what men recognize as merit . . . the value which a person's capacities or services have for us and for which he is recompensed has little relation to anything we can call moral merit or deserts.

Though market society sustains no clear connection between merit and reward, it provides something more important to Hayek (1978, 94): It allows people to "enjoy advantages in proportion to the benefits which their fellows derive from their activities." Market processes, not some "higher power," assess merit (see also Naverson 2004a, 401–2).

Pogge appeals to this sort of "interdependence" of market outcomes to make either a commutative or prudential case for redistribution. But, for Hayek (1978, 97), any non-market assessment of what people are due requires an intrusive intimacy based on a "colossal presumption": "that we are able to judge in every individual instance how well people use their different opportunities and talents given to them and how meritorious their achievements are in the light of all the circumstances which make them possible." No human being has the knowledge to make such assessments. Nor, consistent with Smith, would Hayek be happy with developing extra-market institutions that would make such valuations. Hayek (1978, 98–9) argues that, instead of making "remuneration correspond to merit," we should accept and expose "how uncertain is the connection between value and merit." In a market society as we strive and compete, risking social and biological death, our fate depends on how nameless and faceless strangers assess what we can supply. If such assessments produce radical inequality for large segments of the population, we must stoically accept this as the price we pay to live in what Hayek sees as a free society. What Smith left as a paradox, Hayek "resolves" by short-circuiting claims for any sort of redistribution.

However, in another work, Hayek (1976, 74, emphasis added) admits that such a pill may be too bitter to swallow and too discouraging to those beginning their educational and working lives. He shies from his boldness, implicitly recognizing a dilemma within his own position. He acknowledges that a "market order" requires that "individuals *believe* that their well-being depends primarily on their own effects and decisions," however untrue this may be. Hayek expresses doubts that we should openly acknowledge this gap between merit and rewards, recommending instead that educational institutions continue to foster this misconception about market society. We wonder if fostering this misconception would raise but also require deflecting doubts about the role of merit in the existing global distribution of assets and opportunities by also suppressing knowledge of a connected history of violence, a theme we take up in later chapters. Such noble lies seem necessary to resolve the paradox of capitalist justice.

If Pogge and the cosmopolitan egalitarians fail to adequately address the potential incompatibility of liberty and equality, Hayek and the global libertarians like Naverson ignore that most people in modernity accept inequality *only* if they trust in the connection between merit and reward.[10] Egalitarians underestimate how the redistribution to alleviate radical poverty might be seen by many as coercion and theft, while libertarians are blind to how radical inequality threatens a sense of fairness and thereby the social order altogether. Either way, as we show in chapter 1, we arrive back at an unresolved tension or paradox in liberalism.

DENIAL, SECULARIZED THEODICY, AND DESIRE'S FLOW

Using the Lacanian language we often prefer, we identify such paradoxes as the "Real" of capitalism: that which is necessary to market society, which cannot be fully faced or must be denied, but which continues to fuel our anxieties about justice. Instead of a simple dilemma, we find ourselves confronted with scandals of extreme poverty and radical inequality that express the impossibilities of justice in a global market society. Our reading of Smith, Pogge, Naverson, and Hayek points to three responses to these scandals.

First, libertarians limit the application of egalitarianism to formal, legal equality and deny claims to distributive justice, however vast the inequality and suffering. The space Smith opens for distributive justice is barred. For Naverson, charity remains the only option.

Second, by emphasizing formal equality and legal procedures, libertarians, especially Nozick, make current inequalities susceptible to challenge on the basis of a history of subordination and violent expropriation. Hayek recognizes that the moral force of this challenge must be deflected in order to preserve his free society. Drawing on Hayek and Naverson, we identify two such deflections. On one side, modern citizens and theorists attribute these outcomes solely to competitive markets in which no actor is responsible for the outcomes, and the only sensible response is stoicism. On the other side, citizens and theories may ignore and deny the weight of a connected violent history, an issue we explore in chapters 4 and 5. In either case, inequality is attributed to the relative merits and faults of the competitors as a matter of faith.

Third, even where acknowledging a violent history would emphasize the scandal of radical global inequality, Smith and most modern economists, and some global ethicists like Naverson, respond with a kind of theodicy that claims social evils like poverty and inequality are only seemingly evil.[11] As with Christian and Muslim theodicies, an all-powerful Providence has ways of converting apparent evil to goodness—the complete knowledge of which is unavailable to mere mortals but accepted by the faithful.[12] Capitalism's defenders produce a "secular" theodicy by claiming that capitalism turns self-interest, acquisitiveness, envy, and greed—elements considered malevolent in most places and most times—into the public good. God is replaced by the "invisible hand," while libertarians and (most) economists secure the faith through paeans to liberty or pareto optimality (see Mankiw 2013 as an example). Even though we might be tempted to label global inequality and poverty as injustice, or explain it as a result of unjust processes, we are compelled to stick to the faith of the invisible hand since it leads us to the promised land of a wealthy global society. As Naverson (2004a, 405–6; 2004b, 346–7) notes, efforts to redress injustices are less effective—in the long run—than extending the wonders of the market.

In the face of these challenges, we follow Pogge and continue to defend a right to a share and insist on making the fact of a violent history or processes of domination central to discussions of injustice. However, we are more circumspect about the third point wherein the public good results from dismal motivations such as greed. With capitalism, we move from the *negation* and *suppression* of greed to its *valorization* and *celebration*. Greed's release permits desire's flow. This flow, to employ a Lacanian reading of Smith, Hegel, and Marx, is the prerequisite for creating global structures of wealth production and distribution. We don't mean to participate in "a hypocritical defense of the rich," but to acknowledge the "truth" that under capitalism the well-being of many depends on the actions of self-interested investors (Žižek 2009, 15), even as others are impoverished. However, desire's flow is also worrisome: Smith, Hegel, and Marx believe in the necessity of capitalism, but they also agonize over market civilization's flaws, like alienation, social dislocation, and radical social inequality (Blaney and Inayatullah 2010, chapters 2, 5, and 6). Only Marx saw something beyond capitalism, even if his vision remains opaque.

Despite such real worries, we think there is something powerful in the idea of liberating greed, self-interest, envy, and acquisitiveness from the shackles of old-time repression. Freud teaches us that what we repress comes back in an alternative form. Nightmares, disease, and death wishes serve as examples of the "return of the repressed." If greed cannot be eliminated, better to have a self-conscious relationship with greed that bypasses *repression* but also refuses *celebration*, on the way to a meaningful, if uneasy, accommodation with desire's flow. Though we might look askance at the shallowness and excess of many consumer choices, market society has allowed an expansion and diversification of needs that make possible multiple, meaningful modes of flourishing (Levine 1988, 1995; Levine and Rizvi 2005). Marx (1973, 158) similarly saw capitalism as making possible a rich, developed individuality that might be realized for all in a postcapitalist society.

Such a relationship circles back to where we started—to modern society's acceptance of its production of radical inequality and extreme poverty. On one side, we moderns refuse this relationship by denaturalizing poverty. Thanks perhaps to Adam Smith's (and others') constructivist polemics and structural orientation we can consider this social phenomenon as susceptible to eradication. On the other side, the very same Smith produces arguments that truncate that eradication: the spontaneous operations of the global market disallow the kind of viable human interventions that would affect radical reductions in poverty and inequality; and, in any case, efforts in this direction violate liberty while also decreasing the overall accumulation of wealth. The result is that only in modern times do we find a "necro-economics"—the recognition that a thoroughly human-created system continues to produce extreme poverty (see Montag 2005; Blaney and Inayatullah 2010, chaps. 3 and 6; Ozandu 2013). In its own perverse manner, capitalism has internalized a role for the poor. Biological and social death demonstrates what happens when individuals are unable to "compete" in a market society. Such deaths are the sacrifice necessary for the world's affluent to live in a free and prosperous global society.

Why is this scandal of poverty and inequality given a relatively short shrift in IR theory? We believe our short forays into the work of Pogge, Naverson, Hayek, and Smith may be useful. From Naverson and Hayek we take the idea that the social and biological death of the poor is the price of some living in free and wealthy societies. If this exchange is the basis of our current lives, then we need to find the courage to acknowledge what we usually repress. Despite Fleischacker's historically progressive account, we can ask if we have moved much from believing that poverty is natural or a punishment for sin, that material things matter little, or that without necro-economic threats the poor will only fall into self-medicating idleness. Maybe, like Pogge, who withdraws to weaker stances in the face of liberal objections to egalitarian projects, we become resigned to radical inequality. Or, perhaps, despite our pious reverence for the equality of human beings, we retain certain non- or pre-modern commitments alongside our surrender to the invisible hand.

Such othering of the poor points to a scar deep in the heart of our theoretical consciousness—an element, which Fleischacker, as we pointed out, misses in Adam Smith's analysis. The theoretical revolution Smith catalyzes but fails to realize is his social determinacy—that the differences between people are more the effect than the cause of the division of labor. He suggests that specific characteristics of "units" are the result of their location within the social system. Smith's implicit social determinacy rejects the idea that autonomous individual efforts or merit explain differentials in wealth and poverty. The poor are not alien to others; they are simply fellow earthlings in a different location. There but for the grace of the division of labor go we. Perhaps a fear of the consequences of *this* knowledge pushes us to other the poor. That temptation to other the poor and the possibilities for embracing a social determinacy that brings to light our connection to poverty and suffering are explored more fully in later chapters.

Chapter 3

Liberal IPE as Colonial Science

John Hobson (2012, chap. 9) characterizes the work of contemporary liberal scholars in IPE as subliminally paternalistic and Eurocentric. His prime example is Robert Keohane's *After Hegemony* (1984). Just as in the more openly Eurocentric liberalism of the late- nineteenth and early twentieth century, liberal IPE locates agency in the West—a West that promotes open markets and rules of rational cooperation as parts of a civilizing mission. However, in contrast with earlier periods, this message is delivered only implicitly. The Eurocentric narrative is, in Hobson's (2012, 214) terms, "sublimated rather than exorcised." Hobson's indictment of late- twentieth century liberal IPE is compelling—his documentation careful and the parallels precise. But we are left to wonder how Eurocentrism became sublimated. Hobson (2012, 185) points us to a "significant epistemic shift" that espouses "positivist principles" and prescribes "value neutrality." Though he points us in the right direction, we believe he under-theorizes the sublimation at work. Nor does he capture how Eurocentrism lurks symptomatically in liberal IPE.

We trace liberal IPE's sublimated Eurocentrism to its roots in neoclassical economics. IPE, as Benjamin Cohen (2008, 1, 17–21) tells us, grows out of a bridging of the "gap" between political science and economics in the 1970s, though he locates precursors in the classical political economy tradition. The relative decline of U.S. economic clout and growing international economic interdependence served as the immediate catalyst for renewed interest in political economy (Cohen 2008, 21–4). For Cohen (2008, 24–36), Robert Keohane looms large in the founding of this interdisciplinary space, though Robert Gilpin and Stephen Krasner also merit mention. Though economists were relatively minor players in the emergence of IPE, neoclassical economics offered an appealing model of scientific practice for IPE (see Cohen 2010, 887–8; 2008, 41–2), with its "rigorous" specification of actor choice

and constraint—a bargaining space, in which actors, pursuing their preferences with given endowments, reach a determinant outcome understood as an
equilibrium point (Gilpin 2001, 53; Keohane 1989, 103–4). At the same time,
practitioners of IPE feel uncomfortable with the static character of the neoclassical framework (see Gilpin 2001, 75–6; Keohane 1989, 114). IPE aspires
to a dynamic account, vying for the theory that explains the origins of international institutions and change across time. In liberal IPE, dynamic processes
tend to be incorporated as evolutionary forces, using unit-level demands for
greater efficiency or reducing market imperfections to explain collective and
changing outcomes (as in Keohane 1989, chap. 5). Adopting the framework
of microeconomics allows IPE to associate itself with a "clearly . . . more
rigorous and theoretically advanced field of study" (Gilpin 2001, 75), but
replicating economics burdens IPE with a static method.[1] Their solution is to
meld an equilibrium analysis with an evolutionary scheme.

These two moments of a liberal IPE—an equilibrium model that provides
determinant outcomes but within an evolutionary frame—work together to
produce the sublimated Eurocentrism that Hobson identifies. On the one hand,
IPE explicitly embraces a universalized notion of rational actors, abstracted
from any social relations. All actors appear formally the same—as autonomous
agents, though differentiated by endowments of fungible power. Within liberal
IPE, this assumption of formal equality distinguishes the contemporary international system from the imperial and colonial relations of an earlier era. On
the other hand, the institutional structures of the international system depend
on hegemony (in IPE parlance) and therefore on the inequality of actors. The
possibility of achieving institutional bargains at any particular point in time
requires a leading actor with a concentration of resources adequate to underwrite a regime. A superior actor enforces rules and maintains them across time.
Though the need for a hegemonic actor appears to be derived in the abstract—
as an implication of a theory of bargaining among independent actors who
would gain by cooperation—the accompanying historical, perhaps evolutionary, story assumes, as Hobson notes, the rightful place of Western countries
exercising leadership and providing collective goods. Absented in this story are
relations of social domination that may lead to the sacrifice of some peoples.

Rather than an idiosyncratic feature of liberal IPE, we believe this sublimated Eurocentrism is deeply rooted in the neoclassical economics on which
IPE draws. We turn to the work of Alfred Marshall to help illuminate this
claim.[2] We begin with Marshall because, alongside W. Stanley Jevons, Léon
Walras, and Carl Menger, he invents the familiar apparatus of neoclassical
economics: a theory of value based on the intensity of subjective desire, modeled by the demand curve, which when conjoined with a supply schedule,
produces a market-clearing equilibrium price, achieved in a timeless space.
Equilibrium analysis depends on a "mechanistic metaphor" that Marshall

elaborates in Books III and V of *Principles of Economics* (2009 [1920; 1890]; hereafter cited as *P*).[3] Yet Marshall harbored doubts about the sufficiency of this mechanical analytical edifice. He believed that an economics deploying a biological metaphor can do more: it can explain the emergence of the modern economic actor with modern needs; it can constitute the normal situation on which rigorous economic science depends; and, it can capture the broader evolutionary processes of material and moral progress. In both *Principles* (1890) and, more fully, in *Industry and Trade* (1919), Marshall departs from the abstracted formulations of the microeconomic model. Here, he applies the biological metaphor to the history of material progress and civilizational advance, including the extinction of some peoples and races within world-historical competitive processes. Europe, principally England, and then, by extension, the United States, plays the leading role in civilizational advance. Like liberal IPE, Marshall tries to mix these conflicting metaphors—the mechanical and the biological—so as to produce a universalistic but also an explicitly colonial science. His work sheds light on contemporary IPE's own, though sublimated, Eurocentrism.

IPE, MIXING METAPHORS, AND EVOLUTIONARY MODELS

IPE adopts both of Marshall's metaphors, usually explicitly. It desires the rigor and quantitative determinacy it associates with the application of economics' mechanical apparatus. And it wants a dynamic theory that it hopes to reconcile with the mechanical model of individual decision-making. As we shall see at the close of this chapter, this melding produces similar results: a colonial science where abstract actors and static mechanisms are linked to an evolutionary process in which the interdependence of actors is translated into relations of domination and subordination, however sublimated in the narrative.

We find James Caporaso's (1989) appraisal of IPE's deployment of microeconomic principles particularly insightful. He begins with what he takes as a common- sense observation: our "daily environment" sets limits "within which we act" (1989, 136). Framing the human situation as an allocation problem, it seems natural for Caporaso (1989, 139–40) that IPE would adopt the neoclassical framework. In this framework, "basic behavioral units are joined in a market space, where bargains are struck," and, "given an initial endowment, . . . voluntary transactions will take place among individuals to the extent that they improve the well-being of each individual and, . . . thereby, improve the well-being of the group," an invisible hand move, as described in the previous two chapters.

But Caporaso (1989, 141–2) rightly worries that neoclassical economists give a thin description of the institutions that structure the limits and constraints faced by individual units. He observes that this "atemporal" model treats institutions and structures as "fundamental givens" placed beyond explanation, even as economists require these "noneconomic primitives" to give closure to the behavioral system (Caporaso 1989, 142, 147). IPE compensates for the limits of neo-classical economics, Caporaso (1989, 143) suggests, by placing institutions or "regimes" nearer the center of their work. Regimes set rules and norms that structure behavioral interactions, allowing states, here referencing Keohane and Nye (1989, 19), to manage but also to reshape relations of interdependence. The parallel to markets is precise. As Krasner (1983, 6–7, 11) explains, the "market" serves as "a powerful metaphor for many arguments . . . in international relations." The assumption of a "world of atomized, self-seeking egoistic individuals" (perhaps states) drives claims that international institutions "derive from voluntary agreements among juridically equal actors." A minimally governed, market-like space of IR provides "incentives for cooperation," including attempts by egoistic units to overcome "market failures." For Keohane (1989, 108–10), for example, imperfections in the market-like spaces of IR make overcoming market failure the central dynamic of institution creation and change, so that international economic institutions appear as the result of a cumulative process of reducing the transaction costs that inhibit welfare gains from voluntary exchange.

But providing adequate accounts of institutional evolution requires incorporating a range of "political, social and cultural variables," not reducible to simple market models that assume the equality of actors (Caporaso 1989, 147). One key additional factor is power, the presence of asymmetrical "bargaining or relative capabilities" that shape outcomes. Relative capabilities are central, because, as Caporaso (1989, 150–1) notes, "progressive institutions [that] could benefit society as a whole" depend on "privileged groups" committing their superior resources to such regimes. Without such action by privileged groups, a market process falls far short of pareto optimality, where the whole gains without loss to any actor. Caporaso (1989, 144–6) identifies the creation of rules governing property rights and exchange as key to these regimes since rules promote optimal market performance by reducing uncertainty and transaction costs. In these steps, Caporaso has sketched the features of hegemonic stability theory.

Still, Caporaso (1989, 148–9, 153) remains concerned that liberal IPE falls short of fully capturing the dynamic of institutional emergence and change. Conceiving of institutions as chosen—as reflecting the preferences of actors in a fixed or atemporal market-like bargaining situation—seems implausible. Individual actors do not face "a menu of alternative institutional arrangements," but are embedded in a set of institutions *already in place*, that shape choices and therefore cannot be understood simply as an outcome of choice limited only by one's given endowments. In other words, micro-economic explanations of institutions assume a state of nature, where institutions emerge from choices made within an institutionally empty context (Inayatullah and Rupert 1994, 62–5). Scholars might model institutional change as a sequence of choice situations, but this construction not only is farfetched, as Caporaso indicates, but also it is theoretically incoherent because it claims dynamic properties for an intrinsically static model.

This problem might be finessed, Caporaso (1989, 148–50) explains, by adopting, like Marshall as we shall see, a biological metaphor, an evolutionary perspective that assumes institutions and structures are "adaptive outcomes" produced by "selection pressure" that leads over time to a "fit between individual and institutional environment." Here, institutions are treated as "functional" or "adaptive (efficient)" and attributed to a "choice process that is never observed," and, we might add, could never be. The actual processes or histories of movement between institutions are replaced by the assumption that the functional optimality of institutions is a result of a sequence of atemporal allocative choice situations. An intrinsically static "idea of efficiency . . . provides the central mechanism by which economic history acquires its telos, its direction," its human propulsion to change and progress, as Marshall also suggests. "Without such a dynamic, Caporaso stresses, "history would amount to a series of hapless founderings, with no resultant goal or directional drift." Here, conscious choice plays a secondary role to the unconscious but "differential reinforcements for particular institutions" that "drift toward more efficient institutional outcomes." And in an impressive conclusion, Caporaso suggests that, in this move, "Hegel's world spirit is replaced by neoclassical institutional optimizers equating political costs and benefits at the margin." Marshall, as we shall see, also regards his evolutionary scheme as giving specific content to Hegel's philosophical history.

Though Caporaso (1989, 152–5) expresses some discomfort with the functionalist telos of evolutionary models, he nevertheless embraces social evolutionary thought because it potentially compensates for deficiencies in atemporal microeconomic models. He sees evolutionary thinking moving us to recognize the variability of human sociality, so that we may see "economic man" as "a historical product." It emphasizes "a process of winnowing that is at best partly *ex ante* rational, and is quite possibly governed by accident and difficult-to-reverse path dependencies." Finally, evolutionary thought stresses group survival, without ignoring the potential costs to individuals. There may be species or societal advances but no pareto optimality since some individuals adapt successfully and others don't. Here, Caporaso seems clear-eyed about the implications of this turn to evolutionary models: it is not only institutions that are competitively winnowed: some individuals and groups die from their mal-adaption.

Based on this account, we can isolate three elements at play in liberal IPE. (1) It begins with microeconomics as the foundation, but (2) it ties this atemporal framework to an evolutionary dynamic that (3) requires a competitive winnowing—a non-optimal situation in which the advances by the whole involves sacrificing some individuals and groups in the process. These formulations are not idiosyncratic to IPE (see also Wade 2011, 101–2). They are prefigured by Marshall's evolutional economics and liberal IPE's emulation of economics structures its subliminal Eurocentrism.

MARSHALL AND THE TIMELESS TIME OF NEOCLASSICAL ECONOMICS

In *Principles* (1890), Marshall develops the interplay of supply and demand in equilibrium as the familiar building block of today's economics textbook. An "economic science" begins with such regularities—"manifestations of nature which occur most frequently, and are so orderly that they can be closely watched and narrowly studied" (*P*, xii). Since nature does nothing in jumps, Marshall (*P*, xii, xiv) reminds us, economics can deploy "those methods of the science of small increments (commonly called the differential calculus) to which man owes directly or indirectly the greater part of the control that he has obtained in recent times over physical nature." He recognizes that economics as a science of small increments is "'statical' rather than 'dynamical'," deploying "mechanical analogies." To make any initial headway, he asserts, economists must clear the social field of the "numerous" and unwieldy "forces" at play that had been central for earlier political economists. "Thus," he explains (*P*, xiii), "we reduce to inaction all other forces by the phrase 'other things being equal'." Though Marshall recognizes and exceeds the limits of this static approach, it is the static elements of his thought that define his legacy for most economists (Hart 2012, 6–7; Hodgson 1993, chap. 7).

To uncover "economic laws," even if only as general "tendencies," Marshall (*P*, 27) turns to those human motives which "can be measured by price." It is a law-like behavior organized around these motives that bring social science close to the physical sciences. This emphasis on price shifts the focus of economics to demand and consumption from its earlier excessive emphasis on the cost of production (*P*, 70–1). While Marshall's account of human wants might frustrate today's economist, with his emphasis on the growth of human "activities," more than fixed preferences, and his stress on social distinction, more than isolated consumption acts (*P*, 73–7), he soon turns to the construction of the backward-bending demand curve (*P*, 79–85). A good has utility because individuals desire it. Individuals make decisions based on the good's "marginal utility"—"whether it is worth his while to incur the outlay required to obtain it"—a desire that naturally "diminishes with every increase in the amount he already has." This reasoning produces an individual's demand curve for a particular good, which Marshall displays in a footnote on p. 81, a representation extended to society's demand curve representing an aggregation of all individuals' demand for a particular good in a footnote on p. 83. Marshall recognizes that the problem of constructing these curves is treating human "character or tastes" as fixed or, as he says, "allowing" no "time for any change in his character."

Though Marshall develops a complicated evolutionary account of human beings and industrial organization in *Principles*, to which we turn below, he assumes a fixed supply curve in his account of the "General Relations of Demand, Supply, and Value." In parallel to his discussion of demand, he emphasizes the complex "forces of life and decay" of a people and of industry, but suggests that preparing for a more "advanced study" of these dynamics requires that we "first look at a simpler balancing of forces which corresponds rather to the mechanical equilibrium of a stone hanging by an elastic string" (*P*, 269), a model derived from physics, as Mirowski (1984) famously documents. The complications of the time required for "temporary" balances to form (*P*, 274–5) are set aside for a model of "normal values"—a "stable equilibrium" represented by the conventional picture of intersecting supply and demand curves (*P*, 281–8). Again, Marshall (*P*, 289) stresses that identifying an equilibrium price requires the assumption that a process unfolding in time can be modeled as static: "It is the average value which economic forces would bring about if the general conditions of life were stationary for a run of a time long enough to enable them all to work out their full effect." The tension screams out at us: the "average" depends on stationary conditions but only emerges with changes over time.

It is precisely Marshall's mechanical model that has been carried forward in neo-classical economics, but without his qualifications. As Walsh and Gram (1980, 404–5) explain, neoclassical economics centers on a "static allocation model." An equilibrium price is produced as a "balance of forces affecting supply and demand," forces which are treated as given and external to the model. The supply of goods is set as a parameter, not explained by processes of production, and preferences and endowments are fixed. Though neoclassical economists need a process that leads the market to a market-clearing price, the resort is usually to a fictive auctioneer, who matches the supply and demand of all market participants, *prior* to any actual transactions (Walsh and Gram 1980, 407). This result depends on imagining "competition" as the structure of a bargaining space with many actors, not as an active process where bargains are struck in actual time/space (McNulty 1967, 397–8). Similarly, Weeks (2012, 41–2) argues the market models "exhibit their equilibrating tendency in a single instantaneous moment or not at all." The long run can be incorporated only logically—as a static space extended notionally—and never chronologically as an actual history. Walsh and Gram (1980, 408–9) give this point a sharper edge. Neoclassical economists can do little more than "generalize" their framework "to a finite (or infinite) number of timeless allocations," where supposed "multiperiod" allocations are "defined as a sequence of timeless allocations."

Institutions receive like treatment. The particular institutions that give market processes life and a particular shape might be incorporated as constraints or the specific incentives faced by actors at a particular point, but this slightly less parsimonious account still requires that the constraints and incentives be given— fixed as a timeless bargaining space. Institutions might be thought to shape individual preferences, but this is understood only awkwardly as "movements to and fro in [a timeless] space," as Joan Robinson (1980, xi) suggests. Complex processes of socialization require a duration that escapes the analytical tools of neoclassical economics. If institutions change, this must be the result of the new parameters fixed once again in a timeless space. Initial endowments may be different and may therefore produce a different institutional outcome, but these are simply given by the model, without regard to the earlier processes of interaction that produced them. The difficulty that moments in space and time remain unconnected—exactly what worries both Caporaso and Marshall—seems obvious. But this hardly deters those dedicated to treating market outcomes and institutions *as if* they are the result of a series of optimizing decisions by isolated actors in discrete bargaining contexts—all other things being equal.

Marshall's Biological Metaphor

Marshall himself stresses the limits of mechanistic analogies for understanding economic processes. In a letter to a student in 1906, Marshall (quoted in Hart 2012, 30) suggests that mathematical theorems are unlikely to be good economics. In his inaugural lecture, he suggests that the appeal to "forces" that imply "mechanical and regular action" are insufficient to appreciate the way industry and human beings themselves change (Marshall 1885). Somewhat later, after the first publication of *Principles* (1890), Marshall (1898, 44) responded to critics of the evolutionary elements in the text that "economic problems are not mechanical, but concerned with organic life and growth."

Marshall provides similarly clear, though complicated, guidance for readers at the outset of *Principles*. The scientific power of economics, Marshall insists more than once, stems less from abstract models and more from its focus on "mankind as they live and move and think in the ordinary business of life" (*P*, 12). Since "man's character has been moulded by his everyday work, and the material resources which he thereby procures" (*P*, 1), the "business by which a person earns his livelihood" serves as one of the "great forming agencies of the world's history." Here, Marshall embraces a sociological starting point: with individuals whose character is forged in their work, establishing the conscious and unconscious habits that give economic life a stability, or what Marshall calls "normal conditions" (*P*, xi).

Such normal conditions are not simply given as in the axiomatic structure of the economic theory. Writing in 1920, Marshall (*P*, xi) suggests "normal conditions" obtain only "in the Western World and in Japan," being of "recent date" and realized only via a process of gradual evolution. Therefore, somewhat later in the text (*P*, 33, emphasis added), Marshall notes that a science "greedy of facts" often hits a wall because "the economic conditions of early times are *wholly unlike* those of free enterprise, of general education, of true democracy, of steam, of the cheap press and the telegraph." For economists, Marshall (*P*, xiii) then suggests, the real "key-note is that of dynamics rather than statics." The "Mecca of the economist lies" in the complexities of "economic biology" (*P*, xii), so that "fragmentary statical hypotheses are used as temporary auxiliaries to dynamical—or rather biological—conceptions" (*P*, xiii). This is crucial because Marshall sees human "patterns of conduct and character as flows, not as stocks" (Reisman 1987, 101). As an example, Marshall (*P*, 73–6) gives an account of the transformation of needs that occurs as humans move from the "brute and the savage" to the modern. While the savage's "appetite is limited by nature"; "man rises in civilization" only in conjunction with expanding needs "to gratify the desires of hospitality and display" that arise with social distinctions.

But Marshall's example provides something less than a fully dynamic account. Like Adam Smith, who he often follows, Marshall leaves us with something closer to comparative statics, where the distinction between the savage and the modern is less a theory of development and more a comparison of two contrasting social forms (see Levine 1977, chap. 2). Here, Marshall seems to practice a kind of "discrete dynamics," in which events that are static and partial are joined together so that they appear dynamic and whole. A close look at this kind of social theorizing reveals gaps or a vacuum where a process should be (Inayatullah 2003, 61), a theme we return to in chapters 4 and 5.

THE SURVIVAL OF THE FITTEST IN MARSHALL'S DEVELOPMENTAL TIME

"The main concern of economics" Marshall prominently announces in the 1920 preface to *Principles*, "is with human beings who are impelled, for *good and evil*, to *change and progress*" (*P*, xiii, emphasis added). Unsurprisingly, then, Marshall not only credits authors like Antoine Cournot and Johann von Thünen, who shaped his understanding of the role of "increments of quantities" in creating "stable equilibrium," but also highlights the influence of Herbert Spencer in suggesting the importance of the biological analogy and Hegel for his philosophical history (see Hart 2012, 17–28). Marshall's mention of Herbert Spencer seems key since Spencer likewise serves as an important backdrop to Hobson's (2010) account of nineteenth and twentieth century Eurocentric and racialist international theory. Bell (2007; 2016, chap. 10) similarly identifies Spencer's analogy between biological and social evolution as a predominant intellectual assumption for late-Victorian and early twentieth-century middle-class opinion, much of which Marshall shares (Reisman 1987, chapter 6).

But there is something more at stake than a contextual reading. Marshall's developmental time negotiates universality and difference, equality and inferiority, in a way that we, following Todorov (1984) and Nandy (1983), believe is paradigmatic of modern thinkers' understanding of non-Europeans. The non-European other might be thought of as equal, but only to the extent that they could be seen as the same as Europeans, as with Japan in Marshall's assessment, or as the child-like "brute" or "savage," who might be brought into European adulthood. This framing is egocentric or ethnocentric perspective precisely because it is indifferent to variations in forms of life among people. This might seem preferable to emphasizing the utter difference of non-Europeans, which readily translates into strong claims of inferiority, including placing certain non-European others below the threshold of humanity. However, as both Todorov and Nandy make clear, it is the joint figures of equality/sameness and difference/inferiority that together structure the terrain of colonial ideology and practice, a terrain which swings between genocide and enslavement, on one side, and colonial assimilation and tutelage, more consistent with Marshall's views, on the other (see also Inayatullah and Blaney 2004; Blaney and Inayatullah 2010).

Neoclassical economics occupies this same terrain. By axiom, economists offer a "fixed" and "homogenous" picture of human beings as "equally competent"—a kind of "analytical egalitarianism" (Peart and Levy 2003, 283–4; 2007, 123; 2008, 1) modeled in the timeless space of market transactions. On this basis, Peart and Levy treat modern economics as intrinsically neutral in relation to culture or race and insulate proper economics from charges of complicity in slavery, racism, or colonialism. In their telling, racial or cultural claims that are used to justify conquest, colonization, and exploitation can only originate outside of economic thought properly understood, allowing modern economics to claim an anticolonial and antiracist heritage. This is the moment of sublimation.

Nevertheless, Levy and Peart's efforts to insulate contemporary economists from the racial themes of colonial ideology fall prey to the other side of Todorov's joint figure. Nomothetic laws may abstract from personal names and specific times, but culture and history are kept at bay only by invoking axioms about the economic actor and ceteris paribus conditions. When faced with making sense of systematic inequalities in economic outcomes, for instance, economists often feel the need to introduce additional factors, including the varying traits of the units, often invoking, if not by name, cultural, civilizational, and racial differences (Loury 2007; Darity and Mason 2007, 196; Mankiw 2013; see chapter 4 in this volume). Here, the universal trait, axiomatically assumed, appears as a variable and something that must be achieved or perhaps cultivated with the assistance of the more advanced, usually European or upper class, actors and countries (Escobar 1995; Ferguson 1994). By tightly linking homogeneity/equality, economists and other social thinkers ignore the connection of claims of human universality to colonial projects in which difference is ignored or translated as a failure to fully exhibit or develop these universal traits. If colonial anthropology stresses radical differences, contemporary economics highlights a notion of equality so tied to the homogeneity that difference is repressed. The difference can reappear only as tied to the opposite side of the figure—as inequality. Since economics fails to inculcate recognition of both difference and similarity simultaneously, the sublimated Eurocentrism bubbles to the surface.

Marshall similarly negotiates difference/sameness in relation to an understanding of a *normal* man: the axiomatic figure of economic models that emerges historically, but only, initially, in the West. Though Marshall means to suggest that others may develop toward the normal, this developmental story requires, as we shall see, that some are sacrificed as part of evolutionary advance and others provide leadership that necessarily involves colonial tutelage. He introduces this broad evolutionary story in *Principles*, but he claims *Industry and Trade* best illustrates the application of economic biology (*P*, xi, xii). Here, Marshall's economics becomes explicitly a colonial science.

First, the broad story. Marshall begins Book IV of *Principles* by claiming to combine Adam Smith's account of the division of labor and Spencer's biological analogy to understand human progress. Marshall (*P*, 200) asserts, accurately we believe, that Smith associates advances in division of labor with larger populations able to thrive on a limited territory. But, notably and less accurately, Marshall has Smith claim that "the pressure of population on the means of subsistence tends to weed out those races who through want of organization or for any other cause are unable to turn to the best account the advantages of the place in which they live." In this, Smith is said to foreshadow the insights of Malthus, Darwin, and Spencer on the role of the struggle to survive in promoting the "development of the organism, whether social or physical."

The implication that some races may not survive seems obscured where Marshall (*P*, 200–1) almost immediately thereafter claims that organismic development "involves an increasing subdivision of functions between its separate parts on the one hand, and on the other a more intimate connection between them. Each part gets to be less and less self-sufficient, to depend for its wellbeing more and more on other parts." Likewise the social organism: the "industrial organism" accordingly develops by "differentiation"—"of specialized skill, knowledge, and machinery"—and "integration" or a "growing intimacy and firmness of the separate parts" via improved communications and transportation (*P*, 201). The part and wholes together reproduce the system, as in Smith's division of labor, where the individuals connected by mutual neediness in the market all *seem* to survive.[4]

Marshall recognizes that the image of a starker evolutionary competition might be greeted with shock by some liberal opinion. He hopes the "hard truth" suggested by the "law of the survival of the fittest" might be "softened down" by his theory that those races, whose members exercise cooperation and behave altruistically "are not only the most likely to flourish for the time but most likely to rear a large number of descendants who inherit their beneficial habits" (*P*, 201–2). For Marshall, descendants inherit these cooperative habits by passing on culture, but also via heredity, as in Lamarckian views of evolution that Marshall, like many late-Victorians, including Spencer, favored (Hart 2012, 63–70; see Hobson 2012 and Bell 2016). He argues that any species, no matter how "vigorous in its growth," would not flourish long without a strong measure of "family and race duty." In their "ruder stages," humans render services to others by "hereditary habit and unreasoning impulse," but soon this instinct is supplanted by "deliberate, and therefore moral, self-sacrifice." These moral precepts are refined over time and reinforced by their adaptive success since the "races in which these qualities are the most highly developed are sure, other things being equal, to be stronger than others in war and in contests with famine and disease, and ultimately to prevail." Races who fail to develop altruistic habits perhaps deserve their fate in the evolutionary competition. Linking this struggle directly to economic life, Marshall suggests that individual and group character advances steadily, though never swiftly, under the pressure of competition in the "everyday business of life." The invisible hand operates for Marshall, then, not merely to produce a narrowly conceived collective good—a social optimum at a particular point in time—as in most contemporary accounts. Rather, economic evolution involves a broader process of interconnected material and moral advances that includes genocide and ethnocide as central moments. Some have a world-historical role and others fall prey to the slaughter bench of history. Marshall doesn't use these terms, but the resonance of Hegel's philosophy of history is clear (Collini, Winch, and Burrow 1983, 321, 326–31; Groenewegen 1990; Cook 2009).

As in Hobson's account of liberal IPE, it is the leading countries and classes that play a civilizing role for the backward. Rather than name genocide, liberal theorists try to exculpate Western culture by emphasizing its pedagogical imperative, as we suggested in our reading of the Scottish Enlightenment thinkers in chapter 1. Marshall too shifts our attention, in his last work, *Industry and Trade* (Marshall n.d. [1919]: hereafter cited as *IT* and volume number), to the leading role some industries and nations play in general civilizational advance. The processes at work—the extension of markets, new industries, increasing application of science—all promote continued advance in the previously developed, or "old countries" as Marshall calls them, and lead the "new countries" to "quickly fall into line with the old" (*IT* I, 5). As he notes, "even stagnant peoples gradually modify their habits and their industrial technique," lest, apparently, they die out. Key to this is the triumph of "reason" over "tradition," so that the past is displaced as a "guide for the present" by the possibilities shown by "progressive peoples" (*IT* I, 7–9). Partly we find a growing capacity of the individual to "sacrifice ease" in the present in order to gain more in the future both for himself and "to secure a future provision for his family" (*P*, 566). Paralleling his earlier claims about the adaptability of a duty to the whole for both individuals and collectives, Marshall sees humans becoming gradually "less selfish" and this "economic chivalry," as he sometimes calls it, begins to extend beyond the family: "there are already faint signs of a brighter time to come, in which there will be a general willingness to work and save in order to increase the stores of public wealth and of public opportunities for leading a higher life" (*P*, 566, 599; see also *IT* I, 6–8).

Marshall's account of the industrial and moral advance of humanity makes clear that an advanced country's industrial capacity is never a product simply of its own efforts; it always assumes the mantle of industrial leadership by building on earlier efforts (*IT* I, 6.28–9). Yet, national traits remain critical to Marshall's story of England's leading role. While not discounting natural endowments (and tropical climates appear an insuperable barrier to civilization; *IT* I, 112), Marshall (*IT* I, 30) lays greater emphasis on matters of national character or spirit, in England's case certain "qualities of body and character," including "firm will, self-determination, thoroughness, fidelity and love of freedom" (see also Marshall 1890, 630). Marshall exclaims that England has pursued its course "so independently and steadily," so harmoniously blending economic and political institutions, that the English "stand out now as the leading type of continuous development" (*IT* I, 30). Though the narrative suggests that industrial leadership is relational, his claim is weak.

Marshall still holds onto the idea, central to neoclassical models, that distinct units establish their position competitively in a market or market-like environment (Hodgson 1993, 101). Once in the advanced position, countries like England condition the prospects for others, showing them, perhaps by violent incorporation, the path to civilization.

Autonomous development and relations of domination co-exist uneasily here. England shows that the progress of internal industries develops only along with and largely as a consequence of foreign relations. The traits comprising English "economic nationality" may date to a misty past (*IT* I, 28–9), but the industrial practices of the "Mercantile Age" actually forge the country "into an economic unity" where these national traits could be profitably expressed and industrial leadership arise. The expansion of external markets, including growing access to the industrial goods of "the highly civilized parts of the East" and the natural resources of "ignorant people" globally, was supplemented by the establishment of "Plantations." Colonial plantations created "colonial demand," allowing "a larger and more active home market" and an eventual "internal unity in industry" (*IT* I, 30–3). Though the point is to isolate the English contribution, the connections he traces are not among independent states, but involve colonial relationships.

Relations of domination and subordination suffuse Marshall's narrative of progress. He admits that England's internal progress depended on the dispossession of enclosures that expanded the land and raw materials open to use by industry and diffused a sense of the new opportunities widely in the population; it was "excellent . . . from a broad national view, though the costs were quite high" (*IT* I, 36–7). But, without the enclosures, we sense that England could not have arisen to its position of industrial leadership with the attendant spillover benefits to relatively backward states. Slavery comes in for a similar assessment. What Marshall calls "primitive civilization"—Africa, and parts of Asia and indigenous North America—was largely stagnant, until slavery "came to the aid of progress, by forcibly breaking down the prescriptions of custom." It allowed new ideas "to be realized in practice more quickly than if manual workers had been free, but comatose and unintelligent" (*IT* I, 137). He similarly notes the tendency of "negroes" in the United States to "cling to old habits and customs," instead of "those which are the most effective and economical" (*IR* I, 101). That such peoples, even in an advancing country, might not fair well is consistent with Marshall's belief in the survival of the fittest. This harsh reading is justified when we consider that Marshall, in the sentence that follows his comments on slavery, draws the general lesson: "progress has owed much to the subordination of the masses of the population to the will of a dominant race, whose minds have not been occupied with petty cares." But Marshall immediately promises eventual redemption for common people, since "mankind will not have achieved their destiny till the masses can pioneer for themselves" (*IT* I, 137). He makes the same promise about the working classes: industrial advance will redound to the improvement of their moral character—at least over time *IT* I, 7).

When Marshall becomes more specific, we find that Anglo-Saxon leadership is central to this narrative of human destiny. England's economic advance has had repercussions for the entire globe, but its most extensive impact has been on "England's children beyond the seas" (*IT* I, 63). Marshall argues that England's colonies partly benefitted from an enlightened, increasingly chivalrous or altruistic, imperial policy (*IT* II, 233–4; Marshall 1890, 615–19). When Marshall looks out at the world in his times, he see the mantle of civilizational leadership being passed on to the United States. Its "spirit of youth" (*IT* I, 97), its greater individualism, and the "restless energy and the versatile enterprise of a comparatively few very rich and able men who rejoice in that power of doing great things by great means" (Marshall 1890, 621–2) have made the United States the "chief leader" in industrial production (*IT* I, 97). These "men with high business genius" have been brought to the forefront in a context that allowed the "natural selection of singular efficiency" (*IT* I, 105) to be applied to the mastery of techniques of mass production of standard goods with increasingly standardized capital tools (*IT* I, 97). The new industries find an abundant supply of relatively unskilled, especially immigrant labor to man the factories. "In spite of some racial differences," the "methods of living" of the population is generally homogeneous, especially since the country came "under effective control of an advanced western people" and despite "new strains of immigrants of excitable temperament" (*IT* I, 97–9). With all these advantages, it is now the United States that shows the future to the world and establishes the base on which future industrial advances may rise, a base equally deciding the relative fate of classes and races.

CONCLUSION: INSTITUTIONS, HEGEMONS, AND CIVILIZATIONAL ADVANCE

We can retell Caporaso's and Marshall's story to bring us back to Hobson's account of liberal IPE as a form of sublimated Eurocentrism. Robert Keohane (1989, chap. 5, see also 166–9), who features prominently in Hobson's and Cohen's accounts of IPE, uses a microeconomic "choice-constraint" framework to model the emergence, maintenance, and evolution of the global institutional order. International regimes emerge as a product of the rational choices of independent actors given the constraints they face at a particular point in time. Actors' preferences are conditioned by the imperfections in global markets, creating an aggregate demand for institutions that gradually overcome market failure—the transaction costs and uncertainties "that inhibit mutually advantageous coordination." The potential benefits of coordination that regimes provide suggest the progressive direction that actors' demand seems to give to world politics. In this way, Keohane gives a dynamic gloss to a static model.

Keohane recognizes, however, that actors' preferences confront specific supply conditions. Constraints are found in a constant—the anarchical structure of world politics (Keohane and Nye 1989)—but also in conditions of inequality: the kind and amount of regimes supplied to turn on "relationships of power and dependence in world politics" (Keohane 1989, 105). Though not sufficient as an explanation of the supply of regimes, Keohane (1989, 78–9) argues that the concentration of power in a particular country (hegemony) is necessary to regime creation and stability. Only countries with overwhelming power concentrations can underwrite regimes, define norms and rules and exercise authority in the implementation of norms. And though acting only to secure their own advantage, providing regimes to overcome market failure incidentally secures a public good (see also Gilpin 2001, 93–100).

The need for a hegemonic actor appears to be derived in the abstract—as an implication of a theory of bargaining among independent actors who would gain by cooperation but have neither the incentive nor the capability of providing that public good on their own. Only a concentration of power can fulfill the underwriting role. In the bare structure of regimes theory, the main trait distinguishing the hegemonic player from other actors is the distribution of endowments, which creates the incentive and capability to secure a public good (Gilpin 1981, 12–13; Keohane and Nye 1989, 18–19). The hegemon is otherwise unmarked by culture or history, nor engaged in relations of domination and subordination. Like neoclassical economics, the theory appears neutral: any claim of a special role for the West is incidental and, Keohane (1989, 248) insists, the hegemon's stabilizing function operates in a world populated by formally equal and autonomous actors. This is not a theory of empire or structural domination—at least not on the face of things.

However, we might think of the two countries that have played this functional role—England and the United States—not as culturally unmarked and precisely in terms of empire and structural domination.[5] Marshall's account from the early twentieth century makes clear the serious mischaracterization involved in seeing England as an individual actor that happens to bring a preponderance of industrial capacity to a situation of bargaining among autonomous actors over the shape of international institutions. England is present as an empire and with a dominant role in a colonial division of labor. The details of conquest and the creation of an imperial political economy must be ignored by liberal IPE in order to model nineteenth century world politics as an outcome of choice under constraint. A similar forgetting helps erase processes of domination from the story of the postwar international order.

Even if IPE makes no claim about the pareto optimality of global institutions, as Caporaso explained, it nevertheless embraces the idea that the interests of individual units are harnessed by institutions to produce collective goods. As Boucoyannis (2007, 709) suggests, the IPE "utilitarians" use the edifice of economics—preferences, rationality, a market-like "bargaining space . . . within which solutions can be found to reconcile initially competing demands"—to "imagine a world in which harmony is possible." IPE scholars might resist Boucoyannis' claim, stressing the value-neutrality of an economics-based IPE, but, despite such protest, she stresses that the practitioners of IPE are the "real idealists" in IR. And, after all, Keohane and Nye (1989, 267) describe regime analysis in progressive terms as a "theory of learning." Likewise, Keohane (1989, 10, 114) appeals to a functionalist evolutionary logic in his account of demand-driven regime change. Whatever his specific doubts about the harmony promised by liberal theory, Keohane (1990, 194) concludes one assessment of liberal thought on an extraordinarily hopeful note:

> In the end I return to the emphasis of liberalism on human action and choice. Liberalism incorporates a belief in the possibility of ameliorative change facilitated by multilateral arrangements. It emphasizes the moral value of prudence. For all its faults and weaknesses, liberalism helps us to see the importance of international cooperation and institution building, even within the fundamental constraints set by world capitalism and the international political system. Liberalism holds out the prospect that we can affect, if not control, our fate, and thus encourages both better theory and improved practice. It constitutes an antidote to fatalism and a source of hope for the human race.

Here Keohane appears less a neutral scientist and more an advocate of a liberal order with the United States at the helm.

In Keohane, we find Marshall's progressive telos, but without any acknowledgment of empire or U.S. structural power, and without the costs imposed on some groups and peoples by this evolutionary process. Hobson (2012, 218) calls this "a latent liberal-paternalist neo-imperial posture." Similarly, Kimberly Hutchings (2008, 156) explains that liberal IPE offers "a vision . . . in which the continued (and expanding) hegemony of liberal democracy and capitalism is identified as the outcome of rational foreign policy making." We are offered the choice, then, between "the gradual reproduction of all parts of the world in the image of the west" or "descent into irrationality." That is, assimilation or life and death beyond the pale.

Chapter 4

Levels, Eurocentrism, and Positive Science

John Hobson (2012, 213) remarks that "there are surely few larger and more important things in international politics than Western imperialism/neo-imperialism," yet contemporary international theory tends to treat imperialism as secondary to the main stuff of international affairs. We endorse this view and we are very enthusiastic about the body of work from which it derives. Nevertheless, we believe Hobson's framing understates a key point. He underemphasizes that Western IR theory exists *to deny* the importance and persistence of imperialism. This is not mere oversight or ignorance. We insist that this denial is the gravitational center around which the discipline orbits and to which it turns its back.

Hobson catalogs this denial in great detail. He summarizes his findings by honing in on international theory's embrace of "Eurocentric myths" that: (1) reveal a dark, racist, and imperial core to international theory; (2) transpose a civilization/barbarism binary into the sovereignty/anarchy construction (or subliminally adopts such a translation to create a gradated scale of sovereign capacities with the non-West at the bottom); (3) wrap international theory's presumption of a formal/informal hierarchy of peoples into "great debates" that cover up this imperial/racist disciplinary core; and (4) construct a notion of globalization that ignores the continuities with earlier periods where the West remakes the rest of the world (2012, 14–21). Together these myths produce a world constructed by the West in its own image—a world in which the vitality of the rest of the world is diminished (conditioned on the "*pioneering agency*" of the West in Hobson's terms) or treated as derivative of Western values and visions (Hobson 2012, 7).

Though we might think of the period after 1945 as opening space for anti-imperial thinking, associated perhaps with the Third World movement, "a desire to hide or obscure imperialism from view in the body of international theory" remains strong (Hobson 2012, 320). If anything, this desire has intensified after 1989, where, as Hobson (2012, 325) observes, "the contemporary politics of Eurocentrism is whitewashed and consigned to history, removing it from the present and quarantining it alongside the racism of the nineteenth century." Though perhaps no longer openly racist, much contemporary international theory reproduces the political "content" of earlier racialized conceptions and institutions of international society and thereby "fails to deliver on one of its key promises—specifically to produce positivist, value-free analysis and universalist theories of world politics" (Hobson 2012, 344). Again, and consistent with the previous chapter, we might go a touch further by suggesting that "positivist, value-free analysis and universalist theories" provide the fantasy around which IR and IPE organize their disciplinary identities, substance, and power. It is not the failure to achieve the positivist fantasy that allows Eurocentrism to persist, but the implementation of a positivist, universalist science assembled around unit-level analysis that confers scientific status on Eurocentrism.

We illustrate and defend this argument in four steps. First, we discuss Ghassan Hage's report that providing social explanations for suicide bombing is greeted by incredulity (how dare he treat suicide bombers as ordinary human beings?!) or with the insinuation that failing to simply condemn suicide bombing makes one complicit with terrorism. He acknowledges and embraces the first insight: that "social determinism" performs a humanization of actors otherwise relegated to the category of barbarian and acts otherwise categorized simply as evil. We respond to his puzzle about the imperative to condemn *before* explanation with the suggestion that this "condemnation imperative" works to secure the boundaries of the self in relation to feared or denigrated others. As William Connolly and Terry Eagleton suggest, it closes off avenues of inquiry that locate social evils in the structures or institutions of social life that shape both us and suicide bombers.

Second, we build on Connolly and Eagleton to explore the "individualism imperative" at work in IR, investigating the levels metaphor (of system and units or whole and parts) that is claimed to structure our choices as scholars. We argue that this choice is far from politically and ethically neutral and appears less a choice for scholars than a product of being embedded in a particular academic culture and, further, in a capitalist culture of competition. Following Hayek, we analyze the way privileging individual effort and talent works to justify unequal outcomes by obscuring the whole that conditions the parts. We note that IPE claims scientific credibility via a method that represses the whole in order to formulate science focused on unit-level causal propositions, and that efforts to reach beyond a positivist IPE to embrace a more pluralistic approach, as proposed by Benjamin Cohen, founder of the individualism imperative. It is here that we can see how contemporary international theory produces the political content of Hobson's Eurocentric myths as a scientific practice.

Third, we briefly summarize two works that explicitly challenge atomistic approaches and deploy a social determinist politics/ethics: Francis Jennings' *The Invasion of America* (1975) and Walter Rodney's *How Europe Undeveloped Africa* (1974). These texts found a place in academic discussions in IR/IPE in the 1970s. They were part of a broader interest in theories of dependency and underdevelopment that suggested economic growth and capital accumulation in some locales are intimately intertwined with the marginalization and destruction of others. But work of this kind- faced resistance—what we have described in the previous sections as an involuntary "stutter" or hesitation—rooted in claims that its lumpy, historical, social determinist elements failed the test of an atomistic, positivist science. Or worse, that such scholarship constituted a threat to civilized society.

In conclusion, we return to our central claim that social explanation brings into focus that which the individualism imperative obscures: the whole or totality within which parts are relationally constituted. We follow Hage in seeing this erasure as exhibiting resistance to or fear of facing both our similarity and difference from the other. Similarity because it allows that, given different circumstances, we might be just like those we condemn and, therefore, cannot readily assume the mantle of a "pioneering agency" by which we assure ourselves that we deserve our development and our "advanced" culture. Difference because the difference of others always serves as a latent critique. Social determinism, then, not only destabilizes positions in a hierarchy but also allows us to embrace the simultaneous teacher/student status of both self and others. Though we see inverting the individualism imperative by favoring the whole as a political/ethical advance, we also hesitate and negate that inversion but in a way that does not return us to the unit level. We advocate moving past the language of the mutual constitution of wholes and parts toward the claim that such language reifies what might be described as a simultaneous and continuous process.

SOCIAL EXPLANATION, EXIGOPHOBIA, AND THE INDIVIDUALISM IMPERATIVE

Ghassan Hage (2003, 65–6) ponders why his attempt to explain the emergence of Palestinian "suicide bombers" ran afoul of both his students and fellow academics. Much to his annoyance, he realizes that commentary on Palestinian suicide bombers must begin with a moral condemnation if it is to be heard. Prior to saying anything about their motives, tactics, and circumstances, one must first reject "suicide bombers" as beyond the pale, as absolute otherness outside the realm of explanation, even as evil. Hage (2003, 67) confesses that what he calls the "condemnation imperative" places him in a performative contradiction: before he can explain or assess the actions of Palestinian suicide bombers, he must first judge their actions to be reprehensible and barbaric. He must give the science before the science, as Marx might say. Hage accepts this predicament in order to bring light to the situation and his essay attempts to humanize "suicide bombers," including proposing a hypothetical sociological/anthropological project that he ties to the term "social determinism."[1]

Along the way, he uncovers three insights that intrigue us. Hage discovers: (1) a fear of social explanation, what he calls "exighophobia"; (2) the partisan politics/ethics of social scientific explanation; and (3) a methodological move we will call the "individualism imperative." The last requires further explanation, a task we take up here and in the section that follows. In our reading, these three strands of Hage's discovery are reducible to this question: Why does social science fear the ethics of social determinism? Prior to attempting an answer to this question, we move carefully through the last two sections of Hage's article.

Hage relates an encounter with a student that exemplifies his and our predicament. Having conveyed to a seminar the steps necessary to devise adequate sociology and anthropology of Palestinian "suicide bombers," he notes the discomfort of his students. One of them says, "You've made it as if suicide bombers are ordinary human beings." Hage contemplates this comment and wonders if this conversion of the seemingly extraordinary to the commonplace isn't "what is always at stake in social explanations" (Hage 2003, 83–4).[2] The explanation makes seemingly anomalous events the mundane result of a recognizable process. If x then y; in situations where one party monopolizes the means of violence and subjects a second party to unviable loss of social dignity, the second party will respond by organizing their society so that some living bodies become weapons whose detonation serves to make the present meaningful and the future hopeful (see Abufarha 2009). Such explanations make suicide bombers seem understandable as "ordinary human beings."

More is at stake, however, than familiarity with and understanding "suicide bombers." The deeper and more dangerous implication is that *any* society put in such a situation will respond in a similar fashion. It is this inference that we may fear as we shift locating the cause of an event from the character of the individual actor to the actor's social-historical context. The wager of social explanation and the worry it prompts is that *they and we* are made of similar stuff who when placed in similar situations will respond in a similar fashion. We resist this conclusion and exhibit this "exighophobia," argues Hage, because we fear seeing ourselves in them. Our fear of their difference (they perform suicide bombings, we do not) is secretly a fear of our similarity (we might do just as they do when put in their situation). The truth value of this claim may not be germane. What is important is the anxiety that can be activated when we entertain the possibility of our similarity with them.

This insight is followed by a second and bolder claim: the ordinariness of Palestinian "suicide bombers" is also a claim about the *ethics* of social determinism. Such ethics retrieves the mundane humanity of perpetrators:

> War emphasizes the otherness of the other and divides the world between friends and enemies and good and evil. This war logic is negated in a social explanation that draws on an ethics of social determinism. By proposing that the other is fundamentally like us, social determinism suggests that given a similar history and background we might find ourselves in the other's place. When we explain an act as the product of a particular history and particular social circumstances *we give its perpetrators some of their humanity back.* (Hage 2003, 86–7, emphasis added)

If so, retrieving perpetrators' humanity is what is at stake in social explanation. Whether social explanation makes the other's difference familiar, as in this case, or whether it makes the other's seeming sameness appear as a partial difference, what is at stake is the other's humanity. Again, these "insights" needn't be verified to produce their effects. It is the potential threat of discovering a perpetrator's normality that can produce exighophobia—the fear and condemnation of social explanation.

If what we have argued seems plausible, it brings us to a complex position in relation to the other: the other is not us, but neither is the other not-us. Rather, the other is both *us* and *not-us* at once. Assimilating the other's difference erases the particularity of the other and rejecting others' similarity to us overlooks their universality. Both moves deny the other's humanity. The social explanation can humanize others by embracing together similarities *and* differences. This process, Hage points out, is not an impartial act: "in taking the side of social explanation one is clearly not inhabiting a politically neutral position" (88). Such partiality, Hage quickly asserts, does not preclude our ability to condemn the very actions we are trying to explain. Having retrieved the humanity of suicide bombers, we can still stand opposed to their actions. So long as we are willing to admit that by so doing we also condemn our own potential actions should we find ourselves in a similar situation. As we condemn their actions, we condemn our own—either as forgotten past or potential future (see Nandy 1983, 2002).

Collecting these elements together, we might say that the logic of social determinism seeks a social explanation of particular actions in particular situations via generalization and that doing so requires regarding the other as both universal *and* particular. Simultaneously, social determinism reveals an ethics that abandons both the assimilation and rejection of the other. This is the standard by which we assess social science and to which we hope it might live up to as an ideal.[3]

Despite this logic, social theorists hesitate to embrace such an ethics of social determinism. We resist the humanizing move, the acceptance of the vilified, whether suicide bombers or other "barbarians," as "ordinary people." Perhaps we fear a loss of judgment, an inability to take a stand, and a dissolution into relativism. The tension between the logic of social determinism and our difficulty in accepting its consequences can be seen as a stutter—a seemingly involuntary disruption of speech and thought; a deep-seated phobic reaction to the humanizing role of explanation—that expresses itself as the "condemnation imperative." As Terry Eagleton (2010, 8–11) notes: "No Western politician today could afford to suggest in public that there are rational motivations behind the dreadful things that terrorists do. 'Rational' might too easily be translated as 'commendable'." And, as Hage (2003, 66–7) argues, the failure to condemn in scholarly discussions makes you "a morally suspicious person," associated with, if not culpable for, the evil itself. Both Hage and Eagleton suggest that pursuing social explanation—an explanation that humanizes the other, that refuses to locate the other as absolute difference—associates the scholar with nefarious purposes. This would seem to foreclose social explanation altogether, replacing it with the cant of the condemnation imperative.

But this resistance to the social explanation as a humanizing strategy doesn't simply foreclose social inquiry; it channels it in certain directions. The condemnation of individuals or groups as evil presumes and invokes the idea of autonomous and responsible individuals whose motives and actions are separable from ours. William Connolly (1991, 1–2, 99) emphasizes that the language of evil is "bound up with the issue of responsibility"—"some agent must be responsible for it." If others are responsible for evil acts, then no further social inquiry is required; the motives of individuals or groups or the context of their actions are rendered irrelevant. And, he stresses, by intensifying "our search for responsible agents" at the individual level, we "exclude some injuries from the category of evil." More precisely, as Eagleton (2010, 143) suggests, we exclude those injuries for which an account in terms of individual responsibility is difficult to sustain, such as where "wickedness is institutional"—"the result of vested interests and anonymous processes, not of the malign acts of individuals." These "forms of wickedness are built into our social systems," within which individuals are "deeply conditioned by their circumstances" and in which we may be implicated (Eagleton 2010, 144–5). Connolly and Eagleton are pointing to the kind of social determinism advocated by Hage (2003, 86–7) that attends to "the social conditions of action and the historical conditions of formation of the acting self." They suggest that explanations that humanize others produce the resistance that prevails not only in Hage's seminars or at scholarly conventions, but also in public debate and social theorizing more generally. They also suggest that resistance to "social determinism" is intimately interwoven with a focus on the individual as a separable unit and or locus of agency, as we saw in chapter 2.

The hints provided by Hage, Connolly, and Eagleon imply that we can link this stutter or involuntary disruption in our political/ethical sensibilities to what we call the *individualism imperative*—the tendency to ignore all levels of analysis in favor of the individual or unit level. Here, actions emerge not from context or structure, but from the autonomous will or certain traits of the individual unit. The unit is the locus of the action and this will must be "blamed" for an insufficient reading of what is good, right, and proper in the world. The Western social scientist is thereby caught between the humanizing ethics of social explanation and the ready opportunities to blame the individual for poor decisions. Hence the hesitant muttering or stuttering.

To foreshadow our point of arrival in this chapter, we see two responses to this stutter. One can discount the role of individual will or traits and move toward a full ethics of determinism. Or, one can emphasize the individual units and thereby disavow the ethics of social determinism, or disavow it in the last instance. In the latter case, one moves to essentialize units. This individualism imperative, as we shall see, goes hand in hand in IR/IPE with a refusal and rejection of the "global level." This refusal also facilitates the Eurocentric myths that keep self and other separated, that produce the stutter that resists the humanizing move of social determinism. We trace the work of the individualism imperative in the following two sections, documenting, first, how the individualism imperative has come to define conventional IR and IPE as positive, supposedly value-free sciences, and, second, how work in IPE stutters in the face of social determinism, even as it expresses the desire to engage plural approaches.

LEVELS, THE INDIVIDUALISM IMPERATIVE, AND EUROCENTRIC CONDEMNATION

We think with metaphors; indeed, we cannot think without them (Lakoff and Johnson 1980). In thinking about the planet, we use visual metaphors that organize space. We imagine its three-dimensional *oneness* via satellite pictures of the Earth as a blue globe and we see *differences* within and across that oneness via maps that show how the various continents are divided into states.[4] IR arranges these images via a metaphor of "levels," though IR tends to favor the unit or actor level. This emphasis on unit-level explanations leads IR to neglect the very processes that produce relations of global inequality and domination. Our wager in this section is that a focus on the problem of levels allows us to locate the deeper root of how IR/IPE becomes racist, imperial, and Eurocentric, thereby undermining even well-intentioned efforts to engage others, more diverse viewpoints.

In his classic paper, J. David Singer (1961, 77, emphasis added) begins by admitting that levels create a problem of choice:

> In any area of scholarly inquiry, there are always several ways in which the phenomena under study may be sorted and arranged for purposes of systemic analysis. Whether in the physical or social sciences, the observer may *choose* to focus upon the parts or upon the whole, upon the components or upon the system.

The word "choose" suggests opportunities for pluralism of scholarly perspectives: "For a staggering variety of reasons a scholar may be more interested in one level than another (in parts as opposed to the whole) at any given time and will undoubtedly shift his orientation according to his research needs" (Singer 1961, 90). But, as Onuf (1995, 35) notes, Singer boils the choices down to "two levels—the behavioral and the systematic," and scholars' research problems dictate whether they highlight units or the system.[5]

Robert Cox (1986, 204, emphasis added) usefully shifts the language somewhat by emphasizing the role of convention or engrained habit involved in disciplinary practice:

> Academic *conventions* divide the seamless web of the real social world into separate spheres, each with its own theorizing; this is a necessary and a practical way of gaining understanding. Contemplation of undivided totality may lead to profound abstractions and mystical revelations, but practical knowledge . . . is always partial or fragmentary in origin. Whether the parts remain as limited, separated objects of knowledge, or become the basis of constructing a structured and dynamic view of larger wholes is a major question of purpose and method. Either way, the starting point is some initial subdivision of reality, usually dictated by *convention*.

Cox seems to suggest that one's orientation toward parts and whole is not so much chosen but acquired through disciplinary socialization. To further invert Singer's claims, we might say that level schemes choose the scholar and, having been selected (or initiated into disciplinary conventions), scholars organize their work according to a predecided understanding of levels.[6] And, Cox stresses, our choice of levels is not innocent. We read him to say that a discipline organized around "parts" tends to support a problem-solving mentality that takes existing structures of world order for granted, treating them as given or as exogenous (see chapters 3 and 5). Only when scholars are disciplined to focus on the whole as a kind of totality can they adopt a critical stance toward world orders (Cox 1986, 207–10).

We follow Cox's lead and explore the political and ethical implications of being selected by a level. We read along with Nicholas Onuf, who has done the most thorough and sophisticated work on levels in IR. Onuf (1995, 43) says that "levels schemes are all members of a family of pictures, or framed spaces, within which we see the contents of the field of study we call international relations." Pushing against Singer's notion of a choice of levels following from the selected problem, he seems to indicate the level scheme comes first, not the seeing. As Onuf (1995, 41) puts it, "level is just one in a family of spatial metaphors not the identification of a problem. They tell us how we see, and not what we see." Closer to Cox in his respect, Onuf implies that seeing (or inquiry) begins with a level scheme that shows you how to see the contents of the world. Put more starkly than Onuf might like, we can say that the level conditions how the scholar can see and what counts as an inquiry. Our methods, our epistemological stance, are given to us when we are selected by a level.

But, in apparent contrast with Cox, the implications of levels schemes seem to have little political importance for Onuf. He suggests that levels are free of ethical implication:

> As a family of pictures, levels schemes are horizontally oriented. Top and bottom lines frame the picture. Levels are lines parallel with top and bottom, each functioning as top and bottom for pictures encapsulated in the larger picture. Up and down are locational instructions; only the observer's angle of vision and focus change. *While "up" generally connotes good and "down" bad . . ., levels schemes have no such implications.* (Onuf 1995, 44, emphasis added)

We want to dispute this claim, namely that levels schemes carry no connotation of good or bad or carry no political/ethical weight.[7]

Some of the challenges we can muster using Onuf's own words. For Onuf, levels shape not only how we see but also how we make our disciplines and how humans make the world or maybe various wholes or worlds.[8] As he puts it:

> Levels are not just a taxonomic convenience for scholars, or a methodological convenience. They are a potent metaphor, an ancient convention, for marking, and thus making, wholes. In our culture, as in our field, we would have difficulty getting along without the language of levels. In other cultures people make wholes of their own . . . and mark their significance with conventions we may not even recognize. (Onuf 1995, 53)

For example, Onuf (1995, 48–9) reports that Aristotle locates the "complete good" in the self-sufficient community, or Polis, that stands above its many parts. Similarly, Christian cosmology associated the complete or final good with "with God and the heavenly city" that stands above "social arrangements" that order the human beings which reside below that social order. The cosmos was visualized as a "great chain of being. . ., [o]rdering all things from least to greatest, lowest to highest" (Onuf 1995, 49). As individuals, we look up to locate the good—toward God and the social order sanctified by God. Here, up points to the good.

But, by the seventeenth and eighteenth centuries, "an alternative visualization gained favor"; "after Kant, metaphorically, the great chain tipped over—levels became stages" (Onuf 1995, 49). In place of God's order and God's goodness (descending from on high), we come to see nature as governed by its own laws. So too with humans: God's laws are replaced by those humans make for themselves. And a notion of sovereignty follows. As Onuf (1995, 49) explains, "If nature's design fosters horizontal representation in space, so also does the emergence of autonomous sovereignties . . ."; the "flat territorialities of states" come to replace "overarching claims to hierarchical authority." A modern cosmology challenges the notion that we locate the good above. The locus of the good now shifts to a lower rung on the great chain—to individual members of the community and the independent states that now govern this horizontal space. Down points to the good or the preferred. And social order appears not as a realization of the good of the individuals, but as exogenous, as a potential constraint on the autonomy or responsibility of individual or sovereign actions.

Thus, the "flat territorialities" of states suggests an IR of "like units" (Waltz 1979). The claim of sovereignties suggests an IR of independent actors that appear, in principle, as formally equal. Where the units are privileged as the locus of the good and of creative action, explanatory emphasis is placed on the actions of the units as opposed to the determining effects of the structuring of the whole. Singer (1961, 80–1) captures this opposition in his own discussion of parts and wholes: looking at the world from the level of the individual unit emphasizes the concrete and moves away from abstraction. Looking up, toward the system or the whole, "we tend to move . . . away from notions implying much national autonomy and independence of choice and towards a more deterministic orientation." Perhaps we catch a hint of favoritism: foreshadowing the next section, an emphasis on the whole smacks of the kinds of lumpy historical arguments made by dependency theories that so violate the commonsense notion of the world as looked at from below—from the point of view of the behavior, traits, or free choices of individual actors.

The flat map of formally like-units does not preclude the assumption of graded selves or states, however. The flat map of sovereignties co-exists with the kinds of inequalities of position within a capitalist division of labor emphasized by theories of dependency and underdevelopment. Although these inequalities are taken to indicate higher and lower, where higher suggests more civilized, more developed, etc., the individual units retain the status granted by the flat map. They remain sovereign units, ungoverned or largely undetermined by any social arrangements that might be located at a higher level. This does not mean that the outcomes are without a pattern. Transformed into time, the great chain of higher and lower seems to be reinstated and individual units seem to be graded or valued according to their location along with an array of stages of development (as Onuf's comments about the modern era hint; see also Walker 1993; Inayatullah and Blaney 2004; Blaney and Inayatullah 2010).

Looking from above down onto the component parts of a whole, we see how colonial rule and imperial domination produce an unequal grading of Western and non-Western peoples as natural. This kind of patterned inequality undercuts claims of the autonomy of the units: they achieve their position only in relation to others on the chain of stages of development. And such patterned inequality appears to give the lie to the flat map of sovereignties: social arrangements force the units into a hierarchy of individuals, peoples, and states. Our modern scholarly socialization now disfavors the view from above. Seeing from above has been stigmatized because it suggests the primacy of the patterned inequality of the whole. When seeing from below, from the level of the units, is idealized, patterned inequality is treated as secondary—as an effect of individual traits, not a cause of them.

Thus, even if Onuf is correct that the up and down of levels do not connote good or evil in the sense suggested by a Christian cosmos, levels schemes are not politically and ethically neutral. Rather, a levels scheme that privileges looking from below dovetails with a Eurocentric reading of IR. Hobson (2012, 224–5) explains and as we explore in the section that follows, seeing from the level of individual actors, in this case, Europe or the West, as "self-constituting and exceptional," tempts us to "deny the dialogical notions of an 'other-generated Europe' and the poly-civilization 'logic of confluence' that a non-Eurocentric approach would focus upon." When one neglects the structuring features of the whole, of colonial rule and imperial domination, it is easy to use the claim of non-Western inferiority as an explanation for the relative successes and failures of a flattened planet of autonomous units.

Though explicitly universal and value-free in its aspirations, much of contemporary IPE proudly displays the individualism imperative and reproduces and reinforces the political content of this racist Eurocentrism. The purported scientific achievements of IPE, Benjamin Cohen (2008, 143) claims, have come via a focus on individuated units—"*actor behavior*"—and how these actors, usually states, manage the interdependence generated by their interactions. Cohen's story (2008, 21–3) of IPE begins with postwar recognition of growing independence among national economies, including newly independent countries. International institutions (GATT and the IMF in his account) appear as mechanisms for managing disputes among independent states. In a claimed advance over the work of economists, Cohen announces a new era of inquiry in which "the world economy could be depoliticized no longer." Yet, as he acknowledges, the tremendous gains in knowledge production come via imitation of the "technical sophistication and intellectual elegance" of economists—a kind of "reductionism" (in his terms) which "comes at a price in descriptive and practical credibility" (Cohen 2008, 42–3). The explicit contrast is with earlier Marxist theories of imperialism, dependency theory, and a contemporary "British School" that harks "back to the tradition of classical political economy, [where a] broad comprehension of 'society'— the social context of IPE—is valued more" (Cohen 2008, 18–19, 44). Cohen seems to suggest that we can add some of the "social" to a Eurocentric science of IPE focused on unit-level behavior.

But, as we have seen, "levels" are not neutral or simply abandoned or expanded at will. Being chosen by the unit-level forecloses close attention to the kind of diversity of viewpoints that Cohen (2010) now seeks. Reduction to the unit is connected to a culture of competition that shapes IPE so that an account of imperialism is discouraged if not excluded by convention. In our era at least, competition presumes and expresses the formal equality of the autonomous individuals brought into the competition. At the same time, competitive situations assume and establish a ranking (or hierarchy) of achievement and values. Or, drawing on a key informant on the logic of markets, Hayek (1979, 67–8) describes markets as "discovery procedures" in which competition reveals and values the quantities and qualities of individuals' abilities, efforts, and skills mobilized for the market. Where a ranking is established in relation to individual efforts and achievements, individuals' positions in the hierarchy are taken as a sign of merit and value relative to others. To put the point starkly, the individual establishes his or her value by comparison with other competitors in markets (Lane 1991, 221).

Market competition appears, then, as Hayek (1976, 107) points out, as an expression of and unintended outcome of the particular, independent, and voluntary actions of free and formally equal individuals. By rewarding differential capacities and potentialities, markets simply spur individuals to develop and display these premarket differences. For Connolly (1991, chap. 1), this reflects a key feature of our late modern understanding of social life: because the task of cultivating and managing one's skills and talents falls on individuals, the outcomes of social interactions must equally be born as individual responsibilities. Or as Hayek (1976, 74) puts it: "It certainly is important in the market order (or free enterprise society, misleadingly called 'capitalism') that the individuals believe that their well being depends primarily on their own efforts and decisions."[9]

Like Cohen and IPE, Hayek commits himself to a levels scheme that looks up from autonomous individuals. He rules out any dialectically or mutually constitutive relationship between parts and wholes. Parts exist only as separate, independent entities; the whole is not allowed to be the context within which the part emerges and is sustained. This levels scheme renders inequality a natural outcome of individual interactions, making success and failure an individual responsibility. Since success or failure in markets is where individual fitness is revealed or discovered, a culture emphasizing competition insulates social hierarchy from the political challenge. In this way, levels choose us with serious political and ethical implications.

To return to Hobson, the continued embrace of Eurocentric myths by IR in the twenty-first century need not be taken only as the resurgence of latent racism/Eurocentrism on the part of scholars or a discipline. It is not only Western ignorance or discrimination that leads to the marking of the non-West as legally recognized but relatively failed states or quasi-sovereigns. The West also turns to "evidence." The non-West's failure to develop is "evidence" that reveals and confirms an underlying hierarchy of capacities and potentialities. Civilizational hierarchy or gradated sovereignty merely names this underlying differential in the capacities of autonomous units. Given a methodological individualism that rules out thinking of the whole as the context within with parts and their relations emerge, this naturalized hierarchy can only be re-enforced by the continuing "evidence" of the relative failure of the non-West to develop or live up to civilized standards of governance.

Thus, the political and ethical possibilities of modern life rest on a tension between wholes and parts within an assumed theory of progress. On the one hand, political and economic development is seen as isomorphic with modern Western civilization. Here, modernity is more than just a model; it classifies the past and foretells the future of all cultural spaces. On the other hand, political and economic development is also linked to the principle of sovereignty, a principle that separates political and economic spaces and putatively allows each state to find its own version of meaningful development. IR/IPE concentrate exclusively on one side of this tension by focusing on the spatial demarcation of world space into separable nations or peoples or states or civilizations who follow (or not) or are capable of following (or not) the path pioneered by modern Western states and the international institutions they have created. This atomistic vision posits that realizing the promises of modernity (i.e., political and economic development) depends on the character of the developing (or not) units themselves. We saw similar formulations by Marshall in the earlier chapter. In this way, IR suppresses from our thinking the larger context of historical structures/interactions that follow from seeing down from the whole—from a fuller comprehension of the structuring of the whole. If the Western theorist "chooses" the individual level, he seems always to do so. It serves his belief that he and his state do not exist in deterministic and hierarchical order; that he and his state have earned their status. He need not wrestle with the problem of levels. The conversation ends precisely where it needs to begin.

THE POLITICS/ETHICS OF SOCIAL DETERMINISM

Some scholars have wrestled with the problem of levels, challenging the reductionism, to quote Cohen, that is taken as the epitome of social science. In doing so, they engage in a mode of social explanation that reveals the politics/ethics of social determinism. Our choices might be thought arbitrary since there are numerous authors to whom we might turn. But there is some method here. Francis Jennings' *The Invasion of America* (1975) and Walter Rodney's *How Europe Underdeveloped Africa* (1974) had the good fortune of being written at a moment when protests against Eurocentric social science had gained fleeting acceptance within various fields including IR. This was the age of dependency theory and the rise of world-systems analysis in which the power of social determinism, despite stuttering resistance to such work in the name of positive science, emerged as a segment of the field. And such work began to thrive until IR was recentered around liberal v. realist debates over the precise formulation of unit-level propositions. The space for the politics/ethics of social determinism soon shrunk, but never completely disappeared, as we suggest here and in the chapter that follows.

Like Hobson, Francis Jennings (1975) challenges the myths of the European conquest of North America, where European invaders become agents of civilization. The crudest form of the myth "postulates that America was virgin land, or wilderness, inhabited by nonpeople called savages" (15). Less crude versions point to the inevitability of the demise of Indian societies due to their technological, economic, and political backwardness (19). Jennings rejects both versions of the myth, retelling the story in order to place Amerindians back into the crucial "part" they played "in the creation of modern American society and culture," including documenting the "staggering price in lives, labor, goods, and lands" that the Indians paid for their "part" in an initially more symbiotic relationship with European invaders (41). But he also deploys social explanation in aid of a humanizing purpose: he aims to restore Amerindians as "rational human beings" whose "actions and reactions do not seem so difficult to infer from both circumstances and the available documentary evidence" (14).

If Jennings' Amerindians appear as "ordinary human beings" like us, or similar in most respects to the European invaders, he documents the ways differences were emphasized by Europeans to locate Amerindians as radically other. Native Americans were skilled hunters and lived in part by hunting. Europeans emphasized that facet of material provisioning in order to downplay that Amerindian farming produced an agricultural surplus that allowed gradual population increases until struck by unfamiliar diseases transported by European adventurers and invaders. The importance of hunting was used to suggest economic wastage that would justify the dispossession of the land (Jennings 1975, 62–7, 82–3). Though lands were not owned in a European sense (and therefore labeled as commons available for seizure), native groups "were as tied to particular localities as Europeans" and well understood what the Europeans were after (67, 82).

Similarly, though Amerindians were already connected by continent-wide trade, and were incorporated as energetic actors in the global circuits of the fur trade, Europeans generally imagined Amerindians as indolent. Directly contrary to that image, Indians provided much of the labor involved in trapping, initial processing of hides, and transportation crucial to the world market in furs. And Indian groups invested this labor and skills to produce furs in return for European trade goods, particularly iron and steel implements beyond local technology to produce (Jennings 1975, 85–6, 89–90, 102). Though equally seeking their advantage as traders and consumers in this world market, the trade was, as Jennings points out, "a means of unstable symbioses for two societies": "For Indians the advantages of the trade were local and temporary. Over the long term, the commercial transformation of their society implied its decay." Jennings lists disease and growing conflict as important, but the key is that "the Indians became dependent upon the Europeans who controlled the market's functioning in America" (87–8). As Europeans advanced a process of capital accumulation through the trade, Indians lost assets when hunting areas were depleted and the complexity of the local economy declined: "Indian industry became less specialized and divided as it entered into relations of exchange with European industry." Increasingly subjugated to colonial capitalism, intertribal trade decreased, credit arrangements put Indian producers in permanent debt, and growing European economic prosperity allowed the extension of a property regime that secured legal titles to land for Europeans and the police power to enforce that dispossession on Indian groups (85–7, 102, 129–33). As Jennings puts it: "In legal terms they lost both sovereignty and property" (129). And with dispossession, Indians "lost all hope of finding any niche in the society called civilized, except that of servant or slave" (145).

Indian resistance to Europeans, including by violence, appears in Jennings' story not as some special savagery, but more as the actions (however desperate) of "ordinary human beings." In preinvasion conditions, Indian villages were relatively peaceful by comparison with European cities and towns; justice among parties was negotiated instead of meted out, as in "civilized justice" through civil "revenge" (1975, 147–9). Jennings quips that "Indians never achieved the advanced stage of civilization represented by the rack and the iron maiden" (163). Intertribal warfare occurred along the frontiers shared by groups, though this fell far short of the total war practiced by Europeans (in Mexico, the Thirty Years' War, or in North America in displacing the native groups; see Inayatullah and Blaney 2004, chapters 1 and 2), and territorial boundaries generally survived despite defeat (150–7). Indians proved themselves no more sadistic than Europeans, though cruelty increased in response to European depredations and intertribal wars increased in incidence and ferocity as groups were displaced onto the territories of others and competed for control of shrinking hunting and trapping grounds (159–60, 162–8). These wars only intensified as Indians became allies and "expendable surrogates" in inter-imperial competition in North America (168).

Jennings' account takes on the character of Hage's social determinism. He moves us beyond the imperative to condemn the Amerindians as civilizational backward. Instead, the social and military practices of the Indians appear as aspects of a human drama that we all share. This humanizing moment of social explanation recognizes the Indian groups' own reactions and decisions. Importantly, North American Indians do not simply "fail" as autonomous units in competition with European others now on the continent. Rather, they are incorporated in specific social relations of sovereignty, property, and trade within which they are progressively marginalized and their ways of life disrupted, if not destroyed. These social relations are, as Hage would have it, "the social conditions of action and the historical conditions of the formation of the acting self." Amerindian responses to European contact and domination and their own destruction appear as and in parallel to Hage's analysis of suicide bombers, all too human. Jennings' social determinist argument likewise challenges the Eurocentric myths documented by Hobson, by resisting the heroic accounts of Europe as the agent of civilization that blazes a pioneering, independent, and the natural path that others must follow or risk demise. He shows how these myths obscure past and present interactions or relations among groups that produce wealth and poverty, centrality and marginalization, and, consequently, justify representations of non-Europeans as collectively and separately backward, barbarous, and failed political and economic orders.

Jennings' language is reminiscent of Third World theories of dependency and unequal development that reached prominence in the 1960s and 1970s.[10] As many have emphasized, development economics and allied work in sociology, political science, and economics understood the lack of industrialization and economic growth in newly independent colonies as a function of internal cultural and social conditions and chronic political misrule (Chilcote 1984). Dependency thinkers and theorists of unequal development argued that twentieth-century conditions could not be understood without a clear grasp of the historical development of the relations that made the current international system possible, including the capitalist global division of labor. We take Walter Rodney's *How Europe Underdeveloped Africa* as similarly exemplary.

Rodney (1974) lays out his purpose very clearly. He writes a history of African underdevelopment/European development as inseparable elements of the processes of global, systemic, uneven development (11). For Rodney, theories of uneven development lay siege to the key myths that sustain Eurocentric visions in the international political economy. They overturn the notion of independent development (14, 52, 90) and expose the resort to racist or cultural theories that purport to explain what are treated as Africans' individual and collective failures (21, 88–9).

Rodney details the specific mechanisms producing development/underdevelopment in depth. He begins with the extension of trade relations in the fifteenth century that draws Europe and much of the rest of the world into intensified interactions, including a key circuit of trade in slaves that makes Africans and African supply chains crucial to processes of capital accumulation in the Atlantic. Though our unit-level commitments might tempt us to see the global trading system as an emergent property of individual interactions, we should not ignore, Rodney suggests, the institutionalization of a trading regime, including authorizing the role of Africans as "merchandise" under the governance of (European) international law, and the dynamics of economic and military power that reproduced these social relations. Thus, Africans were crucial to the trading system not only as captives but also as producers of captives via raiding and the transportation infrastructure for delivering them into the European-dominated trading system as property—as owned factors of production (75–85).

Capital accumulation, cultural disruption if not destruction, and political subjugation occurred as connected elements of Africa's role in the global capitalist division of labor. The accumulation of merchant capital under the monopoly control of Europeans gradually concentrates technological advance and industrialization in Europe and key centers beyond Europe, fueling the extension of empires and imperial production and trade. In Africa, existing polities are transformed as they become forcibly or voluntarily incorporated into the emerging imperial world. Conflict among Africans increases along with the circuits of the slave trade, local ways of life and local knowledge are disrupted, and incipient processes of trade and technological advance occurring across the African continental trading system are stymied.

Eventually, most African polities lose any claim to sovereignty and Europeans deepen their political and military role on the continent in order to control and facilitate the production of plantation commodities and minerals central to the industrial revolution and capital accumulation in the capitalist world economy. With African entrepreneurship displaced and African resistance to formal colonization defeated, Africans are "assimilated" into key roles in colonial capitalism. They appear now as cheap labor for colonial infrastructure projects, plantations, and mines and as low-level functionaries necessary to administering empire. And a new "elite" class of merchants, administrators, teachers, and soldiers are incorporated as subordinate players in the structures of imperial rule (24–6, 85–90, 141–2).

Rodney explicitly attends to what Hage calls the "social conditions of action and the historical conditions of the acting self" in his discussion of anticolonial struggles and the emergence of newly independent African states. A colonial African elite grew out of the educational institutions created by the colonial state or by missionary societies (262–7). Rodney identifies the "explosive contradiction" between this educated group's individual aspirations and political vision and the continuation of colonial rule (267–72). Instead of accepting their role in the empire, these elites helped to organize and direct the dissatisfaction of the mass of African small producers and wage laborers into movements directly challenging the colonial rule, including adopting armed struggle when the colonial regime stubbornly refused to grant independence. Rodney references the Mau Mau resistance movement and the Algerian armed struggle as key examples. For refusing to accept their role in empire, Africans participating in movements, whether non-violent or not, found themselves classified as "upstarts, malcontents, agitators, communists, terrorists" (273–4). Like Jennings' "savages," Africa's malcontents and terrorists receive a social explanation from Rodney that restores their humanity.

We can read Jennings and Rodney as examples of an international theory that deploys a social determinist mode of argument. Both challenge the condemnation imperative and restore concerns with the *social conditions* of action and agency to the center of IR.[11] But IR scholars stuttered in the face of this kind of work, relegating it to the margins of the academy by the 1980s.[12] For example, James Caporaso, a generally sympathetic reader of theories of dependency and underdevelopment, in the end, finds the work unsatisfying in scientific terms. He recognizes the "complexity" of thinking involved in theories of Western or capitalist "domination" such that "the units of analysis are no longer ordinary nation-states interacting with and attempting to influence one another." Rather, theories of dependency and underdevelopment see a complex of internal and external processes that operate together as aspects of a single system of forces and relations that produce domination (Caporaso 1978, 19, 24). Describing that complex of forces and relations, Caporaso (1980, 622–3) notes, requires a "lumpy" or "qualitative" historical account that combines an analysis of the capitalist global division of labor and the specific similarities and differences of specific countries and regions.

Yet this is precisely where Caporaso begins to falter. Such lumpy, qualitative analyses inhibit our capacity to provide proper social scientific generalization disconnected from particular times and places (Caporaso 1980, 622–3). More precisely, by situating social explanation in relation to a historically specific capitalist global division of labor simply provides too little variation, too few degrees of freedom, to establish causal patterns subject to disciplinary standards of "falsifiability and verification" (Caporaso 1978, 43; 1980, 615). Caporaso's own effort (1978, 34–5) to translate dependency thinking into causal patterns requires *separating* the actions of individual units, whether individuals, states or corporations, that provide a suitably rich empirical basis for study (a large-n) from the small-n "systemic" analysis that cannot be the basis of a proper social science.

With this separation, Caporaso locates social determinist theories as beyond the pale of acceptable knowledge production precisely because they, like Hage, Jennings, and Rodney, focus on both "the social conditions of action and the historical conditions of formation of the acting self" and thereby ignore the "individualism imperative" or, perhaps more friendly to Caporaso's ear, the unit-level imperative. If Caporaso's words are measured, others resort to stronger language. Those who persist in deploying a politics/ethics of social determinism, like dependency theory, are charged with being "inescapably ideological" or, more harshly, an "intellectual guerilla movement" (Almond 1990, 229–30).

We hear echoes of Hage's exighophobia and the individualism imperative. Much is at stake here. Following Eagleton's hints earlier, we might say that the failures of international theory reach beyond Hobson's diagnosis of the willful ignorance of the history of imperialism. They reach to the active suppression of perspectives that would place systems of imperial domination at the heart of the disciplinary inquiry. And we should not be surprised to find that scholars justify their resistance to a social determinism that explodes these myths in the language of science: the allegiance to a unit-level social science. Eurocentrism becomes the epitome of positivist science.

Concluding Remarks

Explanation always means systematic explanation. The systematic explanation requires exploring or uncovering a system in which wholes and parts are mutually constitutive and both stand in for continuous processes. Wholes and parts are a metaphorical construction that helps us envision the world as a system. Wholes and parts are linked, as we have seen, to another metaphor—that of levels—where the individual level stands in for the part and the system level stands in for the whole. While different levels are acknowledged, that is, the view from the parts and the whole are presented as possible choices, the "individualism imperative" pushes explanation in IR toward the individual or the unit. In the process, the whole, the global level, is either discounted or ignored. The kind of stories told by Rodney and Jennings are barely acknowledged or denigrated outright.

Following Hage, we see this erasure (and the ignorance or stutter that results) as exhibiting a resistance to or fear of similarity—an anxiety that we may be just like them. We cannot allow ourselves to imagine how the other sees the world lest we admit that their vision is already within us—that ordinary human beings, like us, might use our bodies as weapons or might find our sagging prospects in a culture of competition attributed to our genes or deficient culture. Such sameness threatens to undermine our own space/time/cultural distinctions that allow us to claim *our* development and *our* advanced culture. It challenges our specificity, exclusivity, and uniqueness and, in Hobson's terms, any sense of our "pioneering agency." As long as we don't allow ourselves to see the other as another within us, we will resist explaining their actions. Instead, we will impart to them the status of "evil," "the backward," "the underdeveloped," the "yet to be civilized," in a nutshell, "the still lacking." And, to extend Hobson, these hesitations, stutters, erasures—all produced by the individualism imperative—are the most powerful instantiations of Eurocentrism, Orientalism, and racism.

If we can't allow the other to be the same, we also cannot seem to bear the other's difference. The difference is always a latent critique, and we are reluctant to face what it might reveal. We fear what that critique might teach us. Learning from the other inverts the usual hierarchy wherein the other always must learn from us. It is no small miracle that we could imagine reversing this relationship—that we can still learn from the other's difference. Fear of difference, then, is resistance to the need to know beyond oneself to know oneself; particularly learning that none of us are whole on our own, that our feeling of being unique or self-sufficient depends on repressing the similarities and overlaps that make us also the same. In this way, fear of similarity and fear of difference entwine.

Where we adopt a position of social determinism, sameness and difference have more to offer than destabilizing our position in a hierarchy. When the other's humanity is restored, their similarity and difference appear also as resources. To recognize and accept this intimacy with the difference is also to embrace the simultaneous teacher/student status of both self and other. To recognize and accept the intimacy of sameness is also to desire entering the world of the other for the sake of learning. But we hesitate, we stutter, we resist the turn to social determinism. Our trepidation exhibits itself as a fear of the global level, a fear of regarding parts as always in relation to wholes.

In IR/IPE, we often translate holism into an emphasis on the global or systemic level, as we saw in Singer and Cohen. But we wish to translate the global less as a level and more as a system in which wholes and parts are simultaneous moments in continuous processes (see also Oatley 2019). Looking from above, from the system as a whole, does not exclude the parts; indeed, they constitute the whole. But the parts—in this case as particular units—do not exist apart from "the social conditions of action and the historical conditions of formation of the acting self," to quote Hage (2003, 86–7) once more. Still, the usual (conditioned) "preference" of IR/IPE scholars is to see from the parts upward so that these scholars have not reached out much to the systemic thinkers. Though unit-level analysis may require attention to context, so that explanations incorporate "constraints," units are treated as if they can exist apart from the whole, as we noted in chapter 3. Here we have parts without any account of the whole, or as Schwartz (2007, 132) would have it, "incomplete knowledge" that is filled by a "belief in the virgin birth" of the units.

Overcoming the condemnation/individualism imperative requires us to make two seemingly opposed moves: we invert the usual bias and then we negate that very inversion in a way that does not take us back to the unit level. Inversion of the bias toward unit-level explanation involves (1) exposing the politics/ethics of unit-level explanation in justifying and masking violence and inequality and (2) introducing the stories that restore a sense of the whole, the global level. But we also repudiate the dichotomy that separates parts from whole and unit level from the global level. This repudiation calls us to move past the language of the mutual constitution of wholes and parts and levels. It calls us to move toward the claim that such language reifies what might be described as simultaneous and continuous processes, a theme we take up in the next chapter. Taken to its logical conclusion, we would say that there are no parts, no wholes, and no levels. Robert Cox (1986, 204) seemingly pointed us in this direction already. He speaks of the "seamless web" of the social world and about how "contemplating . . . undivided totality may lead to profound abstractions and mystical revelations." We would add: there is only a seamless web of simultaneous and continuous processes whose seeming mystical flow our descriptions cannot but freeze.

Chapter 5

Units, Markets, Relations, and Flow

The social process is really one indivisible whole. Out of its great stream the classifying hand of the investigator artificially extracts economic facts.

—Joseph Schumpeter (1961, 3)

Orthodoxy invokes heterodoxy as its excluded but constitutive other. In parallel to chapter 3, we juxtapose liberal IPE's axiomatic bargaining units with heterodox GPE's commitment to "social process" as an "indivisible whole." Mainstream IPE in the U.S. academy depends on the intellectual apparatus of neoclassical economics—where units act to optimize within given constraints—to lend itself the aura of science and to trade on the prestige of economics as a discipline. While this characterization might construct orthodoxy somewhat narrowly, we argue that the mainstream of IPE since the 1970s is built largely on this foundation, and deviations from neoclassical economics appear as auxiliary statements that leave the fundamental edifice in place (see Oatley 2019). The heterodox thinking that we highlight arose directly alongside liberal institutionalist IPE, though it was quickly pushed to the margins of the discipline as we suggest in the last chapter and other work (Blaney and Inayatullah 2008). Theories of dependence and WST, for example, counter the unit-level bias and oppose the methodological individualism of conventional social scientists. They do so because that bias excludes histories of conquest, colonization, and the violent imposition of a global division of labor thereby conceptualizing development as principally internal (in the case of Western Europe) or as a transfer from the West to the rest of the world (see Anievas and Nişancioğlu 2015). Put differently, and following the opening epigram by Schumpeter, we risk blinding ourselves to the "great stream" of "social process" when we give explanatory priority to individual actors and their interactions.

The works we highlight, K. N. Chaudhuri's *Asia Before Europe* (1990), Eric Wolf's *Europe and the People without History* (1982), and L. S. Stavrianos's *Global Rift* (1981), build on the earlier heterodox efforts. They carefully document the broad historical trajectories of development and underdevelopment, always attuned to global processes and structures of interconnection. While emphasizing the indivisibility of the social process, these thinkers don't ignore the role of the units. Or, perhaps better, they do not ignore the role of parts in comprising complex wholes. Chaudhuri, Wolf, and Stavrianos instead enable us to see the parts not as isolated units, but as richly different and constituted relationally within specific global histories of "social process" that include the violence of conquest, colonization, and ongoing processes of domination and subordination. Finally, their work, following Schumpeter's suggestion, shows us that we need not lose sight of the flow of "social process" as an "indivisible whole," however much we "artificially" extract narrower aspects of social relations and particular time periods from the "great stream" for more detailed attention.

ORTHODOXY

What we call orthodox or mainstream IPE derives from neoclassical economics, especially the latter's parsimonious models of decision-making under constraint. IPE's recourse to these economic models allows it simultaneously to formalize the supposedly common-sense observation that life appears as an allocation problem (Caporaso 1989, 136) and to "model" a "rigorous" specification of actor choice and constraint as a bargaining space: actors, pursuing their preferences with given endowments, reach agreements that achieve an equilibrium outcome beneficial to all (Cohen 2010, 887–8; Gilpin 2001, 53; Keohane 1989, 103–4). As Krasner (1983, 6–7) explains, the "market" serves as "a powerful metaphor for many arguments . . . in international relations," particularly those that begin with "atomized" and "self-seeking" units and explain international institutions as products of "agreements" among actors. In addition, and less often acknowledged, this model of actor bargaining around institutional design, maintenance, and reform supplies an ethical or political judgment: markets and market-like spaces are desirable since the voluntary transactions they allow "take place among individuals to the extent that they improve the well-being of each individual and, . . . thereby, improve the well-being of the group," including through virtuous processes of increasing efficiency, growth, and learning (Caporaso 1989, 139–40, 148–50; Gilpin 2001, 93–100; Keohane and Nye 1989, 267).

By contrast with its neoclassical cousins, IPE offers a fuller account of the character of units and more detailed descriptions of the interacting units' institutional context. IPE thereby claims to produce a more sufficient account of institutional creation and change. We first sketch the "logic" of the neoclassical understanding in order then to draw out IPE's modifications.

By axiom, neoclassical economists begin with a "fixed" and "homogenous" picture of human beings as reasoning or calculating units abstracted from any additional differentiating traits, apart from differing initial endowments of wealth (Caporaso and Levine 1992, chap. 4). These unequally endowed, though otherwise interchangeable, units enter into exchanges in markets *assumed* to have certain minimal features: property rights; a sufficient number of units seeking exchange so that none exerts market power, all being price takers; and some mechanism, perhaps a (fictive) auctioneer, organizing prices so that no exchange takes place except at a market-clearing or equilibrium price (Walsh and Gram 1980, 407).

It is worth highlighting what this textbook account excludes. There is no power, no politics, and no social relations of class, gender, or race. There also is no history or "great stream" of "social process" in neoclassical economics. As Walsh and Gram (1980, 404–5, 407) explain, neoclassical economics centers on a "static allocation model." An equilibrium price is produced as a "balance of forces affecting supply and demand," forces that are treated as externally given. The supply of goods is set as a parameter, not the result of a production process. Likewise, preferences and endowments are fixed, not emerging through social processes. Though neoclassical economists require a process that leads to a market-clearing price (Currie and Steedman 1990, 35; Klein 1997, 209–11), they assume an equilibrium is set (somehow) prior to any actual transactions, not as an active process of bargaining in actual time/space (Walsh and Gram 1980, 407). And they can do no more than "generalize" their framework "to a finite (or infinite) number of timeless allocations," where supposed "multi-period" activity appears, more precisely, "as a sequence of timeless allocations" (Walsh and Gram 1980, 408–9). Put differently, neoclassical economists add time only as a *logical* space, where static moments are extended notionally into a series that can be compared. They rarely look into the actual chronology of events or processes of unfolding (Weeks 2012, 41–2; Klein 1996, 251).

This lack of temporal duration or history impairs economists' capacity to take institutions seriously. Though institutions might be thought important in socializing actors or shaping individual preferences and endowments, to recognize the role of such processes would foreclose identifying an equilibrium point. The condition of locating an equilibrium is fixing a set of parameters, as if they are simply given, ignoring that they unfold across time. Thus, if institutions "change" (or, more precisely, are different at different notional time points), these changes are treated as "new" parameters, fixed once again in a timeless bargaining situation. Initial endowments may differ and may therefore produce a different institutional outcome, but these are simply given by the model, without regard to the earlier processes of interaction that produced them. In this way, gaining mathematical "precision" via equilibrium models systematically trades away more adequate accounts of institutional creation and change (Currie and Steedman 1990, 10–11).

IPE scholars require greater realism. First, by focusing on the particular institutional context of the postwar international system, Cohen (2008, 21–3) suggests that IPE has added the "political" lacking in the economist's models. The "political" appears as the varying character and quality of institutions or "regimes," requiring a thicker description than economists can muster of the particular rules and norms that structure behavioral interactions (Caporaso 1989, 141–3). Providing more adequate accounts of institutional creation and change requires, as Caporaso (1989, 147) explains, incorporating a whole range of "political, social and cultural variables" that indicate that actors are *not* simply like-units, unmarked by specific traits, a particular culture, or position in the international system. Still, IPE scholars mostly formalize difference as differential endowments by abstracting from differences in culture, identity, or social position that might shape identities, interests, and capabilities. Power capability (with wealth as one component and asymmetric interdependence another) is the fungible element in market-like bargaining spaces in IR. It is the distribution of these bargaining capabilities that shape the possibility of and particular character of rules and norms acceptable to actors (Keohane and Nye 1989).

Second, practitioners of IPE rightly worry that the neoclassical framework is dangerously static (see Gilpin 2001, 75–6; Keohane 1989, 114; Caporaso 1989, 142, 147). IPE might model institutional change as a sequence of independent choice situations, as do economists, but this construction is far-fetched, as Caporaso (1989, 148–9, 153) argues: individual actors do not face "a menu of alternative institutional arrangements," but are embedded in a set of institutions *already in place*. This embeddedness shapes interests and decisions and therefore agreements cannot be understood simply as an outcome of choice limited only by actors' given endowments. This problem might be finessed, Caporaso (1989, 148–50) explains, by adopting an evolutionary perspective that assumes institutions and structures are "adaptive outcomes." The "idea of efficiency" gives this process a "direction"—a "drift toward more efficient institutional outcomes."

In Keohane's (1989, 108–10; see also Krasner 1983, 11) well-known formulation, overcoming market failure is the central evolutionary dynamic of institutional creation and change: imperfections in the market-like spaces of IR compel individual and collective efforts to increase efficiency. Keohane does emphasize that actors' preferences/demands are not simply given, but conditioned by the existing imperfections (transaction costs and uncertainties) in the market-like contexts of the international system. He also provides an account of the specific supply conditions the aggregate demand for reducing market imperfections faces, not taking this as given and external, as an economist might, including a constant—the anarchical structure of world politics (Keohane and Nye 1989). But key are the varying conditions of inequality: the kind and amount of regimes supplied turn on "relationships of power and dependence in world politics" (Keohane 1989, 105). Though not sufficient as an explanation of the supply of regimes, Keohane (1989, 78–9) argues that concentrations of power in one or a few countries are necessary to regime creation and stability. Only countries with superior power can provide the resources to underwrite regimes. As they seek their own advantage, they incidentally secure a public good by providing regimes that overcome market failure through securing rules and norms that minimize uncertainty (see also Gilpin 2001, 93–100; Caporaso 1989, 150–1).

The ethical content of orthodox IPE merely hinted at here comes more clearly into focus, when, like so many (political) economists before (from Smith to Hayek and Friedman), IPE embraces the idea that market or market-like institutions harness the self-seeking behavior of individual units to produce collective goods. As Boucoyannis (2007, 709) suggests, the IPE "utilitarians" use the edifice of economics—preferences, rationality, a market-like "bargaining space . . . within which solutions can be found to reconcile initially competing demands"—to "imagine a world in which harmony is possible." IPE scholars might resist Boucoyannis' claim, stressing the value-neutrality of an economics-based IPE, but, despite such protest, she stresses that the practitioners of IPE are the "real idealists" in IR.

As always, idealism also casts a dark shadow. Treating the international system as a kind of market may tempt IPE scholars to assume relative harmony or simply act *as if* this is the case (see chapters 1 and 3). They thereby (must) downplay features of the international system perhaps better characterized as domination or oppression, as emphasized, for example, by theories of dependence (Cardoso 1972; Cardoso and Falletto 1979; Sunkel 1972; Dos Santos 1970; Furtado 1970) and underdevelopment (Amin 1976, 1977; Rodney 1972). These scholars trace the origins of contemporary structures to colonization, not bargaining. They show also that contemporary relations of power produce "bargaining" outcomes that are highly unequal and damaging to some actors. Caporaso himself highlights this unexpressed feature of theories of progressive institutional advance, including Keohane's. Such models, Caporaso (1989, 152–5) explains, require "a process of winnowing" that stresses group survival, but may ignore the potential costs to individual units or peoples. It is not only institutions that are competitively winnowed: individuals and groups also shrivel and die from their maladaptation.

We can summarize the way IPE draws upon but also distinguishes itself from neoclassical economics. IPE gives a thicker description of the particular traits of actors, but it still tends to follow economists in favoring spare models in which bargaining actors are differentiated principally by their varying power capabilities. Scholars in IPE separate themselves from economists by imagining active processes of bargaining that unfold in time and within the context of enduring institutions that shape actor preferences and endowments. Yet, they still generate impoverished accounts of the "social process" as an "indivisible whole." Though outcomes are shaped by the distribution of power, these are treated as voluntary negotiations among formal equals in a market-like space. They are unable to see the role of violence and domination in setting the initial institutional context in which legally equal actors negotiate or in shaping and perpetuating uneven endowments of capabilities. To the extent that powerful actors dominate the system, for liberal IPE, this inequality works to the advantage of all, securing regimes that foster mutually beneficial outcomes. While the market analogy hides all other possibilities, heterodoxy makes its mission to expose what is hidden.

HETERODOXY IN THREE WORKS

The three books we explore here were written in the wake of theories of dependence, Immanuel Wallerstein's account (1976, 1980) of the modern world-system, and the subsequent rise of WST. They are explicit counterpoints to the unit-level bias and Europe-centeredness of IR and IPE. As Denemark (1999) elucidates, WST provides an account of the world system as an emergent whole that structures the relations and incentives of actors within its sweep. Against IR's over-emphasis on the short term and the contemporary, particularly post–World War II events and institutions, WST considers the broad sweep of history, anywhere from 500 to 5,000 years, since world-systems emerge only over long periods of time. And, like others drawing on WST (e.g., Abu-Lughod 1989; Frank 1998; Anievas and Nişancioğlu 2015), our thinkers aim to counter the Eurocentrism of much of IR and IPE by placing the world beyond Europe at or near the center of their narratives.

Our three figures, Chaudhuri, Wolf, and Stavrianos, picture global systemic relationships as a totality that shatters the Eurocentric account of uneven development as driven by internal characteristics and processes. What they achieve, we believe, is something more. They deliver accounts that capture for the reader Schumpeter's "great stream" which makes and is made by the totality or whole. Rather than simply parts and whole or agents and structures, we are treated to "indivisible wholes" and the dynamic of "flow," issues to which we return in the conclusion.

K. N. Chaudhuri, *Asia Before Europe* (1990)

Though influenced by Wallerstein, Chaudhuri defines his project, not as world history, but as "comparative history" (xv), taking much of his lead from Braudel (1972, 1973). A comparative approach requires separable units, with "outer and inner limits" (31), that can be demarcated and compared. But Chaudhuri does not take for granted the units to be compared, as do both economists and the IPE orthodoxy. Rather, such units must be carefully assembled by the scholar from historical evidence, just as the institutions, practices, and material infrastructure that comprise the units were and are assembled and constructed by people over Braudel's *longue durée*. Chaudhuri insists that space and time are intimately connected (28–41; see also chapters 4 and 5), and only by being attentive to the duration of each civilization's articulation of worldview, state, society, and economy can we identify units that co-exist, potentially interact, and that pass into and out of existence (6, 30, 37). He presents what we can think of as a prehistory of the world system that emerges with European expansion, reconstituting time and space into a new global "flow" of social processes.

Chaudhuri constructs his notion of the Indian Ocean as a flowing material and mental unit in order to resist, like the recent critics of Eurocentric social science cited above, any idea of Asia as perennially unchanging, as "people without history" (in direct reference to Wolf), animated only by European intrusions (22–3, 28). Though he believes that we can locate a durable, if differentiated, "totality" made up of Chinese, Indian, Islamic, and Southeast Asian civilizational zones surrounding and interconnected via the Indian Ocean (chapter 2), the boundaries and character of this relatively durable totality are fluid, not fixed (25). Chaudhuri documents the assembling of the Indian Ocean as a region through about 1750 when it is seriously disrupted by the intrusion of European powers. And the key, as we shall explore further, the cultural and material interconnection of these subregions was recognized by many thinkers of the times (e.g., Ma Huan, Ibn Khaldun, and Ibn Battuta), while, "in contrast, Europe and [most of] Africa remained well beyond the limits of immediate perceptions," despite interactions with those regions (29, 36).

Braudel's account of the Mediterranean as a relatively enduring civilizational zone serves as a reference point. As Chaudhuri (5–10) explains, Braudel's careful work revealed the material *and* mental structures that persisted below the surface of everyday life, organizing the patterns and rhythms that governed social activities into a relative unity over time and space. The *longue durée* of persisting material and mental structures serves as the backdrop against which Braudel assesses unities and differences within and across units, charts the interactions of the physical and mental worlds of co-existing units, and identifies processes of gradual change and historical rupture. By emphasizing that these historical unities are an "artificial creation" built by people over the *longue durée,* Braudel refuses any "unilinear narration" or any attempt to establish the necessity of the rise of some particular unit or type (9–10), such as those who construct universal histories of the rise of feudalism and the transition to capitalism (38). But given the weight assumed by "capitalism" as a totality in Wolf and Stavrianos, as we shall see, we need to look closely at Chaudhuri's account of the elements that hang together as a structured, albeit not clearly capitalist, unit of which thinkers of that time and ours might be conscious. We will return to the issue of how to tell the story of capitalism or modernity in the next chapter and the epilogue.

First, as Chaudhuri (29–31) explains, the *climate and geography* of the Indian Ocean shaped the possibilities for assembling an integrated though an internally differentiated social unit of the four Indian Ocean civilizations. Climate, soil, physical barriers to and avenues of transport, especially rivers and the oceans, are the conditions on which the mental activities of humans operate to build systems of agriculture and water management (chap. 8), settlements (chap. 11), systems of industrial production that fed into local and long-distance trade (chap. 10), and systems of rule over urban and rural areas (chap. 3 and across the book).

The point for Chaudhuri, however, is not simply that contemporary historians can identify a whole whose external and internal limits are set by a particular geographical, climatic, and social materiality. Rather, and second, he stresses that individuals of the time could *see themselves* as occupying a whole *in time and space*—a space for which events can be plotted across time. In chapter 4, he argues that in this era people came to be aware of themselves living in civilizations that existed in time, whose activities could be measured in various time units. These time-measures facilitated not only scholarly and popular histories, but also contributed to practices of managing and regulating the various activities of everyday life—from agriculture and water supply to shipping, trade, and taxation. In chapter 5, Chaudhuri suggests that this sense of shared space is constructed partly in terms of origin stories of a way of life or system of rule around which identities might circulate. These ways of life were given a topographical grounding in broadly common systems of cropping of cereal grains and water management that might be counterposed to more nomadic forms of life that set something of an external limit to the Indian Ocean civilizations (see also chapters 8 and 9). The advantages of Indian Ocean industrial producers in cost, quality, and variety over other regions favored their goods for local consumption as well as export into the circuits of trade that flowed across the world from and around production and staging centers. All these gave a centricity to the zone and a sense of shared superiority in these arts. The geographical extension of a sense of identity and difference also was conditioned by possibilities for travel set by the infrastructure established for trade within and beyond the Indian Ocean (31, 117, 147).

Third, Chaudhuri documents in great detail the signs of commonalities and differences in everyday life—of food and drink, clothing, and housing—that were built over time on intersecting patterns of agriculture, industrial technique, climate, and natural resource availability (chapters 6 and 7). "Food and drink," he suggests, "constitute the ground floor of material life"; they offer durability, changing only gradually over time, that make them ideal for locating the limits of a social/economic/political unit (151). Clothing and architecture offer similar and quite visible signs of commonalities within a civilizational space, as well as connections and differences among them. These components of everyday material life also served as generally recognized markers of status, wealth, or position. Despite the variations in food and drink, and so on across the four Indian Ocean civilizations, Chaudhuri finds patterns of congruence in the symbolic role, ritual purposes, and systems of marking social status across the region that he takes to support his reconstruction of an integrated but differentiated whole.

Finally, Chaudhuri's commitment to the idea of the Indian Ocean as a "unit" or "totality" in no way suggests such units are independent atoms, whose growth are determined simply by their own efforts. Rather, the "principles" that he uses to identify the totality made by these Indian Ocean civilizations involve "the reconstruction of historical patterns of articulation between different forms of social activities such as systems of production, distribution, and consumption which *transcend the specific frontiers of each civilization*" (375, emphasis added). This is not a picture of autarchy or autonomous development. Chaudhuri carefully documents patterns of interconnection and influence, brought by trade and travel (see chapter 7 on clothing and chapter 10 on industrial production), and movements of population and the extension and contraction of political rule (383). His story is also one that has an end: a "life-cycle" of relatively stable relationships and patterns of change brought to an end in the eighteenth century, "when British military and naval power fused with the European technological revolution to redraw the civilizational map of the Indian Ocean" (382, 387).

This new civilizational map, he notes, is described by Wallerstein as a capitalist "world-system," composed of center and peripheries defined by relationships of extraction via a market exchange that support capital accumulation and the concentration of power in the cores of the world economy (383). Unlike some others, such as Abu-Lughod (1989) and Frank (1998), Chaudhuri is quite ambivalent about extending this notion of a "world-system" to the totality of Indian Ocean civilizations in the earlier period. He doesn't miss the features of mercantile trading and surplus extraction by the state in the Indian Ocean (385–6), but he claims that it is a political rule, particularly the always tenuous balancing of forces between state and society, urban and rural, that give these civilizational processes a coherence and stability (386–7). The organization of the Indian Ocean more fully around capitalist exchange and production was the product of European imperialism and the consolidation of colonial capitalism.

Eric Wolf, *Europe and the People without History* (1982)

As his title suggests, Eric Wolf aims to restore the peoples beyond Europe to the history of capitalism. This project becomes necessary, he claims, because most social scientists turn "dynamic, interconnected phenomena" into "static, disconnected things" (4). They "disassemble" the "totality into bits" (3), extracting, we might say, elements of Schumpeter's "great stream of 'social process' for analysis, and reduce these processes to effects of 'primitive isolates'" (13). These primitive isolates, or units, are never reassembled into the human whole as "a totality of interconnected processes" (3). The consequence is that some peoples' experiences (e.g., Rome, the countries of Western Europe) are treated as an immanent "unfolding of a timeless essence" (5–6). Other peoples' histories are erased. Or, if noticed, their role is reduced to victimhood. Wolf responds by uncovering "the active histories of "primitives, peasantries, laborers, immigrants, and besieged minorities" (x). To retrieve their role requires a systematic history of "global culture" and a dynamic anthropology of the "social system of the modern world" (ix). Such a history refuses to treat individuals, cultures, or states in isolation. All social entities must instead be seen within worldwide flows of interaction and interconnection.

Wolf begins with a remarkably ambitious chapter that gives us a tour of the "The World at 1400." Much like Chaudhuri's recovery of the dynamic character of Indian Ocean civilizations, he shows that there were no isolated "tribes," cultures, societies, states, or civilizations. All such entities had "linkages," "interactions," and "interconnections" with others, and these encounters shaped and changed the engaging entities. Nevertheless, with the "spread of Europeans across the oceans" the rate of such encounters accelerated and intensified, bringing "regional networks into worldwide orchestration" and subjecting them to a "rhythm of global scope" (385, see also 71). Capitalism drove this "interaction of cultures" after 1492, propelling "Europe into commercial expansion and industrial capitalism" (ix).

To understand capitalist dynamics and to ground a global anthropology, Wolf turns to "political economy" as developed especially by Marx (ix). Political economy provides a theory of the "growth and development" of the "world market in the course of capitalist development." It gives scholars an ability to "relate both the history and theory" of capitalist development to "processes that affect and change the lives of local populations." Most important and in language quite like Chaudhuri's, political economy offers a "theoretically informed history and historically informed theory" that work together to "account for populations specifiable in time and space, both as outcomes of significant processes and as their carriers" (21). Wolf argues that the static and unit-level fixations of our contemporary disciplines that we described above and in earlier chapters, grew out of a rebellion against political economy, with Marx as the "hidden Interlocutor" (19–20).

Armed with a Marx-inflected political economy, Wolf details how "mercantile wealth," as he calls it, "pioneered routes of circulation and opened up channels of exchange" that were transformed with "the rise of industrial capitalism" (88). The English textile industry was key. In "cloth production mercantile wealth was visibly transformed into capital, as it acquired the dual function of purchasing machines and raw materials, on the one hand, and buying human energy to power their operation, on the other" (267). With capitalism proper, "the accumulation of wealth no longer depended on the extraction of surpluses 'by other than economic means'," nor on merchants' marketing surpluses." Now, via the acquisition of machines, "wealth as capital laid hold of technology" and "became proprietor of the material apparatus for the transformation of nature . . . on its own terms." Technology and labor power were used to create greater surplus and the result was to "speed up the pace of technology" and to synchronize "labor power with the requirements of technology" (267).

These English and European developments had worldwide consequences in the form of a global division of labor: Lancashire factories were fed with cotton produced on slave plantations in the American South; peasant production in Egypt was displaced by large cotton-growing estates; and, to furnish Bombay mills, "millions of acres formerly in food crops were given over to cotton in western India" (295). In the process, "whole regions became specialized in the production of some raw material, food crop, or stimulant." These monocultural regions required specialized zones of labor supply or food production (310). And new production patterns at the "level of the world market" led to changes "at the level of household, kin group, community, region, and class" (310, see also 313–24).

Wolf understands that his descriptions disturb received orthodoxy, specifically classical political economists' premise that patterns of specialization work to the advantage of all. The brunt of his critique falls on the assumption of "choice" or voluntary exchange common to contemporary economics and IPE: "When Adam Smith and David Ricardo had envisaged a growing worldwide division of labor, they had thought that each country would freely select the commodities it was most qualified to produce, and that each would exchange its optimal commodity for the optimal commodity of others." Wolf asserts that this vision purges from consideration the "constraints that governed the selection of particular commodities, and the political and military sanctions used to ensure the continuation of quite asymmetrical exchanges that benefited one party while diminishing the assets of another" (314). Even absent military coercion, "forced" choices were dictated by "market domination by more powerful participants." Vindicating Pogge's intuition, coercion and constraint were, for Wolf, the "essence of the process; they were not epiphenomena." With such "forced" choices did Third World peoples "fall under the wheels of the chariot of progress" (314).

Lest we fall into simply reading the Third World as victims, a problem he identifies in the work of WST's leading lights, Gunder Frank and Wallerstein, Wolf calls for greater attention to the "micro-populations investigated by anthropologists" (22), an ethnographic corrective to political economy's emphasis on broad structural relations, gesturing toward fellow anthropologist Anna Tsing's concerns we discuss in the conclusion. Wolf describes how, over three centuries, European tastes for beaver hats dramatically changed the cultures and interactions of virtually all North American nations—even those living in sub-Artic regions (chap. 6). In all of this, and like Jennings, Wolf performs the ethnographic corrective where he demonstrates in painstaking detail how the active labor, knowledge, and planning of Amerindians made this worldwide trade possible. Similarly, he explores how the slave trade reverberated throughout the African continent (chap. 7). Echoing Walter Rodney's insights discussed in the previous chapter, Wolf complains that history written by slavers "has long obliterated the African past, portraying Africans as savages whom only the Europeans brought into the light of civilization" (229). Such a story denies "the existence of the complex political economy before the advent of the Europeans" (229). It also expunges the "organizational ability exhibited by Africans" once the slave trade had begun. For Wolf, "there can be no 'Black history' apart from 'White history'"; each is "only a component of a common history suppressed or omitted from conventional studies for economic, political, or ideological reasons" (19). Nor can there be a history of Europe without a grasp of the role Africa played in its development and expansion: "Leading participants in that growth were not only the European merchants and beneficiaries of the slave trade but also its African organizers, agents, and victims" (231).

Wolf concludes *Europe and the People without History* with what it means to look "at the world as a whole, a totality, a system, instead of as a sum of self-contained societies and cultures" (386). The most important imperative, Wolf suggests, is that we give up our attachment to the idea of societies or cultures as self-contained units. Rather than reading the system as a product of unit-level behavior, the units themselves are understood only "in their multiple external connections" (187). Wolf, therefore, looks somewhat askance at modern nationalists. He rejects nationalist efforts to enshrine a "special spirit or culture" as the basis for imagining narrow state projects. He also worries that nationalism serves as an ideological formation, justifying global inequalities and social suffering as an earned outcome of market competition among juridically equal actors (389–90). If the latter, the state-system appears mostly as an effect of a global capitalist mode of production, with no logic of its own. Wolf situates his critique, then, not from the standpoint of Third World states, as will Staviranos, but that of laboring classes and the "disvalued poor." It is in the opposition of classes that Wolf locates the tensions in the system and detects the basis for the agency in a global conjuncture (chap. 12).

We believe Wolf undervalues the role of the state and interstate competition in the GPE. Notions like "nation," "state," "nation-state," and the "inter-state system" may be dangerous reifications, as Wolf suggests in his critique of unit-level explanations. Yet it is also hazardous to ignore the modern state's organization of economic and cultural life, its efforts to fix national identities, and its engagement with the interstate competition. These elements have become key features of the dynamic *flows* of the "social system of the modern world" (ix), to use Wolf's term. Further, recognizing the role of states and the inter-state system need not mean a retreat to explaining political and economic outcomes as bargains among ontologically separate units. It is perhaps telling that both Chaudhuri and Stavrianos emphasize the role of political rule in shaping the spatial contours of identities and social practices as part of the interactions and interrelations of the global social system as an "indivisible whole."

L. S. STAVRIANOS, *GLOBAL RIFT: THE THIRD WORLD COMES OF AGE* (1980)

Global Rift presents a systematic and relational history of the First and Third Worlds, in which both are constituted by the "structure and dynamics of the whole" (23). Staviranos stresses the unique dynamism of European capitalism: it incorporates all other regions of the world as part of its own logic so that the wealth of Europe and poverty in most of the regions of the rest of the world are interconnected. While Stavrianos invariably explores internal political, economic, and cultural aspects of particular societies, his aim, like Wolf's, is to highlight the neglected "indivisible whole"—the external, interactive, and systemic ways that both wealth and poverty are produced in a GPE. Other theorists and other books, including Wolf's, present similar accounts of the "great stream" of "social process," but none have quite the range and depth of detail of *Global Rift*.

Stavrianos demarcates capitalism both temporally and spatially, according to criteria similar to Chaudhuri's. Temporally, he locates four periods of European capitalist expansion: (1) 1400–1770, in which the European "center" or "core" is engaged in commercial capitalism and colonialism largely confined to the Americas; (2) 1770–1870, in which the center, primarily Britain, is engaged in industrial capitalism and there is a "waning colonialism" in the periphery; (3) 1870–1914, which he describes as the era of "monopoly capitalism" and worldwide colonialism; and (4) 1914–1980 (when the book was published), in which the core must actively defend monopoly capitalism in the face of "revolution and decolonization," with "neocolonialism" as the product (41). These periods correspond to spatial delineations produced by and within spreading capitalist relations: the space which initiates and sustains capitalism (the core); that which the core has incorporated into its own dynamics (the Third World); that which begins to encounter European capitalism but is not yet integrated (the periphery); and spaces that remain external to global capitalism. In short, as capitalism develops and intensifies, more and more of the peripheral and external spaces become internalized as the Third World. It is this dynamic social process and the spatial striations and inequalities it produces that Stavrianos wishes to reveal. By identifying these broad systemic patterns, he allows readers to see how particular places in a particular time are fit into the contours of capitalism as a global phenomenon.

For example, in the initial period of the emergence of West European capitalism, he shows how the Third World originated in the incorporation of Eastern Europe into the trade, investment, and production circuits of Western Europe (chap. 3), a pattern quickly extended into Latin America (chap. 4). Some spaces remain "peripheral" at this stage: Africa, despite the centrality of the slave trade, and the Middle East, meaning the Ottoman empire, remain not yet penetrated by European capitalism (chaps. 5 and 6). Asia, primarily India and China here, were largely spared capitalist penetration and remained an "external area" (chap. 7). Stavrianos performs three more tours of the world like this one that explore the relation of core and periphery in successive periods of capitalist development and more extensive integration of regions in the Third World.

Stavrianos' key and the consistent point is that the First and Third Worlds are not simply products of separable and uneven internal developments. Rather, they are relationally co-constituted within an "indivisible whole," with wealth on one side and poverty on the other. Indeed, "the phrase 'Third World' connotes those countries or regions that participated on *unequal terms* in what eventually became the global market economy" (31–2, emphasis added). For Stravrianos, the co-constituted structural inequalities central to capitalism profoundly distort human development as a whole, though the effects fall most fatally on the Third World, challenging claims of market-induced harmony. While Stavrianos recognizes capitalism's transformative role, including the expanding human productivity released by the restless pursuit of profit, he places greater ethical weight on the devastation wreaked on the economics, politics, and culture of the conquered or marginalized societies (35–7). As in Polanyi's account (that we discuss in chapter 6), capitalism utterly reshapes them: "This was a total and all-encompassing process, for the culture as well as the economies of those societies were profoundly distorted and remodeled in order to satisfy the demands of the global market" (37).

The burden of the text, and picking up the story of European expansion where Chaudhuri ends, is to show how the encounter between European capitalist expansion and the Third World imposes new relationships that incorporate the latter. Here Stavrianos relies, interestingly, on Joseph Schumpeter's distinction between economic development and economic growth (1961, 63). Economic development "calls forth . . . qualitatively new phenomena" that "are not forced upon it from without but arise by its own initiative, from within," whereas "mere economic growth" involves "processes of adaption. . . [of] the same kind as changes in the natural data." Schumpeter's major concern is not the global dynamics of wealth and poverty but to challenge the static character of equilibrium analysis (McNulty 1968; Legrand and Hagemann 2017). But Stavrianos pounces on this distinction between internally created qualitative economic changes (development) versus economic changes that follow from externally initiated and generated processes (economic growth) to organize his narrative.

The distinguishing feature of Third World status besides low incomes, Stavrianos insists, is "growth determined by foreign capital and foreign markets rather than by local needs" (4). Externally determined growth fosters *"vertical economic linkages"* that tie raw material extraction and agricultural production in the Third World to demands in the "metropolitan centers." By contrast, *"horizontal economic linkages"* more fully integrate local production and local needs and support local employment and incomes (39–40, emphasis added). Though the development of the "indivisible whole" of global capitalism may foster some "trickle down" for the First World working classes (267, 270, 439, 794), the dependence of Third World economies on growth via vertical economic ties means that incomes and wealth tend to "trickle up" (794):

> The people of the Third World experienced no corresponding improvement in living standards. For them the impact of the West was a wrenching experience, in which everything was turned upside down and inside out. This was inevitable, for all Third World societies, by definition, were integrated into the world market economy, with unavoidable disruptions and distortion of their traditional institutions. (267)

Thus, Stavrianos arrives at an elegant relational definition of the Third World: "the Third World is not a set of countries or a set of statistical criteria but rather a set of relationships—*unequal* relationships between controlling metropolitan centers and dependent peripheral regions, whether colonies as in the past or neocolonial 'independent' states as today" (40).

In all of this, Stavrianos asserts, the "interests of the colonies were automatically subordinated to those of the mother country" (55). After all, "the purpose of the colonies was to provide markets for manufactures, to supply raw materials that could not be produced at home, to support a merchant marine that would be valuable in wartime and to engender a large colonial population with manpower" (55–6). Colonial underdevelopment appears a natural and automatic corollary of the expansion of capitalism.

But can we be so certain that this subordination is natural and automatic? Why do capitalism's systemic inequalities map largely, if not always neatly, onto a European and North American core and a Latin American, African, and Asian Third World? Creating and sustaining vertical ties with the colony follows an economic logic, certainly, but that seems insufficient. Stavrianos' explanation seems to rely on the additional factors of political competition/chauvinism and practices informed by doctrines of white supremacy. Western Europeans did not imagine their colonies as part of the home nation, territory, or culture. Nor did they consider the peoples of these areas as necessarily or equally human. The peoples of Africa, Asia, and the Americas are thought of as something apart and thereby unworthy of full ethical or legal consideration. Near the end of the book, Stavrianos highlights the consequent limits of worker solidarity across the global relations of capitalism and his narrative makes explicit the role of multiple logics—the logic of capitalism, of the Westphalian state system, and of white supremacy. It is not true that "working men have no country"; "Far from a world dividing along class lines, it is state frontiers that are decisive and meaningful" (631). Indeed, the "evolving world system is dominated not by class interests but by nationalist considerations" (631). Thus, changing our world is not merely a matter of restructuring the global economy. It requires "a comparable restructuring of national units" (812).

This last comment hints at an important narrative shift. Stavrianos, more so than Wolf, begins to show that European capitalism's expansive dynamism is met head-on by Third World resistance and rebellion. Initial rebellions and wars of resistance against European invasions and colonization across the Third World were largely unsuccessful, appearing only as a "gestation phase" of "uncoordinated resistance" (432). But these events were not isolated; they all reacted to the same cause—capitalism's logic of incorporating each space into its own logic and dynamics (424). Yet, these events *were* separated from each other, and the failure to resist "imperialist onslaught"[1] resulted directly from lack of "any international mutual support," while "the imperialist powers aided each other all over the globe." The Twentieth Century brought a change, where, slowly but surely, these movements overcame their isolation and became mutually supportive struggles for national independence and liberation. These struggles' efforts to "break with" a "trauma" created by 500 years of history became the "center of global revolutionary initiative" (431–2).

Of course, capitalist counter-revolutionary forces were not idle. They responded with mobilizations of their own political, economic, cultural counterrevolutionary strategies (433–83). He announces that the future of our world depends on the "nature, strength, and interaction of global revolutionary and counterrevolutionary forces" (432) and his less hopeful prognosis has been vindicated by events already unfolding as he writes the final sections of *Global Rift*. Skyrocketing oil prices, Third world debt, stagflation in the core followed by draconian monetary policy, all combined with assassinations, support of dictators tied to the interests of capital, and intensified counter-insurgency weakened and fractured the Third World movement. The movement's demands for an international order serving and reflecting national needs, ideals, and goals remain unrealized. As reactionary forces gained the geopolitical-economic upper hand, theories diagnosing and protesting global inequality were likewise gradually marginalized in respectable academic discussion in the United States (Blaney and Inayatullah 2008) and neoclassical economics reasserted its predominance, erasing nearly any other voice in universities and policymaking circles. It is at this moment that liberal institutionalist IPE assumed a dominant position in the academy of the U.S. imperial core, obscuring attention to the "indivisible whole" with its privileging of unit-level explanations. Yet, the struggle continues because, according to Stavrianos and as theorized by others (Escobar 1995, 2018; Santos 2007), as we see in the next chapter, the "problem of how to attain autonomous economic development remains unresolved, both in theory and practice" (796).

CONCLUSIONS AND A CAVEAT

Despite the precision and majesty of these works, they have had remarkably little impact on the IPE mainstream in the United States. Cohen, as noted, suggests that U.S. scholars favor more parsimonious, unit-level explanations because of their rigor and scientific status. Reading Chaudhuri, Wolf, and Stavrianos indicates a different conclusion: that social theory is an effect of empire and continuing domination (Wolf 1982, 13, 389–90; Stavrianos 1981, 37–8, 793–4; Chaudhuri 1990, 22–4; Blaney and Inayatullah 2008, 669). More precisely, IPE's methodological individualism and national internalism lend support to existing inequality by erasing attention to colonial conquest and continuing structures of domination from the intellectual agenda. This erasure is as political and ethical as epistemological or ontological, since the unit-level bias informs IPE's strident idealism, specifically its characterization of IR as a market-like space producing collective goods (see our chapters 3 and 4). We can surmise that our authors' attempts to restore colonialism and domination to the agenda of IPE is precisely what produces resistance to their work. As we put it elsewhere, "We can read international relations, then, as the refusal to recognize the denial involved in its own constitution" (Blaney and Inayatullah 2008, 670).

Stressing this point risks downplaying the most important intellectual contribution we identify. What our authors point towards is not the whole over the parts or structure over agency, as it is often put, but dynamic processes or flow. To make this point, we distinguish our view from Anthony Giddens' discussion of the "duality of structure," which we fear retains what Giddens was trying to overcome, namely, the "dualism" of agents and structures. Giddens' turn from "dualism" to "duality" refers to what we have called "flow" (see Inayatullah 2016). Flow is the dynamic interaction that shows how structures are created from the actions of individuals, who themselves act according to these structures, both individuals and structures changing within an interactive process. By employing the term "duality," Giddens rightly concedes that we cannot grasp the totality of dynamic social relations all at once. Therefore, the reified entities called "agents" and "structures" represent truncated but necessary ways of speaking about a dynamic and fluid process. Closer to our IR home, we see Alexander Wendt (1987) drawing on Giddens to produce precisely this misreading in his seminal engagement with the structure-agent problem, sustaining more than overcoming this reified separation of "agents" from "structures."[2] We suggest that analysis and appreciation of these three books starts here—with the herculean theoretical and historical effort to overcome both a "dualism" and "duality" of structure and arrive instead at dynamic interaction, or "flow." In this way, we again counter the methodological individualism of proper economics or liberal IPE with a vision of "the social process" as "one indivisible whole."

To be fair, liberal IPE also imagines a global space, as we indicate in chapter 3. In parallel to social contract theory, IPE begins with units and sees international institutions as a series of bargains in which states exercise rights within limits they themselves set. These institutions allow key human practices to extend beyond boundaries; market production and exchange become parts of an international economy of individuals, firms, and states. Somewhere, also, is the hope that liberal principles of restraint and tolerance will come, eventually at least, to inform the relations of states, just as the rights of individuals should take on a universal or cosmopolitan character (see chapters 1 and 3). In this sense, liberalism and its traveling companions, modernity, and capitalism, are always already international. But still, the presumption of unit-level explanation holds strong. The "individualism imperative" connected to the "levels" scheme in IR resists any turn to social explanation, as we show in chapter 4. We must work hard, as do Chaudhuri, Stavrianos, and Wolf, to make the case for starting with a relational whole.

Both liberal IPE and our Marxism-influenced critics seem joined in *presuming* a universal or cosmopolitan order. We want to acknowledge a caution that we can too easily take the categories of capitalism, global, and system for granted. Anna Tsing (2005, ix) brings the anthropologist's tools to bear on what she calls an "ethnography of global connection" and offers stories about capitalism that cut somewhat against the grain of those provided by Stavrianos and Wolf. Tsing's multilayered stories are about walking through forests as part of hiking clubs, forest dwellers' cultivation practices, a local scheme for classification of biodiversity, and small-scale miners and migrants seeking farmland to squat. She describes geologists and environmental scientists studying the forests as sites for mining or preservation, respectively, government officials registering property, representatives of Indonesian and Japanese firms seeking control of minerals or supplies of rattan, and the ultimate denuding of some forests and the conservation of others, but nearly invariably displacing the forest peoples. Tsing knows these stories are also about supply chain capitalism, dispossession and deforestation, global democracy and environmental movements, national development plans, and international development agencies. She uses these familiar terms and notions, but also refuses to accept them at face value. No global process moves across space without *friction*, the metaphor that informs her narratives.

Tsing's stories also turn the tables against the unit-level or individualism imperative of liberal IPE and disrupt liberal understandings and justifications of inequality. Her actors are embedded in social relations and processes; their stories require attention to "spatially far flung collaborations and interconnections." But Tsing (2005, ix–x) wants to make certain that "diversity" is not "banished" by easy recourse to theories of globalization. Rather, global collaborations and interconnections are made only in relation to local particularities; Tsing (2005, 1) says "they come to life in 'friction'," in "the grip of worldly encounter." Here, we have not so much a world, as worldly encounters. Presumed universals like "capitalism" and "science" travel across space as aspirations not as systems but as "dreams" that we "cannot not want," because they offer "us a chance to participate in the global stream of humanity" (Tsing 2005, 1). These universals appear as both "the yearnings and nightmares of our time." We can't disagree. It is liberal capitalism's appeal to equality, freedom, and property that continues to beguile us, and rightfully so. These aspirations and perhaps partial achievements also point to the "nightmare" (or scandal or wound in our terms) of poverty and inequality that liberal capitalism produces. We see the yearnings and the nightmares both as central to the worldly encounters that comprise the processual flow of liberalism and global capitalism.

We wonder though: what is at stake for Tsing in identifying the apparently widespread desire to "participate in the global stream of humanity"? Tsing (2005, 270–1) suggests that any political project that claims universal relevance "must enter the fray" of encounter. It is in this "fray" that our projects can be realized and, only then, because they find life in connecting to the particularities and diversities they encounter on the ground. We stage such an encounter, in thought at least, in the next chapter, where we explore two competing, but also overlapping readings of Karl Polanyi's *The Great Transformation*. The first locates Polanyi's socialist vision as emergent from the failures of liberalism as a world order. Here, socialism means securing livelihood in order to realize the freedom of individuals in the complex societies and global institutions of the modern era. The second grounds its project in an alternative, anti-modernist ontology. Here, the political project becomes more complicated. A right to a share seems to entail a right to a "world" resistant to and separate from modern societies. And the relations between these worlds and the universalizing modern may be guided by principles of repair and healing more than distributive justice. While the differences appear striking, we believe these political projects overlap. Securing livelihood in a world in which many worlds are possible requires operating at multiple scales and with multiple applications of the principle of a right to a share.

Chapter 6

Complex Societies
and Alternative Worlds

We posed a problem at the end of the last chapter. Accounts of capitalism as a world system can be accused of an indifference to the variety of histories and situations that allows them to take such categories as global and capitalism for granted. An exploration of "global connection," Tsing (2005) argues, allows us to tell multilayered stories that involve the "friction" that emerges when global processes travel across space. Tsing's notion of friction reminds us to attend to the presence of difference even as we stress the presence of a global capitalist system that interconnects the fate of people across the globe. In earlier efforts to address the issue of capitalism and difference, we turned to the work of Karl Polanyi. We will do that again, but this time in relation to a stronger challenge: Arturo Escobar's tendency to locate anticapitalist energies in spaces that appear still somewhat outside of capitalist modernity in order to make a claim for disconnecting the fate of communities from dominant global systems of domination. For Escobar, exploration of ontological difference—of a pluriverse of world-making projects—casts doubt on any political-ethical conclusions drawn simply against a backdrop of liberal modernity or global capitalism. Escobar's move pushes back against thinkers, such as Pogge and ourselves perhaps, who justify redistribution within an interconnected world in the form of a right to a share of global social wealth.

In our earlier treatment of Karl Polanyi in *International Relations and the Problem of Difference* (Inayatullah and Blaney 2004, 161–2), we identify two broad readings of his work. We might think of one as a distinctly IPE reading. The second we might call a postdevelopment reading. Placed together these two readings raise not only interpretive problems in relation to Polanyi's body of work, but also pose intertwined questions about the character of the relational totality, perhaps the world-capitalist system, as Chaudhuri, Wolf, and Stavrianos would have it (see chapter 5), that constitutes a possible object of analysis. We will consider some of these interpretive questions facing Polanyi's thought but largely because they bear on other issues, particularly the political/ethical implications of speaking of the global as a social whole. We sense that something deep is at stake. This deep something cuts to the ontological heart of the relational/processual view we have defended in these essays as an alternative to the methodological individualism of liberal thinkers. In both possible readings, a relational view of human livelihood emerges. We see the limits of liberal thought and practice from the point of view of a social totality. But if the first reading begins with the idea of the social totality as a world system built from capitalist social relations, the latter often challenges that claim in the name of the presence of alternative and, often, localized worlds. In the end, we assess the divergent ideas they offer of what it means to secure the livelihood of people.

The first reading, developed further in the section that follows, is familiar to most scholars who work in IPE. Since the 1980s, progressive liberalization and commodification disembedded markets from social life on a global scale, eroding elements of social citizenship that had been won earlier and newly dispossessing populations of land and resources and dislocating ways of life across the globe. Following Polanyi, scholars argue that deregulating money (or finance) and subjecting land and labor progressively to market discipline necessarily spark a range of local, national, and transnational countermovements. These movements separately and in conjunction demand greater societal self-protection at multiple scales in order to secure labor rights, basic livelihood as a right to a share of social wealth, and more democratic control of economic policy. Together they might constitute the basis for a socialist reembedding of the economy that would institutionalize Polanyi's vision of freedom in a complex regional or global society coterminous with the global scale of capitalist market relations. We develop this line of argument in order to highlight a key implication of Polanyi's vision of freedom: the obligation to secure the right to livelihood.

The second, and less familiar, reading we associate with figures such as Gustavo Esteva, J. K. Gibson-Graham, and Arturo Escobar. These authors emphasize Polanyi's comments on capitalism as a process of cultural dislocation, if not quite a destruction, and they defend difference in the face of a normalizing, if not always fully homogenizing, project of modern development. As we explore in the second section, Escobar reads Polanyi's economic anthropology as a defense and restoration of varied non-modern and non-capitalist modes of the economy or material provisioning, more so than a socialist countermovement on a national, regional, or global scale. As we put it in *Savage Economics*, this emphasis on difference beyond liberal capitalism might "intensify our appreciation of people's connection with local landscapes." We might recognize how "localized ways of life come to see themselves as cultures"—"as distinct ways of life that will survive and adapt, and evolve according to their own decisions, and claim a place among the diverse peoples of the world" (Blaney and Inayatullah 2010, 192–3). The defense of a right to a distinctive way of life connected to a particular place might lay claim less to a right to a share of the social wealth produced in a globalized market society and more to a right to live apart from the modern capitalist world-making project. It is a demand to be freed from compulsory participation in the world system and to the possibility of material provisioning largely delinked from wider social relations beyond those embodied in the localized community/place. The claims by communities to justice may be restorative—a demand to repair what has been damaged by colonialism and capitalism, to redress past dislocations, and to restore a world in which multiple worlds may thrive. The politics/ethics that derive from this reading appears to offer a radical anti-modern alternative to a modernist vision of human freedom in a complex (perhaps global) society, though we also attend to the ways the two may converge or be mutually supportive.

These two readings of Polanyi lead us to reflect a bit more on the question of a right to a share of the world's wealth. We earlier explored Thomas Pogge's claim that a right to a share of the wealth follows from the fact that wealth and poverty are produced as part of an interconnected global process of wealth production and impoverishment (chapter 2). Providing people a secure material basis for a rich and meaningful life can be extended to a global society as a whole because the process of social wealth production is itself a global one. The limits of the application of this argument may be exposed by Escobar's thinking about multiple worlds. Escobar seems to assert a more radical form of difference on behalf of peasant, indigenous, and Afro-descendant communities, and his claims could lead us to support a right of a community to a world (or to a process of worlding) that sees its survival as defending and sustaining itself outside not only capitalism but modernity itself. We take seriously the idea that this gesture to radical separation and difference might challenge the idea of a globally interconnected process of production and consumption that grounds the idea of a right to a share of income or wealth. Yet we also identify the limits of Escobar's claim of difference/separation. We explore the points where the two cases meet or overlap and where they might be put into a fruitful dialogue so that each project might find the other as a necessary, if underemphasized, moment. On the one side, we note that global democratic provisioning requires imagining multi-scalar institutional arrangements that attend to the autonomy of localized communities. On the other, we argue that Escobar's vision of self-organizing communities appears to entail exactly the sorts of multi-scalar arrangements that make democratic provisioning a global project.

POLANYI AND FREEDOM IN A COMPLEX
(GLOBAL) SOCIETY

Polanyi's work has had great appeal in the contemporary neoliberal era, especially his "analysis of the pathogenesis and malign consequences of free-market globalization" (Dale 2010, 2–4, 207). Fred Block (2001, xviii) writes that *The Great Transformation* "remains fresh" for precisely this reason: "it is indispensable for understanding the dilemmas facing global society at the beginning of the twenty-first century." Or, as Silver and Arrighi (2003, 325) put it, Polanyi's "brilliant quotable quotes" serve as ammunition against the "wrong-headedness" of the "promoters of the Washington Consensus and 'neoliberal globalization'." In general, scholars in IPE draw links between Polanyi's analysis of resistance to the cruelties of the liberal creed, including the emergence of the New Deal as a response to the crisis of a world organized around free trade and the gold standard and contemporary antiglobalization movements at various scales.

The basic features of Polanyi's account in *The Great Transformation* (Polanyi 2001; see Inayatullah and Blaney 2004, chapter 5; Dale 2010, chapter 2) are well known. In most times and places, the system by which humans provide their material livelihood (the "economy" in Polanyi's terms) has been embedded in the social values of the community and an embedded economy largely secures the material life of the community and its members. Guided by a new liberal creed, emerging industrial societies subject labor, land, and money to the market. Freed from the social values that had checked the scope of market relations, human livelihood becomes precarious, human habitat is despoiled, and buying power for those relying on the market becomes unreliable. Polanyi suggests that it is only dogmatic liberals with their religious faith in self-regulating markets who are surprised by what he calls the "double movement" or "countermovement"—the complex alliances of social groups working to redress the consequences of the self-regulating market. Actions to protect society from free markets include: regulation of working conditions, food safety, sanitation, and banking; the provision of public libraries, universal education, public works, and income maintenance programs; the implementation of tariff protections and industrial policies; the self-organization of workers and consumers in cooperatives; and struggles for suffrage that allow political parties to speak to and for a mass base. Though largely unconnected, myriad acts redressing specific social ills join together to form a system of societal self-protection, not as a plan, as in liberal attempts to make market society, but as an accretion of concrete efforts to protect the substance of the human community. It is these systems of societal self-protection, eventuating in the New Deal and similar ventures elsewhere, that stabilized modern society after the combined global crises of war, heightened nationalistic economic competition, and depression. This twentieth-century double movement serves as the possible basis for the development of a form of socialism that Polanyi describes in the conclusion to *The Great Transformation* as "freedom in a complex society."

Polanyi's notion of countermovement raises some interpretive difficulties.[1] It is possible, Dale (2010, 226, 230) suggests, to read Polanyi as embracing a "pendular motion of marketization and protection," where what is at stake is only "market excesses" and what is achieved is the stable institutionalization of capitalism. But Dale (2010, 46) worries that this reading places too much emphasis on Polanyi's account of the always-failed nineteenth-century efforts to create self-regulating markets and not Polanyi's attention to the varying responses to the crisis of liberalism in the twentieth century. The great transformation that Polanyi has in mind is *not* the initial transition to industrial capitalism in Britain (though the lessons of that history weigh heavily on Polanyi's present, as he emphasizes). Rather, it is the final collapse of nineteenth-century civilization around which Polanyi believes an era of transformation beyond the liberal creed becomes possible.

Debates unfolding within the IPE literature illustrate Dale's point. On one side, we might locate John Ruggie. Ruggie (1982) famously draws on Polanyi's discussion of the global crisis of the interwar period to explain the Bretton Woods institutions as the "embedded liberalism" bargain. This bargain blended relatively open markets and the protection of national autonomy, allowing international trade to grow dramatically in the postwar period, without great disruption to the autonomy of domestic macroeconomic policy, including social insurance systems, and the existing global distribution of economic power. Following Ruggie, the hope expressed by scholars is that we might locate similar possibilities for re-embedding neoliberalism (see, for example, Hettne 1997; Caporaso and Tarrow 2009; and Helleiner 2007; see the recent surveys by Germain 2019 and Helleiner 2019).

On the other side, Hannes Lacher (1999a, 1999b, 2007) pushes back against the idea that Polanyi offers us no more than a pendulum swing between periods of excessive liberalization of markets and corresponding actions to check those excesses. He stresses that the American-led postwar embedded liberalism was a pale reflection of Polanyi's hope for subjecting markets to democratic control in order to secure humanity's material existence. We see Lacher's version of Polanyi as an important corrective to Ruggie's more famous reading; it prompts us to focus greater attention on Polanyi's vision of socialism (see also Block 2018, 168–9).

Polanyi links his case for socialism to the "reality of society" (Polanyi 1936, 392; 2001, 267). His somewhat varying accounts of *society* share a key commonality: they involve a war against liberal economists' assumption of the individual as the sole unit of analysis and their claim that socialism is contrary to human nature (see also Block and Somers 2014, 228–30). Polanyi develops his sense of the social in relation to a distinction he draws between "substantive" and "formal" meanings of the economy. A "formal" understanding stipulates the economy as "economizing," as a series of individual acts of "economical" behavior (Polanyi 1968, 140), familiar to us from neoclassical economics and liberal IPE (see chapters 3, 4, and 5). The formal understanding imagines an entire and exclusive world in which a particular aspect of human motivation and behavior—maximizing gain—becomes human behavior per se. But maximizing behavior may be universalized *in practice* only by institutionalizing markets "isolated" from other social motives, values, and institutions, including politics itself, so that a market society could "function according to its own laws" (Polanyi 2001, 60, 263). This form of society, if we can call it that, is constituted as an aggregation of every individual's economically rational acts. "For what could such a society be," Polanyi (1977, 13) asks, "other than an agglomeration of human atoms behaving according to the rules of a definite kind of rationality?" It is exactly this "agglomeration of human atoms" that libertarians and liberal IPE take for granted or, perhaps paradoxically, argue that we must intervene to create (Jahn 2019).

The tone of Polanyi's question indicates that generalizing the idea of economizing as a "whole culture" is dangerous or, perhaps by definition, impossible. He ties the simultaneous impossibility and danger to a second, and counter, "substantive" notion of the economy. Polanyi (1968, 139) highlights this "substantive" notion that all societies provide for livelihood as part of a complex social and material interchange that takes various forms in different times and places. With this move, he challenges the normalization of the formal idea of economizing and prompts us to see the diversity of "empirical economies of the past and present" (Polanyi 1968, 140) and consequently the richness and variability of human motives and institutions. Material provisioning achieves a certain "unity and stability" only as "an instituted process" and, thereby only as "embedded" in complex motives, values, and institutions (Polanyi 1968, 146, 148). Attempting to dis-embed or insulate markets from wider social values and processes, as liberals intend, undercuts the stability of human livelihood and, thereby, human society itself. It produces, as Polanyi (2001, 164) puts it, "a social catastrophe" that encompasses cultural as well as economic life.

At one key point, Polanyi (2001, chaps. 10, 17, 20, and 21) also presents "society" as something discovered (or rediscovered?) as a concept for scholars in the nineteenth and twentieth centuries.[2] Society became "a reality" for scholars, activists, and officials when they acknowledged the need to address the growing pauperism and poverty created by the dislocation of vast populations in the face of the industrial revolution and the strident attempt to subject human habitat and human livelihood to the reign of unconstrained markets. As Polanyi tells the story, first, socialist visionaries, Christian social reformers, and national protectionists, and, later, New Dealers, social democrats, and fascists alike used an appeal to the idea of society to resist the imposition of free markets. For all these groups, the *social* served as the counterweight to liberals' attempt to run "society" as an "adjunct to the market" (Polanyi 2001, 60). The twentieth-century countermovement that finally ended nineteenth-century free-market liberalism involved the panoply of "measures which society adopted in order not to be, in its turn, annihilated by the action of the self-regulating market" (Polanyi 2001, 257).

Liberal efforts to dis-embed material provisioning from other values, norms, and institutions "exist only in ideology" (Block and Somers 2014, 219); they ignore the impossibility of such a regime and the inevitable defense of society. Early Scottish proto-liberals, as we saw in the first chapter, mostly recognized and fully exemplified a consciousness of the fantastical quality of unregulated markets. Invisible hands are accompanied by artful and invasive hands and the market appears as much a complex cultural and political system as a mechanical (or amoral) apparatus. But Polanyi more completely inverts the conclusions of liberal economists, including his primary nemeses, Friedrich Hayek and Ludwig von Mises (Özel, n.d.; Lind 1994, 147; Block and Somers 1984; Mendell 1990; Brie 2018), than do our Scottish Enlightenment "liberals." Where the liberal creed sees market exchange and prices as an expression of individual freedom and hence a morally justified outcome, Polanyi sees the laws of the market generating an ethical deformation of individuals and their freedom. In an essay that prefigures many aspects of *The Great Transformation*, Polanyi (1936, 375) deploys a line of argument close to Marx's critique of commodity fetishism: "developed market-society" is treated as a "spectral world," in which relations of cooperation and interdependence are "hidden behind the exchange of goods."[3] But, as in Marx, these "*spectres are real*" in the sense that they take on an "objective guise." As Rotstein (1990, 105) summarizes Polanyi's point in this essay, market society appears as "an alien and eternal network that channels economic life" and the individual is "cast into a situation out of his moral control" (see also Thomasberger 2005). But, Polanyi (1937, 375) asserts, these "human relations are the reality of society." And society can be "humane," a truly "human society," only when this "spectral world" created by modern capitalism is subjected to conscious control.

For Polanyi (1937, 392–3), regaining human ethical self-determination requires actions beyond the most interventionist of our Scottish Enlightenment thinkers: the "extension of the democratic principle from politics to economics" or what he calls "socialism." Socialism reverses the alienating features of capitalism, recognizing both "the fuller realization of the dependence of the whole on individual will and purpose—and a corresponding increase of responsibility of the individual for his share of the whole." The institutional mechanisms for "oversight" of production—"making society an increasingly plastic medium of the conscious and immediate relationship of persons"—requires the cultivation of leadership and capacities for self-government by all. How these democratic capacities would be exercised in the institutions managing material provisioning are not so clearly worked out, but Polanyi finds inspiration in the kinds of cooperative arrangements he associates with Robert Owen and guild socialism more generally, worker education movements, and bargaining by labor unions (see Mendell 1990; Rosmer 1990, 61–2; Dale 2018, 128–30).[4]

Polanyi revisits this theme at the end of *The Great Transformation*. What is at stake, he suggests, is nothing less than human "freedom in a complex society," the concluding chapter in which he highlights "the complex social interconnectedness" of modern life (Block and Somers 2014, 234, see also 227; Bugra 2018). He recognizes, as we do in chapter 2, that liberal fears of violations of human liberty are crucial to the case against socialism (Polanyi 2001, 258). Polanyi (2001, 259–60) freely admits that the untrammeled role of the market in relation to labor, land, and money must be suppressed for the sake of human freedom and well-being. In regards to labor, Polanyi notes that growing public regulation means that the key terms of the labor contract are set outside of the market, including working "conditions in the factory, hours of work," and "the basic wage itself," though he does not promote exact equality or ban profits (see Dale 2018). Similar discussions of land and money follow. Public regulation of land for the provision of food and raw materials dominates his concerns, but he also mentions setting aside places for public use, including parks, libraries, art facilities, and nature preserves. For money, Polanyi envisions the end of the gold standard (and the periodic austerity it forced), making possible national control of the money supply with the purpose of securing buying power. The sense is that finance would cease to be a site of destabilizing speculative activities and money would be limited to its role as means of exchange in material provisioning. Rather than a comprehensive vision of a centrally planned society, Polanyi seems to suggest that socialism is about the *process* of taking "care of these concrete problems" (Rosmer 1990, 58). It is about the continuing human response to the problem of freedom. We might see this process as a form of democratic socialism that unfolds *from* modern liberal capitalism, not simply in opposition to it.[5]

But this vision of socialism moves us away from the liberalism of unrestricted individual freedom. Polanyi (2001, 262–5) acknowledges that certain kinds of freedom of action are lost in these restrictions on the sway of market forces: "regulation both extends and restricts freedom." The freedom of the market claimed by liberals has been achieved only "at the cost of justice and security." With restrictions on labor, land, and money markets, certain freedoms may be lost for the most "comfortable classes." But "more justly spread[ing] out income, leisure, and security" will provide much greater freedom for those previously forced to be "content" with only a "minimum." Here, Polanyi turns quickly to a rousing defense of basic civil liberties—protection of the "right to nonconformity," freedom of "conscience," freedom of scientific inquiry, freedom to protest, the end of "victimization" by the state—as sacrosanct elements of a society dedicated to "an increase of freedom." He suggests that "the passing of market-economy" ends "privilege" in the application of justice and extends freedom to those usually excluded. Making "free enterprise" sacrosanct has effectively denied the possibility of using "democratic rights to gain shelter from the power of the owners of property" (Polanyi 2001, 265). While Polanyi (2014a, 43) accepts the story that our notions of civil liberties arose along with liberal market societies, he finds unconvincing the claim that only market societies can defend these rights.[6] Liberal society's claimed defense of these freedoms proved, Polanyi (2001, 265–6) insists, largely illusory. Liberals staunchly denied the reality of society upon which human freedom depends, with the disastrous consequences he outlined throughout *The Great Transformation*. Unrestricted market freedom brought the liberal order to a succession of wars, economic crises, and ultimate collapse, spawning various forms of authoritarian rule that "reject[ed] the idea of freedom" itself.

If the social control of markets hopes to enhance individual freedom within complex societies, Polanyi (2001, 261–2) imagines that new international arrangements would secure entire countries' or peoples' autonomy from homogenizing market forces. The liberal order unleashed "unrelenting pressure" from global financial and military powers to conform to the market pattern. But with that Old World in "ruin," a New World allowing "economic collaboration of governments *and* the liberty to organize the national life at will" can now emerge. This "collaboration" and "liberty" allows the possibility for substantial "domestic freedom" for the "peoples of the world" who had been "institutionally standardized to a degree unknown before."

Just after he penned this version of the conclusion for the 1957 edition of *The Great Transformation*, Polanyi (2014 [1958], 32) followed out this suggestion further. Here, the collapse of the liberal international system spawns an emerging order characterized by a newly "circumscribed, reduced West." Not the West that offered its utopian illusions of either "unrestricted freedom" or "general regulationism" as competing versions of "universalism." Not the West that was the "bearer of industrial civilization, which, whether as capitalist or socialist, soon comprised almost half of the planet." The spread of this industrial civilization was never a product of negotiation or collaboration between the West and the rest of the world, as it could be in the new world being born; "It was not a conversation, rather a spirited monologue." In what appears to be a recognition of the aspirations generated with the gradual end of colonialism, Polanyi forecasts and embraces possibilities for the practice of diverse forms of the national economy (see also Bugra 2018). Escobar's reading of the modern era and the meaning of Polanyi's work, as we shall see, turn on modernity's foreclosure of such diversity.

When contemporary scholars imagine a socialist world made by a contemporary countermovement, they return to Polanyi's language of freedom and material provisioning.[7] Robert Latham is a prime example (but see also Standing 2007 and Rey Pérez 2007). Latham (1997, 57) suggests that Polanyi's reflections on societal self-protection allow us "to rethink how we approach the organization of material life on a global basis, through states or other political forms."[8] In broad terms, Latham (1997, 58) suggests that we follow Polanyi by recognizing "that there is no one strategy, mechanism, or schema like socialism or localism for contending with the social costs of markets." Polanyi inspires in us a "self-consciously heterogeneous approach," drawing widely from experiences across the globe so that we do not narrow our focus to the European-style welfare state. But such schemes do possess a "central and unifying task": "provisionsim," or *"democratic provisionism."* That task flows naturally from Latham's (1997, 58–9) assertion, following Polanyi, that the "purpose of institutions and activities that shape material life is to provide communities with goods, services or other values necessary to sustain community or group life, free of deprivation." Contemporary "economies and economic systems" do provide livelihood, and at high levels for some in the world, but vast numbers remain "extremely deprived" and, in our times, we can expect "growing deprivation and increasing social insecurity." A counter movement to protect society would require recognizing "that all communities and their constituents have rights of provision and thereby claims on economic transactions and exchanges that draw from, occur within, or simply impact upon them." Or, as we put it earlier in our reading of Pogge (chapter 2), people have a right to a share of global economic transactions and interconnections. We would also place the same demand on each community: that their "own economic systems and institutions should be providing for all."

Latham (1997, 62) wants to reinforce Polanyi's relative "optimistic" account of the possibility of "freedom in a complex society" in our rather pessimistic era. To arrive at this point, he thinks through the array of possible approaches to democratically subjecting markets to control (Latham 1997, 60–2). The question is how the "demos" will effectively "rule" the mechanisms of control. He worries that many activists over-emphasize the local.

Since provisioning today is largely built around "large-scale institutions like states, markets or trade and communications systems," he believes that these must be leveraged for securing "rights to provision." Not surprisingly, then, Latham believes that "the advancement of a democratic provisionism will rest ultimately on the capturing of state power." With the state as the central apparatus of provisionism, we can imagine a countermovement "global in reach, while at the same time locally specific."[9] It is only with "new forms of collaborative regulations between states and societies at the global level" that we can hold "global markets accountable," though these efforts are necessarily "connected with provisionist political and ideological projects implemented in local contexts as well." Without states committed to provisionism, Latham is doubtful that other actors—however grassroots or transnational—have the capacity to forge these "cooperative" arrangements across "different states and societies" and "different local and regional spaces." Latham's view casts some doubt on Escobar's focus on local communities, as we shall see. We also might see Escobar's work as a rejoinder to Latham's reading of Polanyi's vision.

ESCOBAR ON POLANYI AND THE RIGHT TO A WORLD

In *Encountering Development*, Arturo Escobar (1995, 3, see also 11) defines his task as an "anthropology of development." An ethnographic investigation of the discursive and representational practices associated with development reveals its "status of certainty in the [modern] social imaginary" and its power, thereby, to construct Western standards and understandings of the economy as a "benchmark" of human achievement. As a series of benchmarks, development inscribes a distinction between "permissible modes of being and thinking" and those beyond the pale (Escobar 1995, 5, 8). But an "anthropology of development," not unlike Polanyi's perhaps, reveals this distinction as arbitrary, relative to a particular "historically singular experience"—that of Europe (Escobar 1995, 10–11). From the ethnographer's gaze, it is development and its homogenizing and categorizing imperative that appears "exotic," as "peculiar, if not strange." This revelation makes possible a "postdevelopment regime of representation" as an alternative source of social imagination and contemporary practice.

Escobar draws on Polanyi to support his defense of cultural difference in the face of a normalizing, if not homogenizing, project of modern development. He begins the chapter where he performs an ethnography of "economics" with an epigram from Polanyi. Here, Polanyi identifies the liberal notion of "economic" as nearly unique in human history. Later in the chapter, Escobar (1995, 67–8) refers very favorably to Polanyi's account of the utopian character of liberal markets and the inevitable collapse of the liberal order, although he signals something less than enthusiasm for the "technocratic vision of the economy" that emerged with postwar economic institutions that so many in IPE extol. In fact, Escobar (1995, 72) indicates that "'the great transformation,' so admirably described by Polanyi," may have "marked the collapse of some of the most cherished economic principles of the nineteenth century." But that version of the liberal creed simply "gave way to more efficient ways of managing economies and populations." This shift inaugurated the era of development, development economics, and global institutions providing development aid and exercising economic discipline. Escobar's description of the postwar era sounds more like Ruggie's embedded liberalism than Polanyi's hope for socialism. Indeed, Escobar (1995, 61) credits Polanyi with being among those "critical analysts of market culture" who aimed to "remove political economy from the centrality that it has been accorded in the history of modernity." Polanyi's work allows us to "supersede the market as a generalized frame of reference" so that a "wider frame"—one opening to an "anthropology of modernity" and alternative ways of life— might emerge.

We can see Polanyi's value to Escobar's project. Polanyi (1977, 4–5) opens scholars to the greater diversity of the human experience in his refusal of "the economistic fallacy," where a broad "generic phenomenon" of humans providing their livelihood is confused with a "specific form" of the economy where human livelihood is decided by the market.[10] As we saw above, Polanyi (1968, 139–40) uses the distinction between formal economics (or economizing) and the substance of material provisioning to open up the social sciences to the varied "empirical economies of the past and present." Market logic appears as but one form among many, not the category revealing the meaning of logically superseded, if not always temporally prior, forms of economic experience. Here, we can see how Polanyi's characterization of the economy as always "embedded" or as "instituted process" can allow scholars like Escobar to refuse the economists' assumption of the logical priority and the historical sequences ascribed to the Western experience, including perhaps the inevitability of the processes that produced the capitalist world system.[11] This theme motivates much in Escobar's book.

Escobar develops related ideas in material initially dropped from *Encountering Development*.[12] Here, he complicates and historicizes the usual story of the evolution of the "Western economy." Escobar (2005, 139–40, 172, fn. 2) again begins with an epigram from Polanyi and quotes him extensively, explicitly embracing "Polanyi's concept of the economy as 'instituted process'." He repeats Polanyi's three-fold taxonomy of "basic forms" of societal "integration": "symmetry, centricity, and the market" (Escobar 2005, 150). Polanyi (2001, 1968) developed this schema as part of diversifying our understanding of how material provisioning of human livelihood is institutionalized or embedded. The economy may be integrated as practices of redistribution that give society a centricity since there must be a central political organ for collecting and redistributing the goods necessary to social life. Symmetry holds society together via modes of reciprocity very distinct from market exchange. While redistribution is usually associated with the concentration of political power that governs a larger unit, reciprocity may operate at various scales and within and in between groups. While market exchange was present in many times and places, for most of human history these markets were highly localized and were often peripheral to securing the basic livelihood of the population, since securing society was too important to be left up to the vagaries of market exchange. Polanyi also used this scheme, as Escobar (2005, 144–5) notes, to offer an alternative history of the rise of market society. Liberal stories, as we noted in the book's Introduction, and as Escobar (2005, 144) stresses, assume that market exchange is natural, growing from "the natural propensity of individuals to trade and barter," and that isolated individuals necessarily create local, national and, finally, international markets. Polanyi's story about the Western economy in *The Great Transformation* (2001, chapter 4) is much different. Being embedded in values that secure livelihood, localized exchange is highly circumscribed. Long-distance trade may flourish but it deals largely in luxury goods and the reproduction of social relations in much of a political domain is insulated from its effects. Only in modern societies is an economy instituted in a form that subjects individual livelihood to the laws of market exchange.

Though this story connects our two readings of Polanyi, Escobar may be stressing something different than what we find in IPE. When Escobar (2005, 151) describes the disembedding of the market, he associates it with the insti-tutionalization of "an ideology of individualism." Not only are individuals in England and continental Europe subjected to the "stark utopia" of unregulated markets, but they are also constructed as individual subjectivities. What is at stake for Escobar is more than market fundamentalism: it is the imposition of Western cultural patterns themselves. This difference becomes perhaps clearer still when Escobar (2005, 141) invokes a "double movement": on one side, "the extension of the Western economic rationality to the Third World"; on the other side, "various form of resistance to such an extension." Later in the text, Escobar (2005, 165–6) describes this double movement in more detail, though now calling it "dialectics." The "dialectics" of "resistance" to the extension of "capitalist forms" occasions the emergence of "a participa-tory process of political organization and struggle." Escobar depends on the work of several ethnographers to suggest that "peasant resistance to capitalist rationality must be seen as an attempt to preserve not only communal struc-tures but a whole different way of perceiving reality." Resistance is attentive to existing ways of satisfying "wants and needs" but it also finds motivation in "the conflict between two ways of apprehending and evaluating the world." Thus, the dialectic starts "with people's knowledge (not necessarily 'scientific' knowledge), and seeks to build popular counter-power."

Escobar (1995, 215–16) speaks in similar terms in the conclusion to *Encountering Development*, but also seems open about the forms that alternatives to Western capitalism will take. There is no simple Third World *tradition* that resists and "it is too soon even to imagine the forms of representation that this process might promote." He is clear, however, that we are not speaking about "development alternatives but . . . alternatives to development."[13] With mounting challenges to development, he believes that new identities are forming and "nuclei" are emerging "around which new forms of power and knowledge might converge." He warns us not to find in his arguments an appeal to an essentialist "cultural identity"; rather, he invokes the notion of "hybridity" and characterizes these resistance movements' relation to modernity as open, "critical," "transgressive," and "humorous" (Escobar 1995, 218–19). Answers emerge, Escobar (1995, 222–3) claims, not in the abstract, but as localized responses to the "concrete forms that concepts and practices of development and modernity take in specific communities." The character of replacements to "development and modernity" might be revealed by ethnographic research "gleaned from the specific manifestations of such alternatives in concrete local settings."

We can certainly locate echoes of Polanyi here. Attempts to implement the liberal faith in unregulated markets are met by resistance. We might expect that resistance to take the form, initially, of defense of practices that had secured material provisioning in the past, but the forms of societal defense will evolve and vary according to the specific ills being addressed. But we might also sense a difference between Escobar and IPE on the meaning of Polanyi's *Great Transformation*. Most IPE scholars associate the central mechanisms of subjugating capitalism with the institutions of a modern society/state or their extension as forms of global governance. Escobar reads Polanyi mostly against the grain of IPE. And Escobar's dialectic, which pits capitalist rationality against communal structures and alternative ways of being/knowing, presages the key themes of Escobar's most recent work.

Polanyi's idea of embeddedness seems open to these varying readings.[14] Some see Polanyi as embracing and romanticizing nonmarket forms of life (Booth 1994; Katz 1997; Hechter 1981). The charge is that the distinction between embedded and disembedded economies partakes too much of a polarity of community and society proposed by the sociologists and ethnographers who influenced Polanyi. Here, as Booth (1994, 655–7) explains, the idea is that the move to modern society "entailed a loss of a certain vital quality that typified earlier societies." It is modernity that is to be resisted. Fraser

(2014, 544) likewise warns that Polanyi's *Great Transformation* lends itself to a politically retrograde "communitarianism": an excessive focus on "the corrosive effects of commodification *upon* communities" to the neglect of "injustices *within* communities, including injustices, such as slavery, serfdom and patriarchy, that depend on social constructions of labour, land and money precisely as *non*-commodities."[15] Interestingly, Block and Somers (1984, 71, 77) worry that he does something like the opposite, tending to reify the social as modern society and note that the idea of societal self-protection may not follow from his accounts of "precapitalist societies," except in the loosest sense. It is a modern, complex society in which freedom is being secured. Alongside modern society, then, Polanyi seems to assume the modern state as the site of societal self-protection (Holmes 2012, 479). But it would be wrong to suggest that Polanyi takes the nation-state or the national economy for granted. Rather, as we noted, he highlights the predominance in most of human history of local systems of material provision, supplemented by long-distance trade. The state and the national economy appear just as instituted as free markets.[16] However instituted, Polanyi does seem to accept these historical constructions as the institutional basis for negotiating the future of human freedom. Escobar makes the problem of reconciling community and modern society even more difficult when he embraces political ontology and the idea of multiple worlds in *Designs for the Pluriverse* (2018).

Escobar (2018, ix–x) begins his most recent book by linking together a claim of "crisis" and a particular set of resistance movements of "Latin American indigenous, black, and peasant activists." These movements indict not simply capitalism but the entire Western "civilizational model," "an entire way of life and the whole style of world making." While the sources of what he calls "new design thinking" are emerging globally, Escobar finds his "main epistemic and political inspiration and force . . . in the political struggles of indigenous, Afro-descendent, peasant, and marginalized urban groups in Latin America." Their goals center around "defending not only their territories and resources but their entire ways of being-in-the-world," and they justify these struggles in "the name of their collective alternative 'Life Projects'." Escobar (2018, 20, 248 n. 1) draws a parallel between the kinds of "transitions" (or "the great transition") these groups and he advocate and the "the great transformation" Polanyi described and foresaw. But, it appears, and Escobar (2018, x) stresses, that these movements see their freedom as "cultural and political autonomy" in the making of worlds, largely apart from the modern complex societies that Polanyi may assume. Nevertheless, even what appear as stark differences can also suggest parallels.

The stark differences with Polanyi do stand out. Midway in the introductory chapter, Escobar (2018, 8–10) turns to Ivan Illich's critique of modern institutions and modern forms of expertise. Illich's concerns, as Escobar enumerates them, relate both to democratic control of modern practices, like the mass media and education, and also escape from modern, industrial society. In Escobar's words and reflecting his concerns throughout *Designs for the Pluriverse*, Illich links "human creativity" and "people's autonomy for action" with "humans' localization in place and nature" and "humans' right to community, tradition, myth and ritual." All this requires a "radical inversion, away from industrial productivity and toward conviviality." It requires "an agreement to end growth and development," or a commitment to "degrowth" as Escobar regularly calls it (see also 95–6, 144–51).[17]

Polanyi (2001, 36–43) also identified the industrial revolution as a key influence on nineteenth-century European civilization and our own. But it is clear that industrial production and the advances in science and technology that made it possible are not his primary target. The industrial change was disruptive, certainly, but the key problem for Polanyi was the growing belief in "spontaneous progress" that "blinded" thinkers to the necessary role of the state in mitigating the consequences for the masses of the population. And it is the productive improvement that makes possible the achievement of freedom in a complex society so that the industrial civilization remains central to Polanyi's socialist vision. It is "capitalist market society" that was not essential; there is no sense of a necessary historical role for capitalism as you might find in Marx (Brie and Thomasberger 2018, 12).

By contrast, Escobar's condemnation of industrial civilization is expansive and unforgiving. As one of many examples, he draws on feminist thinking to indicate Western modernity's patriarchal desire for mastery and control that produces domination and environmental destruction. He associates these values with the modern state and professional expertise. In opposition to the exclusions performed by modern regimes of expertise, the often "matristic cultures" he embraces highlight "inclusion, participation, collaboration, understanding, respect, sacredness, and the always-recurrent cyclic renovation of life." There is nothing of Fraser's suspicion of community here. What is called for, then, "is a politics of an other civilization that respects, and builds on, the interconnectedness of all life, based on a spirituality of the Earth." This politics invokes "a culture of healing, the revitalization of tradition and the creation of new ones" (Escobar 2018, 8, 12–14) in response to the spread of modern industrial civilization that generated what Escobar (2018, 69, 81; see also 167) calls an "ontological occupation" suppressing other cultures and traditions. The diversity of worlds—of socio-natures, of communal relationships—become "illegible" when globalization extends a vision of the natural world as "inanimate matter" to be worked upon. Or, a bit later, Escobar (2018, 107–8) describes the disturbance of even the "geological time of our planet" as corporations attempt to "bend the Earth into any form or shape." An alternative civilization, Escobar (2018, 71–3, 75) explains, responds to an "ancestral mandate" to recover and recuperate the "memory" of relations that have been disrupted. A "radical struggle for cultural difference" is always also a "recovery and defense of territory and life plans." Only in conjunction with the memory of the place can people perform their role as "effective weavers of the mesh of life." Closely parallel to the dialectics Escobar isolated in *Encountering Development*, the response to industrial civilization takes the form of "ethnoterritorial social movements" that defend "an entire way of life" (Escobar 2018, 45).

We might conclude that Escobar's *Pluriverse* seems to have moved far from any connection with Polanyi. Yet, as part of his defense of difference, Escobar (2018, 145) still finds Polanyi a useful reference. He returns to Polanyi's notion of disembedding the economy to help explain the destructive impacts of markets, economic growth, and the notion of development in the Global South. Further, Polanyi is among the key thinkers who expose the falsity of the economist's assumption of an eternal and universal economy (Escobar 2018, 242 n. 9).[18] Escobar (2018, 100–1) connects this critique of economics to relational methodologies that challenge the "preexistence of distinct entities whose respective essences are not seen as fundamentally dependent on other entities" (as in our relational critique of liberalism and liberal IPE in earlier chapters). A "relational ontology" brings awareness that *"nothing preexists the relations that constitute it."* It is this awareness that is at the heart of the resistance to industrial civilization and the transitions to a world of diverse life projects that Escobar both observes in the making and embraces as a global project.

What this politics of "transitions" means in practice seems closer to Polanyi's countermovement than might be supposed. Like Polanyi, Escobar's description of resistance to liberal capitalism suggests not a singular movement but multiple defensive actions against "extractive globalization": "a defense of seeds, commons, mountains, forests, wetlands, lakes and rivers." Groups attempt to "secure the autonomy" of their communities via "actions against white/mestizo and patriarchal rule," through "urban experiments with art, digital technologies, neoshamanic movements, urban gardens, alternative energy." These actions appear "as manifestations of multiple collective wills" (Escobar 2018, 16). A different summary occurs later in the text, where Escobar (2018, 133–4, 139) draws out the insights from the design literature for responding to the failure of modern industrial civilization. Drawing on the deeply relational ontology he has defended, he points to the new forms of design that are made necessary by widespread "ecological breakdown or shared experiences of harm." These responses bring together "imagination and technology" but reveal "forms of making that are not merely technological." They draw on "the entire range of design traditions (within the West and beyond)," including "ecology, religion and spirituality, alternative science, food and energy, social movements research, and digital technologies," to promote "convivial and communal instrumentations involving human/nonhuman collectives." These movements are less about liberal freedom or expanding choice, and more about "the kinds of beings we desire to be"; here we find ourselves in the domain of the "noncapitalist or postcapitalist or nonliberal."

While he seems to move us beyond Polanyi's complex society, Escobar (2018, 175) describes these "noncapitalist spaces" in ways Polanyi would likely recognize: these spaces involve "the creation of new forms of life (from daycare centers and urban gardens to free clinics, the restructuring of public schools, and the recovery and self-management of abandoned factories)." Or, in a discussion centered upon designs for transitions, Escobar (2018, 139) speaks of this movement, very much like Polanyi, as an alliance of forces, "emerging from a multiplicity of sites, including social movements and some nongovernmental organizations, the work of intellectuals with significant connections to environmental and cultural struggles, and that of intellectuals within alternative or dissenting traditions."

Escobar is aware that the range of actors and actions involved point not simply to movements exclusively centered in the Global South. Rather, he calls for "bridges" across what might be seen as a hard "onto-epistemic border" (Escobar 2018, 205–6, see also 140–50). He observes that movements in the Global North are dynamized similarly by an emerging sense of place, an imperative to relocalize in the face of liberal "decommunalization." Escobar cites as examples the varying efforts to reinvent the "communal through a multiplicity of activities concerning food, the economy, crafts, and care." Growing expertise in "relocalization" developed elsewhere may be invaluable to movements in the Global South, though these movements in the Global North remain relatively insensitive to broader issues surrounding capitalism and decolonization (Escobar 2018, 208). As Escobar (2018, 209) puts it, thinking in the Global North has yet to "entertain seriously the end of modernity."

Escobar (2018, 210–11) does seem to indicate that efforts to "pluralize modernity" might have some purchase, however: the idea of multiple modernities can allow "moderns," who otherwise would face a "fright that is deeply unsettling," like the fright experienced by other worlds facing the existential threat of a homogenizing modernity, to "*effectively activate* their own specific critique of the dominant modern." Instead of being "enemies," self-critical moderns might be "fellow travelers" in relation to the indigenous and Afro-descendant movements for autonomy. Here, Escobar (2018, 128–9, see also 102) employs ideas developed by Ashis Nandy. Nandy calls not simply for an anti-Western stance in the name of some essentialized tradition, a concern that Escobar (2018, 102–4) reiterates: he worries that "narrow-minded traditionalisms" used to "demystify modernity" only remystify tradition. He also follows Nandy in calling for us to recover "alternative Wests" or "lost or repressed" traditions within the West that open a space for a critique of modernity from within the Global North. This space in the Global North overlaps with alternative cosmovisions from Latin America, an overlap creating possibilities for "critical dialogue, interaction, and mutual transformation among cultures within a genuine intercultural communion."[19] As Escobar (2018, 20–1) states early on, the debate around forms of worlding is one that he has been having for some time both with and against Western philosophers. If there is a bridge that must be built, it is one that he is building within himself and his text. If there is a dialogue, it is one internal to his own thinking and that he aims to perform in his writing.

Polanyi might be a key interlocutor in such dialogue since he veers closer to Escobar on the theme of "spirituality" than most economists or political economists. In *The Great Transformation*, Polanyi (2001, 267–8) locates the source of belief in freedom in Biblical traditions. He speaks of "three constitutive facts in the consciousness of Western man: knowledge of death, knowledge of freedom, knowledge of society." And it is from "resignation" in the face of human mortality and "the reality of society" that "life springs." It is a commitment to freedom in the acceptance of limits—not the technological hubris of modernity—that gives humans "indomitable courage and strength to remove all removable injustice and unfreedom." He develops this general theme in greater detail in an earlier essay. Polanyi (1936, 370) refers to the Christian idea of the soul as recognizing "the infinite value" and "equality" of human beings. This idea might work against society, but Polanyi draws out a strongly relational view: individual "personality is not real outside community. The reality of community *is* the relationship of persons." Though Polanyi believes that socialism requires "a different formulation and a stricter interpretation" of these relational "truths," it necessarily begins with "the individual in his religious aspect."[20] Escobar would surely object that Polanyi's spirituality and the relationality he embraces remain distinctly Christian and human-centered. And, as is evident from his commitment to a complex society, Polanyi embraces the human capacity to produce from nature for the end of a thriving social life. Yet it appears that room for discussion of the status of nature is opened up, especially since some scholars associate Polanyi with strong forms of environmentalism (Bernard 1997; Fraser 2017), perhaps in conjunction with protecting indigenous areas (Orihuela 2020). Pursuing this issue would require a deeper investigation of both Polanyi's idea that nature/land is a fictitious commodity and how he sees the human-nature relationship.

Finally, while the IPE reading of Polanyi emphasizes that freedom is realized only within social and political institutions at multiple scales, including the state, Escobar (2018, 172–5) articulates his vision in unremitting opposition to the state. Exercising autonomy doesn't involve taking control of the state, but "taking back from the State key areas of social life it has colonized." In opposition to large processes of "development, modernity, and globalization," for which the state has been an agent, community autonomy involves an expansive notion of local self-determination: norms are changed from within so that traditions are changed traditionally, though without the implication of stasis.[21] At the same time, Escobar (2018, 187, 200) recognizes that this kind of autonomy is connected to claims to rights—rights that apparently would have to be recognized by other communities and wider institutions. Communities demand rights to identity, territory, and the social space to create "the conditions for the exercise of identity"; "the right to their own vision of the future," including "the right to choose their model of development and of the economy according to their own cosmovision"; and "the right to historical reparations."

In contrast perhaps with the democratic provisioning imagined by Latham, Escobar's community-centered idea appeals to a right to a place for communal world making. It is a share in the form of a claim to *a* world—a claim to a specific place and the world-making attached to that place—within the wider globe. Yet, Escobar does not mention that a right to communal world making also requires respect and implementation by other actors, including state or global institutions. Respecting new administrative boundaries that restrict state power involves a transfer or diminution of sovereignty (see Inayatullah and Blaney 2004, chapter 6). Reparations require the transfer of resources and property rights. Escobar knows that such rights can be achieved only via "struggles" that exercise "forms of counterpower." And, he does see acts of counterpower extending across the globe in a form of "mutualism . . . from locality to locality across continents" (Escobar 2018, 45). But he doesn't speak of the changes in the wider political institutions that would be demanded as part of a radical "communalizing and reterritorializing" of now "delocalized and intensely liberal worlds."

Escobar (2018, 227) does locate global energy for his project: a crisis of global order parallel to the one Polanyi sees as the motive force for the twentieth-century great transformation. Against a backdrop of "proliferating extractivism, truly massive displacement and expulsion, [and] xenophobia," the "fields of potential antagonisms multiply" in the twenty-first century. These are the "seeds" of global transformation brought by "cultural-political projects" that reach from the grassroots to the global.

As a way of summary, we end with two divergent images of what Escobar's global transformation entails, both intimately connected to his vision but pulling us in different directions. The first we find is Graham Dunkley's exploration of the ideology of free trade. Nothing, it would seem, signals the dominance of modern liberalism more than the free trade doctrine. But free trade always coexists with resistance to its creedal character. Dunkley (2004, xiv, 15–16; see also Dunkley 1997, chapter 6) documents the persistence of calls for protectionism based on strong claims of difference. These might be associated with a defense of national culture, but he also recognizes justifications for the protection of small communities, a defense of "Community-Sovereignty" he associates with Gandhi. Without such protections, it is difficult to imagine communities exercising autonomy in life plans or modes of development that Escobar imagines. But, again, there is very little in Escobar's work that explains how this form of sovereignty could be recognized without the restraint of actors from outside of the community. While restraint might be exercised voluntarily, it is more likely to occur when mandated by the state or as part of systems of global governance.

A second image we draw from Robbie Shilliam's *The Black Pacific*. Shilliam (2015, 2–3) points to the existence of "a deep, global infrastructure of anticolonial connectivity." Shilliam warns that however powerful or "rich in relationality," this connectivity seems "poor" in "material" terms; it would appear that there is little "possibility of the colonized relating to each other across global spaces." We have raised exactly that concern about Escobar's vision of a new great transition. Yet Shilliam (2105, 3) argues that movements grounded in indigenous peoples and the descendants of the enslaved are effective in "cultivating knowledge 'sideways'." The "spiritual, philosophical, and political standpoints" that connect sideways are powerful because they confer the power to heal, to exorcise a history of racial inequality, to "rebind communities who have and continue to suffer from such exploitation and dispossession" (Shilliam 2015, 11). Relational practices that serve to "bring back—re-bind—that which has been rent asunder" operate along different temporal lines than modern knowledge practices; this is "restitutive justice" more than a focus on distribution that we might associate with Polanyi. What is redeemed is the "deep relation between the manifest and spiritual domains" (Shilliam 2015, 16–17). Thus, these movements pursue something like Escobar's "ancestral mandate" where justice involves returning autonomy to those dispossessed by securing (or resecuring) the community's place in and with the land. This is a redemption performed by the community itself, always in relation to its own past and to other communities. The mediation of the state or global institutions seems unwelcome or unnecessary.

But we hesitate to embrace fully Shilliam's resolution of the conquest of the globe by colonial capitalism. In a "world laden with widespread insecurity of life and livelihood," we should not be surprised, Ayse Bugra (2018, 87) argues, that "people take refuge in communities" and that "the demand for equal respect for cultures comes to overshadow the deficiency of institutional arrangements providing a dignified life for all individuals." We believe Escobar's *Pluriverse* reflects this political mood and we want to honor that element of his work, even as we raise questions about its limits. Bugra (2018,

83–6) also honors this mood by turning to Polanyi, finding in *The Great Transformation* and Polanyi's other writings a deep commitment to *both* universalism *and* diversity. Polanyi saw the "collapse of the old moral landscape of Western universalism" opening up space for various cultures to assert their own "culturally informed aspirations." And he believes these aspirations can never be asserted in isolation, but always as part of a dialogical process by which freedom is achieved and identities are secured within an interconnected world. This requires respect for "communitarian forms of identity" and building global institutions of redistributive justice.

CONCLUSION: INSIDE/OUTSIDE CAPITALISM

Does the countermovement operate within or beyond capitalism? Is resistance grounded in the realization of liberal modernity's promises of individuality and freedom or does it grow from an alternative ontology or cosmovision? Polanyi inspires thinking in both directions, but we are tempted to resist the either/or implied in these questions. We worked through this tension at least twice before. In both cases, we, like Escobar, found inspiration in Ashis Nandy's idea of a dialogue of traditions. In *International Relations and the Problem of Difference* (2004, 162), we locate Polanyi in a liminal space that joins an "immanent critique" of "the modern project of realizing the freedom and equality of the individual" with a critique located "partly *outside* or *beyond* the project of development/political economy." In this overlapping space of "political economy" and "economic anthropology," we may find the resources for a "dialogical critique of capitalism." In this respect, Polanyi may teach us to take "an ethnological stance, finding in the other, both within and outside [modernity], resources for critical reflection on our own understanding of economic life and potential allies in the struggle to create a new civilization" (Inayatullah and Blaney 2004, 182; see also Bugra 2018; Brie 2018). We found a version of that space in the Scottish Enlightenment liberals who think both within and beyond society as organized by the market (see chapter 1). We might now locate such resources and allies in the overlapping space of IPE and Escobar's refusal of modernity in the name of the pluriverse. Escobar seems to acknowledge this overlapping space, particularly when he slips into speaking about hybridity or the co-constitution of movements within and beyond modernity. And he seems to suggest that alternative global visions are emerging from dissenting views within the Global North as much as from indigenous and Afro-descendant movements in Latin America.

We come to a similar conclusion in *Savage Economics* (2010, 197). There, we highlight Polanyi's insistence that the results of market liberalization should be seen less as simply economic deprivation and more as cultural or social: "a catastrophic dislocation of the lives of the common people" as Polanyi (2001, 35) put it. These are transformations in forms of life, where ways of being, working, thinking, and social connection are radically altered. In Polanyi's (2001, 35, 41) evocative phrase: "the old social tissue was destroyed," leaving a "veritable abyss of human degradation." We don't read Polanyi as suggesting that the dislocation of the social embeddedness of these non-modern forms of life is irrelevant to the present. We instead stress that "the times of the savage and the modern overlap" (Blaney and Inayatullah 2010, 199). Modern market society continues to dislocate stable forms of life; it generates insecurity for common people across the globe. These are shared conditions that allow us to draw parallels across the embedded economies of most times and places that Polanyi had documented in order to disrupt the economistic fallacy that demands social dislocation. Traditions of "sharing" in hunter-gatherer societies remind us that "resources and knowledge" are "social" and available to "be pooled or shared." The communal commitment to "social solidarity" found in many societies suggests we strengthen contemporary mechanisms of social insurance and income transfers that move society toward greater equality and security. Recognizing the importance of connection to place, we might respect the importance of "stability" and "resist treating individuals as easily movable factors of production" and forbid capital complete freedom of mobility (Blaney and Inayatullah 2010, 193).

Though we don't ignore the persistence of the non-modern in our world, our message is more for those of us who occupy modern or hybrid spaces. We stress the possibility of learning from those voices unheard because they have been relegated to a superseded past. Escobar wants us to listen more fully to the demands for communal autonomy as part of realizing an "ancestral mandate" to memory and place in the making and remaking of worlds. For us, Polanyi leads us toward that space where we can listen. And, as in the earlier book, we argue for finding in overlapping of times and places the resources for redeeming ourselves (Blaney and Inayatullah 2010, 193).

But we acknowledge that Escobar's pluriversal vision might also call us to rethink what we mean by a world-capitalist system (Blaney and Inayatullah 2010, 194). Enrique Dussel (2002, 236–7) provides us guidance where he pictures the world-system as a form of "transmodernity" in which multiple "universal cultures" now take their place alongside "European and North American culture." Transmodernity, he claims, is a vision of a "more human and complex world, more passionate and diverse, a manifestation of the fecundity that the human species has shown for millennia." Dussel's vision comes close to Escobar's at those points when Escobar (2018, xvi) associates the "pluriverse" with the Zapatista goal of "*a world where many worlds fit.*" We cannot be sure that Escobar would accept this notion of "transmodernity," though his references to hybridity and the co-constitution of places in relation to modernity suggest the possibility. But this idea might move us too quickly away from the more localized movements he makes central.

Polanyi appears to open us to Dussel's reading of the world system where he embraces the postwar possibility of global institutions supportive of a multiplicity of economic forms. We worry that Escobar to his peril ignores the important role of global institutions in his account of "transitions." As in our previous books, we doubt that the varied and localized reactions from the margins of capitalism could effectively curtail capitalism's power. At the very end of our work with Polanyi in *International Relations and the Problem of Difference* (2004, 184–5), we suggest that "we should not lose sight of Polanyi's insight—derived from the juxtaposition of the European and colonial experiences—that reembedding the logic of economy depends on a wider and effective set of social and political institutions." Hence, "the importance of the state and regional and global institutions," with the proviso that scholars continue to "imagine . . . more generous forms of federalism, allowing greater local autonomy, but nested within regional and world schemes of overlapping political authority." If there is to be a pluriverse in Escobar's sense, it appears to require a multi-sited, transnational countermovement that works at multiple scales to bring into being multileveled institutions that support diverse forms of life. The ambiguity in the Zapatistas' slogan and Escobar's own formulations appear pertinent: a world fit for many worlds remains, in an important sense, a singular world.

Our reading of Polanyi suggests that his work authorizes attention to both the world and many worlds. Jamie Peck (2103, 228–9, emphasis added) similarly praises Polanyi for being "one of the original theorists of the diverse economy" and also for his "axiomatic concerns with part-whole connections." His Polanyi gives "no receipt for the study of the 'others' of the market, in detached isolation." Rather, Peck claims, he highlights the "diversity" of local and regional responses to markets and, importantly, to the "multiplicity of [local and regional] *relations with enduring 'alternative' socio-economies.*" Polanyi, in Peck's account, saw that the failures and excesses of markets "spawned a *range* of 'double-movement' responses which in turn would foster codependent modes of development, contradictory hybrids, and all manner of out-of-equilibrium gyrations." For Peck, countermovements unfold not from isolated places confronting markets, but from diverse and hybrid "socio-economics." Escobar comes close to this formulation in *Encountering Development* but less so in *Pluriverse*. Alternative forms of world-making are recognized as hybrids within, though resistant to the central character of, the world system. It is only the relational co-constitution of different worlds in direct response to liberal modernity's homogenizing project that makes it possible to imagine a world of many worlds. We might read Escobar's project, then, as implementing what Peck sees as "the Polanyian principle of recognising economic diversity while attending to the demands of meth-odological holism" that firmly reject the possibility of places existing in "detached isolation."

But Escobar might resist any relational view that makes the modern world system the object of inquiry. We sympathize with Escobar's suspicion. The holistic vision of modernity has swallowed up much of the world, destroying ways of life in the name of progress and rendering the radical difference that remains invisible (see chapters 3 and 4). Not surprisingly, Escobar's dialectic of resistance unfolds in opposition to modernity. Polanyi's democratic provi-sioning might, then, appear as part of a continuing "ontological occupation." However humane systems of social protection might be, they still assume the problem of democratic provisioning is best seen as securing a share from a global system of production and consumption. It may be that escaping existing global interconnection is the precise desire of indigenous and Afro-descendant movements in Latin America. It is autonomy—not more equal participation in the whole—that defines their demands.

These demands also reflect the lack of reciprocity involved in liberal modernity. The extension of industrial society occurred not as a collabora-tive project, but, as Polanyi noted, like a monologue, as colonization. More sharply, the rise of global capitalism is a story of violence, political subjuga-tion, expropriation of resources, imposition of an unequal division of labor, unequal exchange, and cultural destruction (see chapters 4 and 5). Demo-cratic provisioning might work to counter that history if our idea of securing a share is sufficiently adaptable to varying conditions and responsive, as Polanyi suggested, to myriad problems unleashed by unregulated markets. A global society might fulfill its obligation to secure the livelihood of its members as a right to income and employment for those who are integrated into wider economies. *And* it might secure something like a right to property/ sovereignty in a local place for communities who can use this "right" in order to resist the violent integration of their region into wider economies. Put differently, multi-level global institutions might secure access of all people to the commons of knowledge and wealth but would also need to limit the unequal access of outsiders by aiding communities in defending and cultivating their own commons connected to place. We might see these moves as redistributive on one side and restitutive on the other. And we can imagine global institutions performing some combination of both as part of democratic provisioning.

Epilogue

These essays highlight three themes in liberalism and liberal IPE. First, liberalism produces a scandal when paired with capitalism. It promises liberty, equality, and accompanying prosperity. But it does so by alienating working conditions for many, delivering abject poverty for a startlingly large number and fostering deep social inequalities that undercut the social order by foreclosing liberty for many. Our claim is not only that liberalism fails to deliver according to its own standards, though this is important. Liberalism is also an account of justified inequality, justified colonial tutelage, and the justified sacrifice of some for the purported good of the species. Still, we want to avoid the temptation to treat liberal principles of freedom and equality merely as ideology. We mean to suggest something different and something more. Liberalism calls forth its other: critical responses from within and alternative traditions that pit themselves against liberalism and place themselves beyond it.

Second, liberalism constitutes a particular political-economic world. It creates a realm in which we (in part) imagine and conduct ourselves as autonomous individuals and in which our reactions are conditioned by what we term the individualism and condemnation imperatives. It makes a world in which our political/ethical options are circumscribed by the idea that people are naturally isolated units, that they receive their "just desserts" as decided by (fair) market competition, and, even if they don't, any redress of historical injustices and contemporary suffering impairs liberty and the mechanisms producing wealth. Liberalism also reinforces a colonial world imaginary that transposes unit-level assumptions and the condemnation imperative onto countries, peoples, races, and civilizations, grading their achievements and explaining their relative successes and failures as products of their own cultural/racial character traits and lagging efforts. Forgetting and erasing the history of colonial violence is necessary to sustain the paired individualism and condemnation imperatives and to preserve the impression that unequal outcomes are merited.

Third, liberalism pushes us beyond the bounds of liberalism itself. A liberal world transforms social space and activates political/ethical thinking that necessarily moves beyond any narrow libertarianism. From the beginning, many liberals accepted that to secure a prosperous and stable social system, markets require not just the invisible hand but also visible hands that are invasive, artful, regulatory, and reforming. We now see that liberal modernity depends on and intensifies a deeply relational and global economic space that defies characterization as the product of autonomous bargaining units. Here, we have pulled away from the individualism imperative and toward ideas of social determination—that the differences between Smith's porter and philosopher emerge from the division of labor, not as its cause; that poverty and wealth are products of an interconnected process. We are drawn toward a Marxist scholarship that sees global capitalism as structuring of social relations that emerge from violent subjugation and continue as processes of domination and subordination. We are similarly drawn to postdevelopment thought that embraces worlds built on alternative relational ontologies that resist colonial capitalism. We stress that enshrining methodological individualism as a method tempts liberals to blame the poor for their poverty, presume that groups deserve their subordinate place in social hierarchies, and justify the eradication of "backwardness." Following Eagleton and Connolly, social determination shifts "blame" to institutions, to social processes of structural domination. We follow Smith, Pogge, and Polanyi in suggesting that the appeal to a social process—the interconnections of the division of labor, a history of violent acquisition, and what Polanyi calls "the reality of society"—prompts an obligation to redress absolute poverty, to secure the livelihood of citizens of complex societies, and to recognize the ties of people and land that allow enacting alternative worlds.

We wonder if we don't presume too much in that final sentence. After all, we concluded chapter 2 on a much more ambiguous note. There, we are less certain than is Pogge (and perhaps Polanyi in chapter 6) that recognizing the trajectory of historical injustice or the reality of societal interconnection necessarily leads people to embrace an obligation to redress poverty, to secure the livelihood of fellow citizens, and to recognize the rights of peoples to enact alternative worlds. Our doubts in chapter 2 rest on the lingering scholarly and popular libertarian faith in the necessity of market incentives, the persistence of pre-modern views of natural inequality, and the value placed on denial and suffering. Here we want to think again about the language of "social determination" that we use, following Hage, to talk about the unfolding processes of social relations. We know that some react negatively to this term, precisely because it appears on its face to erase any strong role for human will.[1] Our initial response is that claims about human will or agency may be much exaggerated, that the emphasis on the agency is driven by the perceived political "needs" of the present more than a careful understanding of the possibilities laid down within existing social relations. This issue of human will or agency requires some attention because, as we shall see, it leads to real perplexities when we think about the responsibility of the West (Europe and North America principally) for the conditions of masses of people in the Third World.[2]

SOCIAL DETERMINATION

We are attracted to the language of "social determination" because it strikes at the heart of methodological individualism and the condemnation imperative. Following David Levine (1997, 7), when we begin with the idea that the "person" or "self" is "a socially constructed and recognized entity," we can more readily distance ourselves from naturalistic claims about social behavior and the presocial traits of individuals. Rather, we can only understand a person or self "within a *determinate context of interaction*" that gives individuals and behavior their "meaning and significance" (Levine 1997, 7; emphasis added). The individual is not primordial, nor can its behavior or traits be specified apart from a particular "social determination"—a "specific system of social relations" (Levine 1978, 6–7). In this way, the notion of social determination unseats the "unit status of the self" as pregiven; rather, the self as a unit arises only "within a determinate set of social institutions and interactions." Though it may make some sense to speak of individuals as self-determining agents, this status arises only within social life—not prior to it—and only as particular modes of action meaningful within particular forms of social life (Levine 1997, 9). Though not presupposed or pregiven, the individual or self may be particular. But its particularity or individuality can be understood only in relation to a determinate context of interaction. Its particularity is intertwined with what we might call its socially constituted "universality" (Levine 1997, 20)

The idea of social determination also guides us in understanding social relations as a process, as we stress at the end of chapters 4 and 5. Since the status of the human as a self-determining individual only arises as socially determined, we cannot convincingly explain social institutions and interactions as a product of autonomous units (Levine 1997, 9). If we are to see human action as more than unique instances of individual behavior, actions must be placed within a conception of the processes and relations of a social system as a whole (Levine 1978, 10), including, for example, the whole of global capitalism. The implication is that understanding social actions or processes "cannot be made from historical 'facts,' since taken on their own, in the form of isolated instances, events or data, they must remain mute." Instead, as with Marx and the Marxist scholars' accounts of global capitalism, we survey in chapters 4 and 5, the "inner connection" of otherwise isolated facts can be revealed only within specific systems of social relations (Levine 1978, 12). Thus, the notion of "social determination" refers us to whole *and* parts, where processes unfold within structures that are "built through the interaction of its elements" (Levine 1981, 3). Social determination resists those modes of explanation that turn processes into isolated atoms that might be aggregated and declared a pattern displayed by the interaction of the intrinsically isolated elements. As we suggest, following Hage (see chapter 4), social determination also conveys a political/ethical message about individual and group responsibility.

Hage offers "social explanation," though we might prefer "social understanding,"[3] as an ethical mode of social-scientific engagement with terrorism. Instead of immediately turning to vilification or identifying individual or group failings or limits, we begin by understanding the position of actors in a specific system of social interaction. Suicide bombing appears comprehensible in particular contexts, not evidence of particularly evil individuals or groups. The position of the porter and the philosopher—the rich and the poor—similarly reflect less the merits or achievements of individuals, except as those are shaped and judged within social processes. Extending the principle of social determinism to capitalism as a system of social relations raises questions also about the tendency to vilify capitalists and those who benefit from capitalist social relations, though this issue was not our explicit concern in that chapter. Wouldn't our first step be to understand the role of capitalists within capitalism, who are constituted within particular social relations as much as their relational pair, the proletariat? We find this point made clearly by Marx, despite his application of often vivid and ghoulish imagery to the capitalist. Our response might best be less personal condemnation and more a recognition that the capitalist exercises a particular and determinant social power. The capitalist's behavior appears less an individual act of free will or the particular expression of some unique (and especially ethically flawed) self, and more as a social "universality" within a determinant set of social relations. Inequality, poverty, and alienation appear then as integral features of the relations of domination and subordination that individuals inhabit as social actors and less a matter of personal moral failings of the dominant or the subordinated. Fiery language singling out capitalists as individuals behaving reprehensibly may be politically motivating, but we doubt that it is sociologically illuminating unless individual behaviors or "facts" are understood in terms of their "inner connection" within a system of social relations.

THE RISE OF CAPITALISM AND
THE WEIGHT OF STRUCTURES

Equipped with the idea of social determination, we can turn to a recent debate about the question of agency and blame in the rise of capitalism.[4] At the beginning of chapters 3 and 4, we express our enthusiasm for the work of John Hobson. We admire his nearly exhaustive account of Eurocentrism in IR (Hobson 2012) and his vigorous and unfailing efforts to document the usually ignored agencies in world history originating beyond the West (read Europe), including in the history of capitalism (Hobson 2004, 2021). Hobson corrects the myth of Western self-creation, where modernity and capitalism emanate from the internal genius and energy of Europeans and European culture. As we suggest in chapter 4, this heroic understanding appears as a variant of the individualism imperative, which sees countries' and regions' positions in the global capitalist system as a reflection of their individual and separable efforts and merits. We applaud how Hobson's work confronts such claims with a more variegated historical story. We also value his attention and fidelity to the historical record.

Despite our praise and embrace, we differentiate our project from his. Hobson means to deny European claims to (undue) credit for the achievements of the modern world, including capitalism. This narrows his attention and focus. He thereby puts less weight on the pervasive violence, suffering, and relations of domination integral to the social relations of colonial capitalism. By emphasizing these features of capitalism, we don't mean to deny that it has produced real achievements. We draw on Marx himself as a corrective to push back against contemporary Marxian arguments that ignore these achievements (Blaney and Inayatullah 2016; Inayatullah and Blaney 2016).

We do mean, however, to highlight a feature of Eurocentrism that differs from the one Hobson stresses. We highlight the way Eurocentric stories deny the role of violent imposition and colonization as key features of the rise of modern capitalism (see chapters 4 and 5). Hobson's narrower focus on defeating claims of heroic European agency with the corrective of adding substantial Eastern agency risks, we believe, playing into the hands of those who want to erase the history of European violence and imposition: "it permits a kind of complicity to creep into the actions of the East—or rather it assumes the East to be equally complicit in its own exploitation and destruction" (Sajed and Inayatullah 2016, 202). Hobson thereby risks downplaying the story of "the West's structural force and power" (Sajed and Inayatullah 2016, 203).

Hobson (2016, 213) recognizes that he and his critics have different worries. The critics conceptualize Eurocentrism, he notes, as an "ideology that seeks to deny the role of Western capitalist imperialism in the world." But he worries that, in their desire to lay full blame on the West for the violence and destruction of colonial capitalism, their formulation ascribes the very "hyper-power" to the West that Eurocentric stories use to explain the emergence of modern capitalism in and by the West.[5] We believe we can work our way out of this impasse.

All parties to the debate agree that the Eurocentric story of the rise of capitalism ties itself to the presence of pregiven, autonomous units. In this Eurocentric story, some units advance (first), and others fall behind, perhaps permanently. These two patterns of "facts" about the units—either as advanced or backward—are *not* connected causally or constitutively. Economic advanced doesn't cause backwardness nor is backwardness a source of the advantage of others within a shared set of social relations. The only connection is that the two conditions are revealed by a "common" measuring stick of development or economic growth provided by liberal modernity. In this story, these social patterns appear necessarily as aggregates of individual behavior, such as patterns of successful or failed behaviors or unfavorable or favorable traits characterizing the actors. Any social institutions that shape the interactions of units are treated as the product of bargains struck among autonomous units, as we saw in chapter 3, not as a system of social interaction within which individual actors arise and their behaviors and positions are given social form and meaning. So far, Hobson and Salina/Inayatullah are on the same page.

Following Chakrabarty's useful distinction between the history of the emergence of capitalism and the logic of the social relations of capitalism (Chakrabarty 2000),[6] we can recast the impasse and locate further common ground. The two strategies, as reflected in the work of Hobson and Sajed/Inayatullah, might be seen as individually incomplete and complementary, not opposed, since one emphasizes the *historical emergence* of modern capitalism and the other the *social determinations of a system* of colonial capitalism. Not being fully cognizant of this difference in stress, the disputants partly mischaracterize the other's argument. Hobson foregrounds Eastern agency in the history of the emergence of modern capitalism, which pushes into the background the structuring of social powers integral to the system of colonial capitalism that emerges over time. Sajed and Inayatullah foreground the latter and therefore fault Hobson's history of the agencies involved in the emergence of modern capitalism as an insufficient account of the relations of domination and subordination that emerge with the determinant system of colonial capitalism. When we attend to a distinction between claims about the history of the emergence of capitalism, on the one side, and the character of colonial capitalism as a system of social determinations, on the other, the impasse appears to dissipate.

In a first step, Hobson works to defeat claims that the "unit" Europe monopolizes the traits that confer historical agency in the rise of modern capitalism. He deploys vast amounts of evidence, particularly from East and South Asia, of the presence of industry, science, technological innovation, and enabling social institutions, including mechanisms that mobilize finance, manages risk, and protect accumulated property (Hobson 2004, 2016, 211–13; 2021).[7] Hobson (2016, 217) claims that his account avoids a "zero-sum conception" of the history of capitalism. He rejects the idea of a hyper-capable Europe as a sufficient source of capitalism. He substitutes a story informed by a distinctly "relationalist ontology" in which modern capitalism arises as an emergent property of the interactions of the East and West. Hobson's story is about the agencies involved in the *emergence* of modern capitalism, not an account of the actors and powers structured by the social relations of colonial capitalism with its fuller formation.

Emphasizing the history of emergence, Hobson rightly foregrounds the actions and events necessary to that history, but that forces into the background an account of the relations of domination and subordination integral to fuller-fledged colonial capitalism. The interactions from which capitalism emerges cannot be determined strictly by colonial capitalism, since these interactions unfold within and out of geocultural spaces not yet fully integrated into a determinant global social system. Hobson's story, particularly in his most recent work, makes this clear (see Hobson 2021). The industrial, financial, and technological agencies that East and South Asians display all unfold within pre-existing systems of social interaction that look more like Chaudhuri's account (see chapter 5) of the Indian Ocean space as a determinant system and less as an expression of the emerging global capitalism.[8] Though not fully isolated, even if they operated largely autonomously for several centuries, East and West do not appear as undetermined units coming into interaction as in the Eurocentric state of nature story. From their socially determined interactions, modern capitalism emerges and with that emergence capitalism develops into the "weighty" structure of colonial capitalism that Sajed and Inayatullah highlight.

In Sajed and Inayatullah's reading, Hobson allows capitalism to appear as a negotiated outcome of interacting units and, therefore, the violence and destruction of colonial capitalism appear as something the East imposes upon itself. In their version of resisting Eurocentrism, they direct attention to the structuring of social powers by colonial capitalism in the face of stories about the emergence of capitalism that appears to undercut the "weight" of those structures. Their effort should be read not as an inflation of the weight of the structure, a "hyper-structuralism" about which Hobson (2016, 217) worries.[9] Rather, they highlight the playing out of social powers—of forms of

domination and subordination—within the emergent system of modern colonial capitalism. They believe that Hobson's emphasis on Eastern agency and
the mutual or dialectical creation of modern capitalism reads too much like
liberal IPE in under-emphasizing the weight of domination and subordination.

We can read Hobson more generously if we don't equate his story with
the kind of tales favored by liberal IPE, where institutional outcomes reflect
the interests of isolated bargaining units. We need not see Eastern agency, to
use Hobson's terms, as the free expression of unit interests. We might treat
Eastern agency, as we believe Hobson does, as the expression of determinant
social powers—as actions given meaning and significance within particular
systems of social relations existing in South and East Asia prior to the emergence of colonial capitalism. We don't need to embrace all of the details of his
historical account. We might highlight more fully actions by leaders that play
into the hands of European trading companies or by Eastern industrialists that
subject many residents to oppression. We might note the growing violence
that Europeans mobilize. Hobson would likely recognize all of these points.
To draw once again on Chakrabarty's distinction, whether we emphasize the
history of the emergence of modern capitalism from interactions of East and
West, or emphasize the logic of the structured system of domination and subordination that results, the weight of structures is always present.

A return to the work of Jennings and Rodney discussed in chapter 4 reinforces the importance of the distinction between the emergence and logic of
modern capitalism.[10] Both Jennings and Rodney combine attention to: (1) the
actions of Amerindians and Africans in the face of European intrusions into
their respective continents; and (2) the resulting structure of domination that
results. On the one hand, neither the rise nor the character of the pelt and slave
trades can be attributed simply to European agencies. Native American and
African planning and labor were crucial to and partly constitutive of these
trading systems. Many Amerindians and Africans participated freely and their
identities and motives were conditioned within their own social systems. But
the gains from these interactions favored Europeans, who increasingly pressed
their advantage through both economic and military means. The result in both
cases was increasing loss of sovereignty and property and a new political-
economic dispensation we might call colonial capitalism. There was certainly
strong resistance to colonial rule, but this was defeated by overwhelming
force.[11] We read Jennings and Rodney to suggest that it is important not to
attribute to European actors powers that they did not possess during the early
phases of the European intrusions into North America and Africa. Certainly,
every interaction changes the context of interaction and begins to reshape the
identities and powers of the actors, but there would have to be some threshold passed before we could describe the system of social interaction that
Jennings and Rodney describe as full-fledged colonial capitalism. Beyond

that threshold, it is clear that interactions begin to assume the form of the structured determinations of colonial capitalism, not systems or institutions created by the interactions of or bargains amongst Amerindians, Africans, and European intruders/invaders. As long as we respect this distinction between the history of the emergence of modern global capitalism from earlier forms of social organization and the logic of the structured relations of colonial capitalism as a global social system, we can give due attention to the weight of structure and Eastern agency. We think Hobson could agree.

RESPONSIBILITY FOR VIOLENCE, POVERTY, AND INEQUALITY

We can now return to Smith, Pogge, and Polanyi. Specifically, we return to the issue of our responsibility in reducing extreme poverty and securing livelihood. All three thinkers tie economic justice to the idea that all our fates are deeply embedded in social relations that produce systematic advantages and disadvantages. It is not just that we share social space in some generic sense or that we owe something to others simply because they are human beings. Smith, Polanyi, and Pogge (in the end) rest the obligation to others on the claim that our very status and abilities are a function of our position in the interactions structured by a determinant system of social relations. And, importantly, that social position is relational: status and social power (riches and poverty, domination and subordination) exist in relational complexes. Some might claim that liberal moral philosophers, such as Rawls, are motivated by relations of domination and subordination to try to formalize an airtight case for the obligation of citizens to others. But liberals, including Rawls, tend to start with the interests or preferences of individuals. We doubt that starting with premises about individual interests or personal moral preferences leads to a recognition of deep responsibility. Beginning with premises about unit traits tends to reinforce the idea that we exist as individuals who are only contingently connected to others. The damage we do to others is likewise contingent, not a feature of a system of social relations. Similarly, we find unconvincing any social theory that regards moral agency as a trans-historical power existing apart from the determinations of specific systems of social relations. We worry, further, that appeal to universal rights in the abstract rings hollow without deeply connecting our sense of obligation to the history and logic of colonial capitalism.[12] It is within, against, and beyond capitalism that the question of a right to income and a right to livelihood is being fought out.

In these essays, we have argued for starting with the social process as a whole—with both parts and whole in a determinant relationship. Though we hope that our essays are persuasive, we know we have not constructed an airtight case, deductively deriving obligation from social determination. The most convincing evidence we provide of the weight of social determination is the widespread presence of the condemnation or individualism imperative. We highlight that our sensitivity to the weight of structures binds us to a collective responsibility that *calls forth* a deflection of that responsibility. If we didn't sense the weight of social connection, how do we explain the imperative to deny that connection? Social thinkers, IR theorists, economists, and most of us in our everyday lives sense the weight of structures that calls us to collective responsibility, despite living in a world largely ordered by liberal modernity. Conditioned to conduct ourselves as individuals, we are, nevertheless, always weighted by doubts about the story that we are individually responsible for our own fate and that those who suffer deserve theirs. We repress these doubts. We espouse doctrines of merit as a matter of faith. We construct the market as an abstract and timeless entity as if the determinant relations of social life do not exist. We treat suffering as the inevitable result of capitalist competition and accept that some groups are naturally uncompetitive. We erase the history of colonialism and slavery from the official record and try to wipe it from our consciousness. We read Adam Smith one-sidedly as an ontological individualist. We deny the "reality of society" as Polanyi puts it.

Yet the reality of society cannot be denied. Living in a liberal world means also living beyond liberal verities: Energies for social reform inevitably arise where markets are given freer reign; a socialist vision of the world coexists and intertwines with liberal imaginaries; and those whose ways of life have been colonized by liberalism calls for the recognition of worlds beyond capitalism. Liberalism remains unstable and incomplete; it calls forth its other. In this book, we began with liberalism and liberal IPE as a way of finding our way to the other Marxist analyses of the structure of global capitalism and to postdevelopment perspectives that seek a rebinding of people to land dispossessed and a revalorization of denigrated ways of life. In earlier work, we were more attuned to the latter, the critique from space before and thereby beyond liberal modernity (Inayatullah and Blaney 2004; Blaney and Inayatullah 2010). In future work, we plan to begin with Marx and the Marxist tradition itself.

Notes

CHAPTER 2

1. Though we describe Pogge's proposals as modest, we recognize that he pushes beyond the "conservative" reading Rawl's gives to his own principles, taking the argument in a more "progressive direction" and extending it beyond national borders (Pogge 1989, 7–10).

2. This admission reflects Hayek's ongoing engagement with socialist and social democratic thinkers. Though not requiring validation by the latest statistical techniques, the socialist view of capitalism as radically unequal is supported by recent simulations showing that, without interference to counter inequality, markets invariably concentrate income and wealth in a very few hands. Market imperfections (like asymmetries in initial endowments) simply speed up the process. See Boghosian (2019). These simulations were done by physicists, not economists.

3. See Himmelfarb (1991) on late-Victorian social reformers and Escobar (1995) and Cammack (2004) on international development practices.

4. We can link Smith's commitment to distributive justice to the role the notion of subsistence plays in his work. Classical political economy was drawn to the idea of subsistence, Levine (1998, 8–20; 1997, 37–9) notes, because it gave them an objective, perhaps an invariable, measure of the cost of labor—the cost of material reproduction. Subsistence can be invariable only if it is fixed prior to and apart from any form of society, including apart from the market. But Smith, Ricardo, and Marx also recognized that subsistence contains moral and cultural elements: people reproduce themselves as part of definite forms of life and market relations alter the character of needs or wants and desires. Interestingly, like Fleischacker, Levine (1998, 9) suggests that the category of subsistence worked in classical political economy to imply an "obligation": "the obligation of the group to assure that its members have the means to maintain the way of life appropriate for them."

5. We take up this theme again in the conclusion. See also Blaney (2018) on Smith and theodicy.

6. Pogge might be correct. Duncan Bell (2019) introduces a collection of essays that makes historical injury and restitution central. These essays collectively display little confidence in claims for distributive justice made in terms of universal human rights, turning instead to arguments rooted in historical injustices of violence and dispossession. We remain unsure that claims of historical injustice will be more telling in terms of political impact.

7. From the point of view of the present, it seems difficult to argue with confidence that enlightened self-interest is sufficient to turn societies towards reform. But we understand Pogge's recourse to this claim when other avenues seem foreclosed.

8. Despite this, Hayek (1976, 405–6, 424) does embrace a guaranteed minimum income, but it feels half-hearted given his argument in *The Constitution of Liberty*. It may be more prudential—an accommodation of public opinion—than principled.

9. That Nozick opens liberal ideas of justice to challenge in this way is stressed by Forrester (2019). We find a similar argument in another founding father of economics, Léon Walras (2010 [1936], 104, 110–11). The economy as a system (of general equilibrium in his case) rewards each according to the value of their contribution in precise mathematical terms. The justice of these outcomes is subject to claims of "commutative" injustice that the "general conditions" of society gave undue advantages to some and created "obstacles and barriers" for others. See also Nichols (2019) on indigenous land claims.

10. Mijs (2016, 2018, 2019) carefully documents the popular belief in meritocracy. For a defense of this orthodoxy by prominent economist and editorialist, see Mankiw (2013).

11. See the previous chapter and Blaney (2016, 2018) and Blaney and Inayatullah (2010) on Smith, Hegel, and contemporary economists. Aee Harvey-Phillips (1984) on Malthus and Christiaens (2019) on Hayek.

12. See Foucault's reading of the invisible hand as indicating the "invisibility" of the economy to the state or prospective planners (Foucault 2008, 278–81).

CHAPTER 3

1. See the related criticism of the "open economy model" by Oatley (2019).

2. Cohen's account of the rise of IPE ties it both indirectly and explicitly to Alfred Marshall. Cohen (2008, 4, 18) describes the work in liberal IPE as rooted in "partial equilibrium analysis," precisely where Marshall is given founding-father status and he mentions Marshall by name when he speaks of the effective segregation of the economy from politics on which economics is founded.

3. Marshall's *Principles* displaced John Steuart Mill's *Principles of Political Economy* as the standard text in economics in the United Kingdom. It maintained that position until finally displaced by the work of his noteworthy student—John Maynard Keynes.

4. Smith is not consistent in guaranteeing the survival of the population. See chapter 1 and Blaney (2018) on the role of infant mortality in setting the natural wage and the market's rationing of life during times of famine.

5. The "world market of the free traders" emerges out of British military victories that allow it to subsume earlier mercantile economies into a system with its industrial production at the center; "forcible conquest" more than the seductions of material gains secured England's institutional commitments explain the free trade regime of the nineteenth century (Skidelsky 1976, 150–7). Formal empire may be finished, but "imperialism remains embedded in the structures and ideology of the current global order" (Bell 2016, 107, 196–203).

CHAPTER 4

1. Nevertheless, Hage (2003, 76) eventually enunciates the very condemnation that he initially and productively resists. There is a paper to be written on how and why he succumbs to the "condemnation imperative." Our work here is only suggestive.

2. Presumably, Hage would agree that the opposite, turning the commonplace into the extraordinary, is also part of social explanation.

3. See our discussion of the possibilities for IR as a study of difference (Inayatullah and Blaney 2004, epilogue).

4. Other actors are possible, of course. Individuals, classes, races, industrial sectors, communities, and empires all make an appearance in the chapters of this book.

5. Singer (1961, 92) does argue that the development of "systematic" generalizations about IR depends on resolving the problem of parts and wholes, though he does not settle on any particular resolution by the end of the article.

6. How a disciplinary schema or a social context selects the scholar varies, perhaps, by the scholar's location and movement within the global political economy or what we might otherwise call her/his biography. See Inayatullah (2011, 1–12).

7. In recent correspondence, Onuf seems to give some ground, at least on the idea that "the [levels] scheme is itself not value-neutral."

8. We explore this issue of world making in chapter 6.

9. As we mentioned in chapter 2, Hayek's stress on the importance of this *belief* is not a slip of the pen. Before the paragraph is out, he admits that market societies have an "exaggerated confidence" that market outcomes reflect individual skill and effort. But this misleading idea seems necessary to making the unequal rewards meted out by competition acceptable:

> It is . . . a real dilemma to what extent we ought to encourage in the young the belief that when they really try they will succeed, or should rather emphasize that inevitably some unworthy will succeed and some worthy will fail—whether we ought to allow the view of those groups to prevail with whom the over-confidence in the appropriate reward of the able and the industrious is strong and who in consequence will do much that benefits the rest, and whether without such a partly erroneous beliefs the large numbers will tolerate actual differences in rewards which will be based only partly on achievement and partly in mere chance. (Hayek 1976, 74)

Hayek does not elaborate the meaning of "mere chance," but *mere* chance seems to indicate processes beyond anyone's control.

10. The most prominent Latin American dependency theorists, at least because their work was available in English, include Cardoso and Falleto (1979), Sunkel (1969, 1973a and b), Furtado (1969, 1970), and Dos Santos (1970). Theorists of unequal development, such as Amin (1976, 1977) and Ake (1972), make closely associated claims.

11. Hobson (2012, 240–2) argues that World Systems Theory and related neo-Marxian arguments (that might be thought to include dependency theories) reproduce elements of Eurocentrism by over-stressing the agency of Europe in shaping the world system and the naturalness of autonomous national development on a Western model. While there is something to these criticisms, we suggest a more sympathetic reading that stresses dependency theories' emphasis on non-Western difference (Inayatullah and Blaney 1995; Blaney 1996). We return to this issue in the epilogue.

12. We draw here on earlier work (Blaney and Inayatullah 2008).

CHAPTER 5

1. Apart from Japan (chap. 17).

2. We see this duality of structure reproduced again in Jackson and Nexon (2019) as holism and agency.

CHAPTER 6

1. This is not to mention concerns, outlined by Dale (2010, 8, 78–9), that Polanyi's description of the "countermovement" is, on one side, overly "deterministic" or "naturalistic," and, on the other side, overly "voluntaristic." Polanyi (2014 [1949], 40) explicitly contrasts his view with both "Marxist determinism" and "*laissez-faire inevitability*." Perhaps, then, the charge of voluntarism sticks better. Some Marxist-leaning scholars indict Polanyi for underplaying the role of class in theorizing social transformation (Halperin 2004; Selwyn and Miyamura 2014; Fraser 2017). Polanyi would turn the tables and suggest that the Marxist emphasis on class was overly determininistic. Whatever the case, Dale's point is that Polanyi does not give an adequate account of how the countermovement operates; he ignores the complex "mediations" necessary to move from individual or social needs to action for societal self-protection, including the fields of power that shape the field of action. We won't tarry much with this concern here. We will take up related questions in our unfolding work on Marx and the labor theory of value.

2. The language of re-discovery seems justified since Polanyi (1957) had argued that Aristotle, who began with the assumption of socially embedded material provisioning, discovered the market economy as the antithesis of a Polis as a deliberative body of citizens.

3. Polanyi's use of and response to Marx seems to depend greatly on Marx's 1844 manuscripts which he read early on in his intellectual development, well before they were translated into English (Block 2018, 170).

4. Marxists might lump Polanyi's socialism with the utopian imaginings that Marx relentlessly criticized. Of course, Marx's critique assumed that he had correctly identified class struggle as the sole agency of radical transformation. It might be that Polanyi's account of societal self-protection and the socialism it allows is more realistic. Block (2018, 174, 171) contrasts Polanyi's "empowerment without hubris" favorably with doctrines of revolutionary transformation and considers this "nonutopian utopia" more attuned to an agnostic and open view of human potential.

5. Polanyi may share with Marx a sense of the necessity of the historical tragedy of modern liberal capitalism. Brie and Thomasberger (2018, 10–13) treat the industrial revolution as the factual backdrop of Polanyi's thinking. Humans are now fated to face "the social implications of the machine." What is undecided is how humans will respond to this challenge. On Marx, see Vogel (1996). It may be Escobar simply refuses to share a modernist sense of the necessity of the destruction of alternative ways of life.

6. Other judgments of the loses and gains are possible, of course. Carlson (2008, 37) quotes Peter Drucker's comment that Polanyi was not willing to accept the "adequate, bearable, but free society" that Drucker defended: "In such a society—and it may be the best we can hope for—we would maintain freedom *by paying a price: the disruption, the divisiveness, and alienation of the market*" (Drucker 1978, 136). We note that Polanyi's assessment is not only a personal preference. Rather, he observes that people and leaders have not been willing to pay these prices on a consistent basis and will turn against free markets and, sometimes disastrously, against freedom itself.

7. The term "provision" is potentially problematic in what it assumes about the relationship between the object and the method of its provision. David P. Levine (1981, 278) argues against what he terms the "principle of separability." This "viewpoint implies that the needs and objects which satisfy them on one side, are independent of the method of circulation on the other . . . We can discern in this a kind of separability that require that we think about the method of circulation as a technique applicable to any set of . . . objects, so that we can separate the method [of circulation] from the objects." Levine (1981, 278–9) concludes that "it would be a mistake to think of this principle of separability as in any way self-evident." The principle of separability also vexes Marx's analysis, an issue we address in our next volume.

8. Helleiner (2000, 21–5) suggests that just such "multi-leveled" activities are necessary to a contemporary countermovement, though he claims that Polanyi restricted his analysis to "a national form of politics." In a later article, Helleinner (2019, 4–6, 21) suggests that the embedded liberalism" of Bretton Woods was meant to create space for "diverse forms of public management," from the welfare state to the developmental state and central planning. Hettne (1997, 2000) disagrees, noting that Polanyi (1945) took up the need for regional organization in an essay written roughly at the same time as *The Great Transformation*, a theme explored by Caporaso and Tarrow (2009) as well. Like Helleneiner, Bienefeld (2007, 28) concludes that re-embedding the global financial system requires that "the struggle must proceed

at every level." Even more expansively, Peter Evans (2000, 2015) treats Polanyi as inspiration for reading contemporary transnational social movements that operate simultaneously at international and national scales as examples of the countermovement appropriate for a globalized age.

9. Standing (2007, 88–9) sees countermovements in play at various scales. He links the idea of re-embedding markets and de-commodifying labor with proposals for Basic Income that provide economic security and always "coupled with a set of universal citizenship rights to insure individual dignity." These proposals presume states and some state-level jurisdiction.

10. Richard Ashley refers to this as "historical economism." Ashley is paying homage to Marx's critique of the kind of political economy that eternalizes capitalist categories.

11. We make similar arguments elsewhere (Blaney and Inayatullah 2010, 173; Inayatullah and Blaney 2004, 171–2, 178–9). Peck (2013, 228) develops this same claim. Polanyi inspires a "substantivist economic geography" that attunes scholars to "multiple modes of economic organization" that are differently positioned culturally, historically, and geographically. Polanyi also pushes back against "teleology, in favour of historical analyses duly cognizant of the diverse forms and pathways of socio-economic development (including paths blocked or not taken), which question singular and unidirectional readings of progress and modernity."

12. This chapter from his dissertation was dropped from the final version of *Encountering Development*. See Escobar (1995, 233, fn. 5).

13. We wonder if we can do without the notion of development altogether—if development is something that we cannot not want as Anna Tsing notes (see previous chapter). Our position on this issue fluctuates somewhat. It is clear that we are deeply suspicious of the way that liberal theories of progress limit our political economic imagination by placing certain values and visions beyond consideration as part of a superseded past. We also cannot ignore Marx's insight that capitalism develops the conditions for a rich individuality, even if it cannot realize that richness for most people. See Blaney and Inayatullah (2010, chapter 6).

14. Bugra (2018), Dale (2010, 90–5; 2016, 28), Watson (2014), and Holmes (2012) all highlight the ambiguities in Polanyi.

15. Escobar (2018, 104), as we shall see, links patriarchy directly to modernity. Community is the hero that must be rekindled.

16. Only with the emergence of industrial society are internal or domestic markets brought into being via "the intervention of the state" (Polanyi 2001, 61–7). Polanyi (2001, 207) documents a sedimentation of the state around the advent of central banking that allowed the currency to be an object of policy. A national policy towards currency reflects the simultaneous transformation of "liberal nationalism" into "national liberalism, with its marked leaning towards protectionism and imperialism abroad, monopolistic conservatism at home." It was this protectionism that "fused societies into new forms"—into the "hard shell of the emerging unit of social life" that IR scholars applying Polanyi tend take for granted (Polanyi (2001, 209, 211). Polanyi insists that these processes of institutionalizing the national economy have been systematically ignored by liberal economists: "The *constitutive* importance of the

currency in establishing the nation as the decisive economic and political unit of the time was as thoroughly overlooked by the writers of the liberal Enlightenment as the existence of history had been by their eighteenth-century predecessors" (Polanyi 2001, 211). Polanyi (2001, 212) calls out David Ricardo, J. S. Mill, Alfred Marshall, and Knut Wicksell.

17. At another point, Escobar (2018, 62) suggests that this transition seems to require the substitution of "craft practices" for "manufacturing."

18. He also recommends J. K. Gibson-Graham's decentering of modern capitalism and their scheme identifying a range of nonmarket practices that already make up much of economic life and that support imagining possible "nonmodern" or perhaps "antimodern" subjectivities (Escobar 2018, 210). For their part, Gibson-Graham (2006, 56–7) link their thinking back to Polanyi's critique of the economistic fallacy and the "impoverished . . . economic language" now on offer. Market logic appears, then, as but one form of economy among many, but never the category revealing the meaning of other forms.

19. Escobar draws largely on Nandy (1987). The conclusion to this paper also is informed, as we note, by a reading of Nandy.

20. This is not to suggest that Polanyi was a believer in some conventional sense. See Bishop and McRobbie (1994) and Rotstein (1990, 99–100).

21. David Gow (2008) documents the variety of choices "indigenous" communities may make. While some certainly opt to separate themselves from wider markets and state institutions as fully as possible, others will decide to try to integrate completely into market society or adopt a more cautious, partial participation in these wider processes. We also would note that Escobar veers close to a line that reifies the indigenous as the authentic opposition to a homogenized West or modernity (see Vieira 2019).

EPILOGUE

1. We would remind readers that it is important not to confuse the idea of social determination with predetermination or full predictability. We do mean to suggest that agency unfolds within systems of social relations and, even when operating against those social relations, still within the contours of the tensions and possibilities laid down by those social relations.

2. We recognize that we are mixing relational pairs, here. We continue to prefer the Third World to the Global South because it references explicitly the relational link—the co-constitution of first and third worlds—in a way that Global South does not. East also has no terribly helpful geographic or cultural demarcation, though the West as a geographic and cultural space has been constituted relationally in opposition to a notional East or Orient. See Said (1978) and Neumann (1999). Still, we worry about trading in terms like East and West that treat complex spaces as homogeneous actors (see Vieira 2019). By Third World, we point to the interconnection and differentiation of spaces within the social relations of colonial capitalism, not to a homogeneous Third World condition.

3. We know that we risk overdrawing this distinction, despite its canonical status (Hollis and Smith 1990).

4. For one of us, this is a return to the debate. See Sajed and Inayatullah (2016).

5. Hobson (2016, 217) in no way denies the role of Western imperialism at least in the later stages of the rise of modern capitalism.

6. We have discussed Chakrabarty's point at some length elsewhere: Blaney and Inayatullah (2010, chap. 6), Blaney and Inayatullah (2016), and Inayatullah and Blaney (2016). We worry that some scholars, in the name of providing a more encompassing account of the evils of capitalism, ignore this distinction altogether. See Anievas and Nişancioğlu (2015).

7. See also, for example, Abu-Lughod (1989) who we reference in earlier chapters.

8. We don't mean to suggest that those industrial, financial and technological agencies simply disappear with the emergence of modern capitalism. Hobson's recent work documents their survival and sometimes expansion and enhancement within colonial capitalism. It is to say that their significance and meaning, including their position as social powers, become determined within the structures of the global capitalist system.

9. Though Hobson is largely concerned with Wallerstein (1997).

10. We could return to Wolf's effort to restore history to people beyond Europe for the same purpose. See also Inayatullah and Blaney (2004, chap. 2) for a suggestive account of the process of encounter from which the imaginaries of colonial capitalism emerge.

11. Stavrianos, we might recall, stresses that this was simply the first phase of resistance.

12. A recent collection of essays edited by Duncan Bell (2019) indicts the standard liberal fare on global justice for its blindness to the history of empire, settler colonization, and race. The implication—and a wager played out across all twelve authors—is that we can better confront issues of poverty and inequality if we eschew the arid abstractions of analytical Rawlsianism and instead cultivate sensitivity to historical injustices surrounding colonialism and slavery. We have no doubt about the exhaustion of most liberal accounts of ethics. We only worry that the authors are not adequately sensitive to the imperative to deny a history of violence and the weight of structures that we document in chapters 4 and 5.

Bibliography

Abufarha, Nasser. 2009. *The Making of the Human Bomb*. Durham, NC: Duke University Press.

Abu-Lughod, Janet L. 1989. *Before European Hegemony: The World System A.D. 1250–1350*. New York: Oxford University Press.

Ake, Claude. 1972. *Social Science as Imperialism: The Theory of Political Development*. 2nd ed. Ibadan: Ibadan University Press.

Almond, Gabriel. 1990. *A Discipline Divided: Schools and Sects in Political Science*. Newbury Park, CA: SAGE.

Amin, Samir. 1976. *Unequal Development: An Essay on the Social Formations of Peripheral Capitalism*. New York: Monthly Review Press.

———. 1977. *Imperialism and Unequal Development*. New York: Monthly Review Press.

Anievas, Alexander, and Kerem Nişancioğlu. 2015. *How the West Came to Rule: The Geopolitical Origins of Capitalism*. London: Pluto Press.

Aristotle. 1995. *The Politics*. Translated by Ernest Baker. New York: Oxford University Press.

Ashley, Richard. 1983. "Three Modes of Economism." *International Studies Quarterly* 27 (4): 463–96.

Barkawi, Tarak, and Mark Laffey, eds. 2017. *Democracy, Liberalism, and War: Rethinking the Democratic Peace Debate*. Boulder, CO: Lynne Rienner.

Bell, Duncan. 2007. *The Idea of Greater Britain: Empire and the Future of World Order, 1860–1900*. Princeton, NJ: Princeton University Press.

———. 2016. *Reordering the World: Essays on Liberalism and Empire*. Princeton, NJ: Princeton University Press.

———. 2019. "Introduction: Empire, Race and Global Justice." In *Empire, Race and Global Justice*, edited by Duncan Bell, 1–21. Cambridge: Cambridge University Press.

Benton, Ted. 1990. "Adam Ferguson and the Enterprise Culture." In *The Enlightenment and Its Shadows*, edited by Peter Hulmeand and Ludmilla Jordanova, 101–20. London: Routledge.

Bernard, Mitchell. 1997. "Ecology, Political Economy, and the Counter Movement: Karl Polanyi and the Second Great Transformation." In *Innovation and Transformation in International Studies*, edited by Stephen Gill and James H. Mittelman, 75–89. Cambridge: Cambridge University Press.

Berry, Christopher. 1997. *Social Theory of the Scottish Enlightenment*. Edinburgh: University of Edinburgh Press.

Berthoud, Gérald. 1990. "Toward a Comparative Approach: The Contribution of Karl Polanyi." In *The Life and Work of Karl Polanyi: A Celebration*, edited by Kari Polanyi-Levitt, 171–81. Montreál: Black Rose Books.

Bienefeld, Manfred. 2007. "Suppressing the Double Movement to Secure the Dictatorship of Finance." In *Reading Karl Polanyi for the Twenty-First Century: Market Economy as a Political Project*, edited by Ayse Bugra and Kaan Agartan, 13–32. Houndsmills, UK: Palgrave Press.

Bishop, Jordan, and Kenneth McRobbie. 1994. "How Karl Polanyi's Moral Economy Can Help Religious and Other Social Critics." In *Humanity, Society and Community: On Karl Polanyi*, 143–61. Montreál: Black Rose Books.

Blaney, David L. 1996. "Reconceptualizing Autonomy: The Difference Dependency Theory Makes." *Review of International Political Economy* 3 (3): 459–97.

———. 2016. "Theodicy and IPE: A Sketch." *Critical Studies on Security* 4 (3): 312–18.

———. 2017. "Late-Victorian Worlds: Alfred Marshall on Competition, Character, and Anglo-Saxon Civilization." In *Political Power and Social Theory*, edited by Tarak Barkawi and George Lawson, 32: 127–52. Bingley, UK: Emerald Publishing.

———. 2018. "Adam Smith's Ambiguous Theodicy and the Ethics of IPE." In *Routledge Handbook of Ethics and International Relations*, edited by Brent J. Steele and Eric A. Heinze, 503–17. London: Routledge.

———. 2020. "Provincializing Economics: Jevons, Marshall and the Colonial Imaginaries of Free Trade," *Review of International Political Economy*, published online 27 July 2020.

Blaney, David L., and Naeem Inayatullah. 2008. "International Relations from Below." In *The Oxford Handbook of International Relations*, edited by Christian Reus-Smit and Duncan Snidal, 663–74. Oxford, UK: Oxford University Press.

———. 2010. *Savage Economics: Wealth, Poverty, and the Temporal Walls of Capitalism*. London: Routledge.

———. 2016. "The Stakes of Uneven and Combined Development." In *Historical Sociology and World History: Uneven and Combined Development over the Longue Durée*, edited by Alexander Anievas and Kamran Matin, 239–50. London: Rowman & Littlefield.

Block, Fred. 2018. "Karl Polanyi and Human Freedom." In *Karl Polanyi's Vision of a Socialist Transformation*, edited by Michael Brie and Claus Thomasberger, 168–84. Montreál: Black Rose Books.

Block, Fred, and Margaret R. Somers. 1984. "Beyond the Economistic Fallacy: The Holistic Social Science of Karl Polanyi." In *Visions of Method in Historical Sociology*, 47–84. Cambridge: Cambridge University Press.

———. 2014. *The Power of Market Fundamentalism: Karl Polanyi's Critique*. Cambridge: Cambridge University Press.

Boghosian, Bruce M. 2019. "The Inescapable Casino." *Scientific American* 321 (5): 70–7.

Booth, William James. 1994. "On the Idea of the Moral Economy." *American Political Science Review* 88 (3): 653–67.

Boucoyannis, Deborah. 2007. "The International Wanderings of a Liberal Idea, or Why Liberals Can Learn to Stop Worrying and Love the Balance of Power." *Perspectives on Politics* 5 (4): 703–27.

Boyd, Richard. 2008. "Manners and Morals: David Hume on Civility, Commerce, and the Social Construction of Difference." In *David Hume's Political Economy*, edited by Carl Wennerlind and Margaret Schabas, 68–85. London: Routledge.

Braudel, Fernand. 1972. *The Mediterranean and the Mediterranean World in the Age of Phillip II*. Vol. 1. New York: Harper & Row.

———. 1973. *The Mediterranean and the Mediterranean World in the Age of Phillip II*. Vol. 2. New York: Harper & Row.

Brie, Michael. 2018. "Karl Polanyi and the Discussions on a Renewed Socialism." In *Karl Polanyi's Vision of a Socialist Transformation*, edited by Michael Brie and Claus Thomasberger, 241–62. Montréal: Black Rose Books.

Brie, Michael, and Claus Thomasberger. 2018. "Introduction." In *Karl Polanyi's Vision of a Socialist Transformation*, edited by Michael Brie and Claus Thomasberger, 5–16. Montréal: Black Rose Books.

Broadie, Alexander. 2001. *The Scottish Enlightenment: The Historical Age of the Historical Nation*. Edinburgh: Edinburgh University Press.

Brown, Wendy. 2001. *Politics Out of History*. Princeton, NJ: Princeton University.

Buchan, Bruce. 2006. "Civilisation, Sovereignty and War: The Scottish Enlightenment and International Relations." *International Relations* 20 (2): 177–8.

Bugra, Ayse. 2018. "Revisiting 'Freedom in a Complex Society': A View from the Periphery." In *Karl Polanyi's Vision of a Socialist Transformation*, edited by Michael Brie and Claus Thomasberger, 77–90. Montréal: Black Rose Books.

Bull, Benedicte. 2012. "The Global Elite, Public-Private Partnerships and Multilateral Governance." In *Global Governance, Poverty and Inequality*, edited by Jennifer Clapp and Wilkinson Rorden, 209–34. New York: Routledge.

Burchell, Graham. 2005. "Peculiar Interests: Civil Society and Governing 'The System of Natural Liberty.'" In *The Foucault Effect: Studies in Governmentality*, edited by Graham Burchell, Colin Gordon, and Peter Miller, 119–50. Chicago, IL: University of Chicago Press.

Burrow, J. W. 1988. *Whigs and Liberals: Continuity and Change in English Political Thought*. Oxford, UK: Clarendon Press.

Cammack, Paul. 2004. "What the World Bank Means by Poverty Reduction, and Why It Matters." *New Political Economy* 9 (2): 189–211.

Caporaso, James A. 1989. "Microeconomics and International Political Economy: The Neoclassical Approach to Institutions." In *Global Changes and Theoretical*

Challenges: Approaches to World Politics for the 1990s, edited by Ernt-Otto Czempiel and James N. Rosenau. New York: Lexington Books.

———, ed. 1978. "Dependence and Dependency in the Global System: A Structural and Behavioral Analysis." *International Organization* 32 (1): 13–43.

———. 1980. "Dependency Theory: Continuities and Discontinuities in Development Studies." *International Organization* 34 (4): 605–28.

Caporaso, James A., and David P. Levine. 1992. *Theories of Political Economy*. New York: Cambridge University Press.

Caporaso, James A., and Sidney Tarrow. 2009. "Polanyi in Brussels: Supranational Institutions and the Transnational Embedding of Markets." *International Organization* 63 (4): 593–620.

Cardoso, Fernando H. 1972. "Dependent Capitalist Development in Latin America." *New Left Review* 74: 83–94.

Cardoso, Fernando H., and Ernesto Falletto. 1979. *Dependency and Development in Latin America*. Translated by M. M. Urquidi. Berkeley: University of California Press.

Carlson, Allan. 2006. "The Problem of Karl Polanyi." *The Intercollegiate Review* 41 (1): 32–9.

Carmody, Chios., Frank Garcia, and John Linarelli. 2012. *Global Justice and International Economic Law*. Cambridge: Cambridge University Press.

Chakrabarty, Dipesh. 2000. *Provincializing Europe: Postcolonial Thought and Historical Difference*. Princeton, NJ: Princeton University Press.

Chandler, James. 1998. *England in 1819: The Politics of Literary Culture and the Case of Romantic Historicism*. Chicago, IL: University of Chicago Press.

Chaudhuri, K. N. 1990. *Asia Before Europe: Economy and Civilisation of the Indian Ocean from the Rise of Islam to 1750*. Cambridge: Cambridge University Press.

Chilcote, R. H. 1984. *Theories of Development and Underdevelopment*. New York: Sage.

Christiaens, Tim. 2019. "Hayek's Vicarious Secularization of Providential Theology." *Philosophy and Social Criticism* 45 (1): 71–95.

Cohen, Benjamin J. 2008. *International Political Economy: An Intellectual History*. Princeton, NJ: Princeton University Press.

———. 2010. "Are IPE Journals Becoming Boring?" *International Studies Quarterly* 54 (3): 887–91.

Collini, Stefan, Donald Winch, and John Burrow. 1983. *That Noble Science of Politics: A Study in Nineteenth-Century Intellectual History*. Cambridge: Cambridge University Press.

Connolly, William E. 1991. *Identity/Difference: Democratic Negotiations of Political Paradox*. Ithaca, NY: Cornell University Press.

———. 2008. *Capitalism and Christianity, American Style*. Durham, NC: Duke University Press.

Cook, Simon J. 2009. *The Intellectual Foundations of Alfred Marshall's Economic Science*. Cambridge: Cambridge University Press.

Cox, Robert. 1986. "Social Forces, States, and World Orders: Beyond International Relations Theory." In *Neoliberalism and Its Critics*, edited by Robert O. Keohane, 204–54. New York: Columbia University Press.

Crane, George T., and Abla Amawi, eds. 2010. *The Theoretical Structure of International Political Economy: A Reader*. New York: Oxford University Press.

Currie, Martin, and Ian Steedman. 1990. *Wrestling with Time: Problems in Economic Theory*. Ann Arbor: University of Michigan Press.

Dale, Gareth. 2010. *Karl Polanyi: The Limits of the Market*. Cambridge, UK: Polity Press.

———. 2016. *Reconstructing Karl Polanyi: Excavation and Critique*. London: Pluto Press.

———. 2018. "Karl Polanyi and the Paradoxes of Freedom." In *Karl Polanyi's Vision of a Socialist Transformation*, edited by Michael Brie and Claus Thomasberger, 126–40. Montreál: Black Rose Books.

Darity, William A. Jr., and Patrick L. Mason. 2007. "Racial Discrimination in the Labor Market." In *Race, Liberalism, and Economics*, edited by David Colander, Robert E. Prasch, and Falguni A. Sheth, 182–204. Ann Arbor: University of Michigan Press.

Davie, G. E. 1967. "Anglophobe and Anglophile." *Scottish Journal of Political Economy* 14 (3): 291–301.

Denemark, Robert A. 1999. "World System History: From Traditional International Politics to the Study of Global Relations." *International Studies Review* 1 (2): 43–75.

Deudney, Daniel. 2007. *Bounding Power*. Princeton, NJ: Princeton University Press.

Dickey, Laurence. 1987. *Hegel: Religion, Economics and the Politics of Spirit, 1770–1807*. Cambridge: Cambridge University.

Donnelly, Jack. 2013. *International Human Rights*. Boulder, CO: Westview Press.

Dos Santos, Theotonio. 1970. "The Structure of Dependence." *American Economic Review* 60 (2): 231–60.

Doujon, Ruhdan. 1994. "Steuart's Position on Economic Progress." *The European Journal of the History of Economic Thought* 1 (3): 495–518.

Drucker, Peter F. 1978. *Adventures of a Bystander*. New York: Harper & Row.

Duke, Michael J. 1979. "David Hume and Monetary Readjustment." *History of Political Economy* 11 (4): 572–87.

Duncan, Bell. 2016. *Reordering the World: Essays on Liberalism and Empire*. Princeton, NJ: Princeton University Press.

Dunkley, Graham. 1997. *The Free Trade Adventure: The Uruguay Round and Globalism—A Critique*. Melbourne: Melbourne University Press.

———. 2004. *Free Trade: Myth, Reality and Alternatives*. London: Zed Press.

Eagleton, Terry. 2010. *On Evil*. New Haven, CT: Yale University Press.

Edkins, Jenny. 1999. *Poststructuralism and International Relations: Bringing the Political Back In*. Boulder, CO: Lynne Rienner.

Escobar, Arturo. 1995. *Encountering Development: The Making and Unmaking of the Third World*. Princeton, NJ: Princeton University Press.

———. 2005. "Economics and the Space of Modernity." *Cultural Studies* 19 (2): 139–75.

———. 2018. *Designs for the Pluriverse: Radical Interdependence, Autonomy, and the Making of Worlds*. Durham, NC: Duke University Press.

Evans, Peter. 2000. "Fighting Marginalization with Transnational Networks: Counter-Hegemonic Globalization." *Contemporary Sociology* 29 (1): 230–41.
———. 2015. "Pursuing a Great Transformation: National and Global Dynamics." *Sociology of Development* 1 (1): 3–19.
Falk, Richard A. 2000. *Human Rights Horizons: The Pursuit of Justice in a Globalizing World*. New York: Routledge.
Ferguson, Adam. 1995. *An Essay on the History of Civil Society*. Cambridge: Cambridge University Press.
Ferguson, James. 1994. *The Anti-Politics Machine: "Development," Depoliticization, and Bureaucratic Power in Lesotho*. Minneapolis: University of Minnesota Press.
Fleischacker, Samuel. 2004. *A Short History of Distributive Justice*. Cambridge, MA: Harvard University Press.
Forbes, Duncan. 1967. "Adam Ferguson and the Idea of Community." In *Edinburgh and the Age of Reason: A Commemoration*, edited by Douglas Young, et al., 40–7. Edinburgh: Edinburgh University Press.
Forrester, Katrina. 2019. "Reparations, History and the Origins of Global Justice." In *Empire, Race and Global Justice*, edited by Duncan Bell, 22–51. Cambridge: Cambridge University Press.
Foucault, Michel. 2008. *The Birth of Biopolitics: Lectures at the Collège Be France*. New York: Picador.
Frank, Andre Gunder. 1998. *Re-Orient: Global Economy in the Asian Age*. Berkeley: University of California Press.
Fraser, Nancy. 2014. "Can Society Be Commodities All the Way Down? Post-Polanyian Reflections on Capitalist Crisis." *Economy and Society* 43 (4): 541–58.
———. 2017. "Why Two Karls Are Better than One: Integrating Polanyi and Marx in a Critical Theory of the Current Crisis." Working paper. */paper/Nancy-Fraser-Why-two-Karls-are-Better-than-One-%3A-in-Fraser/ca001162d4478e474915ff02ac2b58af9e7cb1de*
Frieden, Jeffrey A., and David A. Lake, eds. 1995. *International Political Economy: Perspectives on Global Power and Wealth*. 3rd ed. New York: St. Martin's Press.
Froebel, Folker, Jurgen Heinrich, and Otto Kreye. 1980. *The New International Division of Labor*. Cambridge: Cambridge University Press.
Fuller, Lisa. 2008. "Poverty Relief, Global Institutions, and the Problem of Compliance." In *The Global Justice Reader*, edited by T. Brooks, 454–64. Oxford, UK: Blackwell.
Furtado, Celso. 1969. "U.S. Hegemony and the Future of Latin America." In *Latin American Radicalism: A Documentary Report on Left and Nationalist Movements*, edited by Irving Louis Horowitz, Josué de Castro, and John Gerassi. New York: Random House.
———. 1970. *Obstacles to Development in Latin America*. Garden City, NY: Anchor Books.
Gauri, Varun, and John Sonderholm. 2012. "Global Poverty: Four Normative Positions." *Journal of Global Ethics* 8 (2–3): 193–213.
Geremek, Bronislaw. 1994. *Poverty*. Cambridge, MA: Blackwell.

Germain, Randall. 2019. "International Political Economy." In *Exploring the Thought of Karl Polanyi*, edited by Gareth Dale, Christopher Holmes, and Maria Markanto-natou, 27–48. New York: Columbia University Press.

Gibson-Graham, J. K. 2006. *The End of Capitalism (as We Knew It)*. Minneapolis, MN: University of Minnesota Press.

Giddens, Anthony. 1984. *The Constitution of Society: Outline of the Theory of Structuration*. Berkeley: University of California Press.

Gilpin, Robert. 1987. *The Political Economy of International Relations*. Princeton, NJ: Princeton University Press.

———. 2001. *Global Political Economy: Understanding the International Economic Order*. Princeton, NJ: Princeton University Press.

Gleditsch, Nils Petter. 2008. "The Liberal Moment Fifteen Years On." *International Studies Quarterly* 52 (4): 691–712.

Gould, Carol. 2004. *Globalizing Democracy and Human Rights*. Cambridge: Cambridge University Press.

———. 2007. "Coercion, Care, and Corporations: Omissions and Commissions in Thomas Pogge's Political Philosophy." *Journal of Global Ethics* 3 (3): 381–93.

Gow, David D. 2008. *Countering Development: Indigenous Modernity and the Moral Imagination*. Durham, NC: Duke University Press.

Griswold, Charles L, Jr. 1999. *Adam Smith and the Virtues of Enlightenment*. Cambridge: Cambridge University Press.

Groenewegen, Peter. 1990. "Marshall and Hegel." *Economie Appliquèe* 43 (1): 63–84.

Haakonssen, Knud. 2005. *Natural Law and Moral Philosophy: From Grotius to the Scottish Enlightenment*. Cambridge: Cambridge University.

Habermas, Jürgen. 1970. *Toward a Rational Society: Student Protest, Science and Politics*. Boston, MA: Beacon Press.

Hage, Ghassan. 2003. "'Comes a Time We Are All Enthusiasm': Understanding Palestinan Suicide Bombers in Times of Exighophobia." *Public Culture* 15 (1): 65–89.

Halperin, Sandra. 2004. "Dynamics of Conflict and Systems Change: The Great Transformation Revisited." *European Journal of International Relations* 10 (2): 263–306.

Hart, Neil. 2012. *Equilibrium and Evolution: Marshall and the Marshallians*. London: Palgrave Macmillan.

Harvey-Phillips, M. B. 1984. "Malthus' Theodicy: The Intellectual Background of His Contribution to Political Economy." *History of Political Economy* 16 (4): 591–608.

Hayek, Friedrich. 1960. *The Constitution of Liberty*. Chicago, IL: University of Chicago Press.

———. 1976. *Law, Legislation and Liberty. Vol. 2: The Mirage of Social Justice*. Chicago, IL: University of Chicago Press.

———. 1979. *Law, Legislation and Liberty. Vol. 3: Political Order of a Free People*. Chicago, IL: University of Chicago Press.

Hechter, Michael. 1981. "Polanyi's Social Theory: A Critique." *Politics and Society* 10 (4): 399–429.

Helleiner, Eric. 2000. "Globalization and Haute Finance—Déjà Vu?" In *Karl Polanyi in Vienna: The Contemporary Significance of The Great Transformation*, edited by Kenneth McRobbie and Kari Polanyi-Levitt, 12–31. Montreál: Black Rose Books.
———. 2002. "Economic Nationalism as a Challenge to Economic Liberalism? Lessons from the 19th Century." *International Studies Quarterly* 46 (3): 307–29.
———. 2019. "The Life and Times of Embedded Liberalism: Legacy and Innovations since Bretton Woods." *Review of International Political Economy* 26 (6): 1112–35.
Hettne, Björn. 1997. "The Double Movement: Global Market versus Regionalism." In *The New Realism: Perspectives on Multilaterialism and World Order*, edited by Robert W. Cox, 223–42. Tokyo: UN University Press.
———. 2000. "Re-Reading Polanyi: Towards a Second Great Transformation." In *Karl Polanyi in Vienna: The Contemporary Significance of The Great Transformation*, edited by Kenneth McRobbie and Kari Polanyi-Levitt, 60–72. Montreál: Black Rose Books.
Hill, Lisa. 1997. "Adam Ferguson and the Paradox of Progress and Decline." *History of Political Thought* 18: 677–706.
Himmelfarb, Gertrude. 1984. *The Idea of Poverty*. New York: Knopf.
———. 1991. *Poverty and Compassion*. New York: Vintage Books.
Hirschman, A. O. 1997. *The Passions and the Interests: Political Arguments for Capitalism before Its Triumph*. Princeton, NJ: Princeton University Press.
Hobson, John M. 2004. *The Eastern Origins of Western Civilization*. Cambridge: Cambridge University Press.
———. 2012. *The Eurocentric Conception of World Politics: Western International Theory, 1760–2010*. Cambridge: Cambridge University Press.
———. 2016. "The 'R-Word' and 'E-Word' Definitional Controversies: A Dialogue with My Five Interlocutors." *Postcolonial Studies* 19 (2): 210–26.
Hobson, John M. 2021. *Multicultural Origins of the Global Economy: Beyond the Western-Centric Frontier*. Cambridge: Cambridge University.
Hodgson, Geoffrey M. 1993. *Economics and Evolution: Bringing Life Back into Economics*. Ann Arbor: University of Michigan Press.
Hollis, Martin, and Steve Smith. 1990. *Explaining and Understanding in International Relations*. Oxford, UK: Clarendon Press.
Holmes, Christopher. 2012. "Problems and Opportunities in Polanyian Analysis Today." *Economy and Society* 41 (3): 468–84.
Hont, Istvan. 1983. "The 'Rich Country-Poor Country' Debate in Scottish Political Economy." In *Wealth and Virtue: The Shaping of Political Economy in the Scottish Enlightenment*, edited by Michael Ignatieff, 217–315. Cambridge: Cambridge University Press.
Hulme, David. 2012. "Governing Global Poverty? Global Ambivalence and the Millennium Development Goals." In *Global Governance, Poverty and Inequality*, edited by Jennifer Clapp and Rorden Wilkinson, 135–61. New York: Routledge.
Hume, David. 1807. *The History of England*. Vol. 2. London: J. McReery.
———. 1985. *Essays: Moral, Political and Literary*. Edited by Eugene F. Miller. Indianapolis, IN: Liberty Fund.

Hutchings, Kimberly. 2008. *Time and World Politics: Thinking the Present*. Manchester, UK: Manchester University Press.

Ikenberry, John G. 2015. "The Future of Multilateralism: Governing the World in a Post-Hegemonic Era." *Japanese Journal of Political Science* 16 (3): 399–413.

———. 2018. "The End of Liberal International Order?" *International Affairs* 94 (1): 7–23.

Inayatullah, Naeem. 1997. "Theories of Spontaneous Disorder." *Review of International Political Economy* 4 (2): 319–48.

———. 2003. "Bumpy Space: Imperialism and Resistance in Star Trek: The Next Generation." In *To Seek Out New Worlds: Science Fiction and World Politics*, edited by Jutta Weldes. London: Palgrave Press.

———. 2011. "Introduction." In *I/IR: Autobiographical International Relations*, edited by Naeem Inayatullah, 1–12. London: Routledge.

Inayatullah, Naeem, and David L. Blaney. 1995. "Realizing Sovereignty." *Review of International Studies* 21 (1): 3–20.

———. 2004. *International Relations and the Problem of Difference*. New York: Routledge.

———. 2009. "The Rites of Dispossession: Medieval and Modern." In *Silencing Human Rights: Critical Engagements with a Contested Project*, edited by Gurminder K. Bhambra and Robbie Shilliam, 63–84. Houndmills, UK: Palgrave Macmillan.

———. 2015. "A Problem with Levels: How to Engage a Diverse IPE." *Contexto Internacional* 37 (3): 889–912.

———. 2016a. "Global Capitalism, (In)Equality, and Poverty." In *International Relations Theory Today*, edited by Toni Erskine and Booth Ken, 2nd ed., 161–74. London: Polity Press.

———. 2016b. "The Costs of Weaponizing Emancipatory Politics: Constituting What Is Constitutive of Capitalism." *Spectrum: Journal of Global Politics* 8 (1): 46–69.

———. 2017. "Tea and Text: Cultivated Intuition as Methodological Process." In *Critical Methods in Political and Cultural Economy*, edited by Johnna Montgomerie, 23–7. London: Routledge.

Inayatullah, Naeem, and Mark Rupert. 1994. "Hobbes, Smith, and the Problem of Mixed Ontologies." In *The Global Economy as Political Space*, edited by Stephen Rosow, Naeem Inayatullah, and Mark Rupert, 61–85. Boulder, CO: Lynne Rienner.

Isaak, Robert A. 2000. *Managing World Economic Change: International Political Economy*. Upper Saddle River, NJ: Prentice Hall.

Jackson, Patrick Thaddeus, and Daniel H. Nexon. 2019. "Reclaiming the Social: Relationism in Anglophone International Studies." *Cambridge Review of International Affairs* 32 (5): 582–600.

Jahn, Beate. 2005. "Kant, Mill, and Illiberal Legacies in International Affairs." *International Organization* 59 (Winter): 177–207.

———. 2013. *Liberal Internationalism: Theory, History, Practice*. London: Palgrave Press.

———. 2019. "The Sorcerer's Apprentice: Liberalism, Ideology, and Religion." *International Relations* 33 (2): 322–37.

Jennings, Francis. 1975. *The Invasion of America: Indians, Colonialism and the Cant of Conquest*. Chapel Hill: University of North Carolina Press.

Jones, Gareth Stedman. 2004. *An End to Poverty?* London: Profile Books.

Kamola, Isaac. 2019. *Making the World Global: U.S. Universities and the Production of the Global Imaginary*. Durham, NC: Duke University Press.

Katz, Claudio. 1997. "Private Property versus Markets: Democratic and Communitarian Critiques of Capitalism." *American Political Science Review* 91 (2): 277–89.

Keohane, Robert O. 1984. *After Hegemony: Cooperation and Discord in the World Political Economy*. Princeton, NJ: Princeton University Press.

———. 1989. *International Institutions and State Power: Essays in International Relations Theory*. Boulder, CO: Westview Press.

———. 1990. "International Liberalism Reconsidered." In *The Economic Limits to Politics*, edited by John Dunn, 165–94. Cambridge: Cambridge University Press.

Keohane, Robert O., and Joseph S. Nye. 1989. *Power and Interdependence*. 2nd ed. New York: HarperCollins.

Kettler, David. 1965. *The Social and Political Thought of Adam Ferguson*. Columbus: Ohio State University Press.

Klein, Judy L. 1997. *Statistical Visions in Time: A History of Time Series Analysis*. Cambridge: Cambridge University Press.

Kordela, Kiarina. 2007. *Surplus: Spinoza, Lacan*. Albany, NY: SUNY Press.

Krasner, Stephen D. 1983. "Structural Causes and Regime Consequences: Regimes as Intervening Variables." In *International Regimes*, edited by Stephen D. Krasner, 1–21. Ithaca, NY: Cornell University Press.

Lacher, Hannes. 1999a. "Embedded Liberalism, Disembedded Markets: Reconceptualizing the Pax Americana." *New Political Economy* 4 (3): 343–60.

———. 1999b. "The Politics of the Market: Re-Reading Karl Polanyi." *Global Society* 13 (3): 313–26.

———. 2007. "The Slight Transformation: Contesting the Legacy of Karl Polanyi." In *Reading Karl Polanyi for the Twenty-First Century: Market Economy as a Political Project*, edited by Ayse Bugra and Kaan Agartan, 49–64. Houndsmills, UK: Palgrave Press.

Lakoff, George, and Mark Johnson. 1980. *Metaphors We Live By*. Chicago, IL: University of Chicago Press.

Lamy, Steven, John Masker, Steve Smith, and Patricia Owens. 2019. *Introduction to Global Politics*. 5th ed. New York: Oxford University Press.

Lane, Robert. 1991. *The Market Experience*. Cambridge: Cambridge University Press.

Latham, Robert. 1997a. "Globalisation and Democratic Provisionism: Re-Reading Polanyi." *New Political Economy* 2 (1): 53–63.

———. 1997b. *The Liberal Moment: Modernity, Security, and the Making of Postwar International Order*. New York: Columbia University Press.

Latour, Bruno. 2004. "Whose Cosmos, Which Cosmopolitics?: Comments on the Peace Terms of Ulrich Beck." *Common Knowledge* 10 (3): 450–62.

Law, John. 2015. "What's Wrong with a One-World World." *Distinktion: Journal of Social Theory* 16 (1): 126–39.

Legrand, Muriel Dal Pont, and Harald Hagemann. 2017. "Do Productive Recessions Show the Recuperative Power of Capitalism? Schumpeter's Analysis of the Cleansing Effect." *Journal of Economic Perspectives* 31 (1): 245–55.

Levine, David P. 1977. *Economic Studies: Contributions to the Critique of Economic Theory*. Boston, MA: Routledge and Kegan Paul.

———. 1978. *Economic Theory. Volume 1: The Elementary Relations of Economic Life*. London: Routledge and Kegan Paul.

———. 1981. *Economic Theory. Volume 2: The System of Economic Relations as a Whole*. London: Routledge and Kegan Paul.

———. 1988. *Needs, Rights, and the Market*. Boulder, CO: Lynne Rienner.

———. 1997a. *Self-Seeking and the Pursuit of Justice*. Brookfield, WI: Ashgate.

———. 1997b. *Wealth and Freedom: An Introduction to Political Economy*. New York: Cambridge University Press.

———. 1998. *Subjectivity in Political Economy: Essays on Wanting and Choosing*. London: Routledge.

Levine, David P., and S. Abu Turab Rizvi. 2005. *Poverty Work and Freedom: Political Economy and the Moral Order*. Cambridge: Cambridge University Press.

Levy, David M. 2002. *How the Dismal Science Got Its Name: Classical Economics and the Ur-Text of Racial Politics*. Ann Arbor: University of Michigan Press.

Lind, Christopher. 1994. "How Karl Polanyi's Moral Economy Can Help Religious and Other Social Critics." In *Humanity, Society, and Community: On Karl Polanyi*, edited by Kenneth McRobbie, 143–61. Montreál: Black Rose Books.

Loury, Glenn. 2007. "The Anatomy of Racial Inequality: A Clarification." In *Race, Liberalism, and Economics*, edited by David Colander, Robert E. Prasch, and Falguni A. Sheth, 238–55. Ann Arbor: University of Michigan Press.

Mankiw, N. Gregory. 2013. "Defending the One Percent." *Journal of Economic Perspectives* 27 (3): 21–34.

Manzer, Rovert A. 1996. "The Promise of Peace? Hume and Smith on the Effects of Commerce on War and Peace." *Hume Studies* 22 (2): 369–82.

Marshall, Alfred. 1885. *The Present Position of Economics*. London: Macmillan.

———. 1890. "Some Aspects of Competition." *Journal of the Royal Statistical Society* 53 (4): 612–43.

———. 1898. "Distribution and Exchange." *The Economic Journal* 8 (29): |37–59.

———. 1919. *Industry and Trade*. 3rd ed. Vols. 1 and 2. Kissimmee, FL: Signalman.

———. 2009. *Principles of Economics*. 8th ed. New York: Cosimo.

Marx, Karl. 1973. *Grundrisse: Foundations of the Critique of Political Economy*. New York: Vintage Books.

McNulty, Paul J. 1967. "A Note on the History of Perfect Competition." *Journal of Political Economy* 75 (4, Part I): 395–9.

———. 1968. "Economic Theory and the Meaning of Competition." *Quarterly Journal of Economics* 82 (4): 639–56.

Meek, Ronald L. 1965. *The Rise and Fall of the Concept of the Economic Machine*. Leicester, UK: Leicester University Press.

Mendell, Marguerite. 1990. "Karl Polanyi and Feasible Socialism." In *The Life and Work of Karl Polanyi: A Celebration*, edited by Kari Polanyi-Levitt, 66–77. Montreál: Black Rose Books.

Merikoski, Ingrid. 2002. "The Challenge of Material Progress: The Scottish Enlightenment and Christian Stoicism." *Journal of the Historical Society* 2 (1): 55–76.

Mijs, Jonathan J. B. 2016. "The Unfulfillable Promise of Meritocracy: Three Lessons and Their Implications for Justice in Education." *Social Justice Research* 29 (1): 14–34.

———. 2018. "Visualizing Belief in Meritocracy, 1930–2010." *Socius: Social Research for a Dynamic World* 4 (1): 1–2.

———. 2019. "The Paradox of Inequality: Income Inequality and Belief in Meritocracy Go Hand in Hand." *Socio-Economic Review*, 1–29.

Milbank, John. 1990. *Theology and Social Theory: Beyond Secular Reason*. Oxford, UK: Blackwell.

Millar, John. 1979a. "Advancement of Manufactures, Commerce and the Arts." In *John Millar of Glasgow, 1735–1801: His Life and Thought and His Contribution to Sociological Analysis*, edited by William C. Lehman, 326–39. New York: Arno Press.

———. 1979b. "The Origins of the Distinction of Ranks." In *John Millar of Glasgow, 1735–1801: His Life and Thought and His Contribution to Sociological Analysis*, edited by William C. Lehman, 175–322. New York: Arno Press.

———. 1997. *A Historical View of the English Government*. Vol. 4. Bristol, UK: Thoemmes Press.

Miller, David. 1976. *Social Justice*. Oxford, UK: Clarendon Press.

Mills, Charles W. 2019. "Race and Global Justice." In *Empire, Race and Global Justice*, edited by Duncan Bell, 99–119. Cambridge: Cambridge University Press.

Mingst, Karen A., Jack L. Snyder, and Heather Elko McKibben, eds. 2019. *Essential Readings in World Politics*. 7th ed. New York: W.W. Norton.

Mirowski, Phillip. 1984. "Physics and the 'Marginalist Revolution.'" *Cambridge Journal of Economics* 8 (4): 361–79.

Mitchell, Timothy. 2000. "The Stage of Modernity." In *Questions of Modernity*, edited by Timothy Mitchell, 1–34. Minneapolis: University of Minnesota Press.

Montag, Warren. 2005. "Necro-Economics: Adam Smith and Death in the Life of the Universal." *Radical Philosophy* 134 (1): 7–17.

Nandy, Ashis. 1983. *The Intimate Enemy: Loss and Recovery of Self under Colonialism*. Delhi: Oxford University Press.

———. 1987. *Traditions, Tyranny, and Utopias: Essays on the Politics of Awareness*. Delhi: Oxford University Press.

———. 2002. *Time Warps: Silent and Evasive Pasts in Indian Politics and Religion*. New Brunswick, NJ: Rutgers University Press.

Naverson, Jan. 2003. "We Don't Owe Them a Thing! A Tough-Minded but Soft-Hearted View of Aid to the Faraway Needy." *The Monist* 86 (3): 419–33.

———. 2004a. "Is World Poverty a Moral Problem for the Wealthy?" *Journal of Ethics* 8 (4): 397–448.

———. 2004b. "Welfare and Wealth, Poverty and Justice in Today's World." *Journal of Ethics* 8 (4): 305–48.

Neumann, Iver. 1999. *Uses of the Other: 'The East' in European Identity Formation.* Minneapolis: University of Minnesota Press.

Nichols, Robert. 2019. "Indigenous Peoples. Settler Colonialism and Global Justice in Anglo-America." In *Empire, Race and Global Justice*, edited by Duncan Bell, 228–50. Cambridge: Cambridge University Press.

Nozick, Robert. 1974. *Anarchy, State and Utopia.* New York: Basic Books.

Oatley, Thomas. 2019. "Toward a Political Economy of Complex Interdependence." *European Journal of International Relations* 25 (4): 957–78.

O'Brien, Robert, and Marc Williams. 2004. *Global Political Economy: Evolution and Dynamics.* London: Palgrave Macmillan.

Onuf, Nicholas G. 1995. "Levels." *European Journal of International Relations* 1 (1): 35–58.

Onuf, Nicholas G., and Peter Onuf. 2006. *Nations, Markets, and War: Modern History and the American Civil War.* Charlottesville: University of Virginia Press.

Oriheula, José Carlos. 2020. "Embedded Countermovements: The Forging of Protected Areas and Native Communities in the Peruvian Amazon." *New Political Economy* 25 (1): 150–5.

Ozandu, Christopher. 2013. "Theorizing Necro-Ontology, Resisting Necro-Economics." *Atlantic Studies* 10 (3): 323–49.

Özel, Hüseyin. n.d. "The Road to Serfdom in Light of *The Great Transformation*: A Comparison on the Basis of Unintended Consequences." University of Hacettepe, Ankara.

Oz-Salzberger, Fania. 1995. *Translating the Enlightenment: Scottish Civic Discourse in Eighteenth-Century Germany.* New York: Oxford University Press.

Peart, Sandra J., and David M. Levy. 2003. "Denying Human Homogeneity: Eugenics and the Making of Post-Classical Economics." *Journal of the History of Economic Thought* 25 (3): 261–88.

———. 2007. " 'Not and Average Human Being': How Economics Succumbed to Racial Accounts of Economic Man." In *Race, Liberalism and Economics*, edited by David Collander, Robert E. Prasch, and Falguni A. Sheth, 123–44. Ann Arbor: University of Michigan Press.

———. 2008. "Introduction." In *The Street Porter and the Philosopher: Conversations on Analytical Egalitarianism*, 1–15. Ann Arbor: University of Michigan Press.

Peck, Jamie. 2013. "Excavating the Pilbara: A Polanyian Exploration." *Geographical Research* 51 (3): 227–42.

Pocock, J. G. A. 1975. *The Machiavellian Moment: Florentine Political Thought and the Atlantic Republican Tradition.* Princeton, NJ: Princeton University Press.

Pogge, Thomas. 1989. *Realizing Rawls.* Ithaca, NY: Cornell University Press.

———. 2007. *Freedom from Poverty as a Human Right.* Oxford, UK: Oxford University Press.

Polanyi, Karl. 1936. "The Essence of Fascism." In *Christianity and the Social Revolution*, edited by John Lewis, Karl Polanyi, and Donald K. Kitchin, 359–94. New York: Charles Scribner's Sons.

————. 1945. "Universal Capitalism or Regional Planning." *London Quarterly of World Affairs* 10 (3): 86–91.

————. 1957. "Aristotle Discovers the Economy." In *Trade and Market in the Early Empires: Economies in Theory and History*, edited by Karl Polanyi, Conrad M. Arensberg, and Harry Pearson, 64–95. Glencoe, IL: Free Press.

————. 1968. "The Economy as Instituted Process." In *Primitive, Archaic, and Modern Economies: Essays of Karl Polanyi*, edited by George Dalton, 139–74. Garden City, NY: Anchor Books.

————. 1977. *The Livelihood of Man*. New York: Academic Press.

————. 2001. *The Great Transformation: The Political and Economic Origins of Our Time*. Boston, MA: Beacon Press.

————. 2014a. "Economic History and the Problem of Freedom." In *For a New West: Essays 1919–1958*, edited by Giorgio Resta and Mariavittoria Catanzariti, 39–46. London: Polity Press.

————. 2014b. "For a New West." In *For a New West: Essays 1919–1958*, edited by Giorgio Resta and Mariavittoria Catanzariti, 29–32. London: Polity Press.

Poovey, Mary. 1998. *A History of the Modern Fact: Problems of Knowledge in the Science of Wealth and Society*. Chicago, IL: University of Chicago Press.

Rawls, John. 1971. *A Theory of Justice*. Cambridge, MA: Harvard University Press.

Redman, Deborah. 1996. "Sir James Steuart's Statesman Revisited in the Light of Continental Influence." *Scottish Journal of Political Economy* 43 (1): 48–70.

Reisman, David. 1987. *Alfred Marshall: Progress and Politics*. London: Macmillan.

Rey Pérez, José Luiz. 2007. "The Right to Work, Way of Social Exclusion: Basic Income as a Guarantee to the Right to Work." In *Reading Karl Polanyi for the Twenty-First Century: Market Economy as a Political Project*, edited by Ayse Bugra and Kaan Agartan, 95–113. Houndsmills, UK: Palgrave Press.

Risse, Thomas, S. Ropp, and Katherin Sikkink, eds. 1999. *The Power of Human Rights: International Norms and Domestic Change*. Cambridge: Cambridge University Press.

Robinson, Joan. 1980. "Introduction." In *Classical and Neoclassical Theories of General Equilibrium: Historical Origins and Mathematical Structure*, by Vivian Walsh and Harvey Gram, xi–xvi. Oxford, UK: Oxford University Press.

Rodney, Walter. 1974. *How Europe Underdeveloped Africa*. Washington, DC: Howard University Press.

Rosenberg, Justin. 1994. *Empire of Civil Society: A Critique of the Realist Theory of International Relations*. London: Verso Books.

Rosmer, Peter. 1990. "Karl Polanyi on Socialist Accounting." In *The Life and Work of Karl Polanyi*, edited by Kari Polanyi-Levitt, 55–65. Montreál: Black Rose Books.

Rotstein, Abraham. 1990. "The Reality of Society: Karl Polanyi's Philosophical Perspective." In *The Life and Work of Karl Polanyi*, edited by Kari Polanyi-Levitt, 98–110. Montreál: Black Rose Books.

Ruggie, John. 1982. "International Regimes, Transactions, and Change: Embedded Liberalism in the Postwar Economic Order." *International Organization* 36 (2): 379–415.

Sahlins, Marshall. 1972. *Stone Age Economics*. New York: Aldine Press.

Said, Edward W. 1978. *Orientalism*. New York: Pantheon Books.

Sajed, Alina, and Naeem Inayatullah. 2016. "On the Perils of Lifting the Weight of Structures: An Engagement with Hobson's Critique of the Discipline of IR." *Postcolonial Studies* 19 (2): 201–9.

Santos, Boaventura de Souza. 2007. *Another Production Is Possible: Beyond the Capitalist Canon*. London: Verso Books.

Schumpeter, Joseph A. 1961. *The Theory of Economic Development*. Translated by Redvers Opie. New York: Oxford University Press.

Schwartz, Herman. 2007. "Dependency or Institutions? Economic Geography, Causal Mechanisms, and Logic in the Understanding of Development." *Studies in Comparative International Development* 42 (1): 115–35.

Selwyn, Ben. 2017. *The Struggle for Development*. Oxford: Polity Press.

Selwyn, Benjamin, and Satoshi Miyamura. 2014. "Class Struggle or Embedded Markets? Marx, Polanyi and the Meanings and Possibilities of Social Transformation." *New Political Economy* 19 (5): 639–61.

Sen, S. R. 1957. *The Economics of Sir James Steuart*. Cambridge, MA: Harvard University.

Silver, Beverly J., and Giovanni Arrighi. 2003. "Polanyi's 'Double Movement": The Belle Époques of British and U.S. Hegemony Compared." *Politics and Society* 31 (2): 325–55.

Simon, Robert L. 1974. "Equality, Merit, and the Determination of Our Gifts." *Social Research* 41 (3): 492–514.

Singer, David J. 1961. "The Levels of Analysis Problem in International Relations." *World Politics* 14 (1): 77–92.

Skidelsky, Robert J. A. 1976. "Retreat from Leadership: The Evolution of British Economic Policy, 1870–1939." In *Balance of Power of Hegemony: The Interwar Monetary System*, edited by Benjamin M. Rowland, 147–92. New York: New York University Press.

Skinner, Andrew. 1965. "Economics and History—The Scottish Enlightenment." *Scottish Journal of Political Economy* 12 (1): 22.

Skinner, Quentin. 1998. *Liberty Before Liberalism*. Cambridge: Cambridge University Press.

Smith, Adam. 1976a. *An Inquiry into the Nature and Causes of the Wealth of Nations*. Chicago, IL: University of Chicago Press.

———. 1976b. *The Theory of Moral Sentiments*. Indianapolis, IN: Liberty Fund.

———. 1982. *Lectures on Jurisprudence*. Indianapolis, IN: Liberty Fund.

Smith, Paul B. 1996. "Conjecture, Acquiescence, and John Millar's History of Ireland." *The European Legacy* 1 (8): 2227–48.

Standing, Guy. 2007. "Labor Recommodification in the Global Transformation." In *Reading Karl Polanyi for the Twenty-First Century: Market Economy as a Political Project*, edited by Ayse Bugra and Kaan Agartan, 67–94. Houndsmills, UK: Palgrave Press.

———. 2017. *Basic Income: And How We Can Make It Happen*. London: Penguin Books.

Stavrianos, L. S. 1981. *Global Rift: The Third World Comes of Age*. New York: William Morrow.

Steuart, James. 1966. *An Inquiry into the Principles of Political Oeconomy: Being an Essay on the Science of Domestic Policy in Free Nations*. Chicago, IL: University of Chicago Press.

Sunkel, Osvaldo. 1969. "National Development Policy and External Dependence in Latin America." *Journal of Development Studies* 6 (1): 623–48.

———. 1973a. "The Pattern of Latin American Dependence." In *Latin America and the International Economy*, edited by V. Urquidi and R. Thorp, 3–34. New York: John Wiley & Sons.

———. 1973b. "Transnational Capitalism and National Disintegration in Latin America." *Social and Economic Studies* 22 (1): 132–76.

Teichgraeber, Richard F. 1986. *'Free Trade' and Moral Philosophy: Rethinking the Sources of Adam Smith's Wealth of Nations*. Durham, NC: Duke University Press.

Thomasberger, Claus. 2005. "Human Freedom and the 'Reality of Society.'" *The History of Economic Thought* 47 (2): 1–14.

———. 2018. "Freedom, Responsibility and the Recognition of the Reality of Society." In *Karl Polanyi's Vision of a Socialist Transformation*, edited by Michael Brie and Claus Thomasberger, 52–66. Montreál: Black Rose Books.

Todorov, Tzvetan. 1984. *The Conquest of America: The Question of the Other*. Norman: University of Oklahoma Press.

———. 2005. *The New World Disorder: Reflections of a European*. Cambridge, UK: Polity Press.

Trouillot, Michel-Rolph. 1991. "Anthropology and the Savage Slot." In *Recapturing Anthropology: Working in the Present*, edited by Richard G. Fox, 17–44. Santa Fe, NM: School of American Research Press.

Tsing, Anna Lowenhaupt. 2005. *Friction: An Ethnography of Global Connection*. Durham, NC: Duke University Press.

Urquhart, Robert. 1996. "The Trade Wind, the Statesman and the System of Commerce: Sir James Steuart's Vision of Political Economy." *The European Journal of the History of Economic Thought* 3 (3): 379–410.

Vernon, Raymond. 1966. "International Investment and International Trade in the Product Life Cycle." *Quarterly Journal of Economics* 80 (2): 190–207.

Viera, Marco. 2019. "The Decolonial Subject and the Problem of Non-Western Authenticity." *Postcolonial Studies* 22 (2): 150–67.

Vogel, Jeffrey. 1996. "The Tragedy of History." *New Left Review* 220: 36–61.

Wade, Robert. 2011. "Beware What You Wish For: Lessons for International Political Economy from the Transformation of Economics." In *International Political Economy: Debating the Past, Present and Future*, edited by Nicola Phillips and Catherine E. Weaver, 92–103. London: Routledge.

Walker, R. B. J. 1993. *Inside/Outside: International Relations as Political Theory*. Cambridge: Cambridge University Press.

Wallerstein, Immanuel. 1976. *The Modern World-System: Capitalist Agriculture and the Origins of the European World-Economy in the Sixteenth Century*. New York: Academic Press.

————. 1980. *The Modern World System II: Mercantilism and the Consolidation of the European World-Economy, 1600–1750*. New York: Academic Press.

————. 1997. "Eurocentrism and Its Avatars: The Dilemmas of Social Science." *New Left Review* 226: 93–108.

Walras, Léon. 2010. *Studies in Social Economics*. Translated by Jan van Daal and Donald A. Walker. New York: Routledge.

Walsh, Vivian, and Harvey Gram. 1980. *Classical and Neoclassical Theories of General Equilibrium: Historical Origins and Mathematical Structure*. Oxford, UK: Oxford University Press.

Waltz, Kenneth N. 1979. *Theory of International Politics*. Reading, MA: Addison-Wesley.

Watson, Matthew. 2014. "The Great Transformation and Progressive Possibilities: The Political Limits of Polanyi's Marxian History of Economic Ideas." *Economy and Society* 43 (4): 603–25.

Weeks, John. 2012. *The Irreconcilable Inconsistencies of Neoclassical Economics: A False Paradigm*. London: Routledge.

Wendt, Alexander. 1987. "The Agent-Structure Problem." *International Organization* 41 (2): 335–70.

Winch, Donald. 1996. *Riches and Poverty: An Intellectual History of Political Economy in Britain, 1750–1834*. Cambridge: Cambridge University Press.

Wokler, Robert. 1995. "Anthropology and Conjectural History in the Enlightenment." In *Inventing Human Science: Eighteenth Century Domains*, edited by Christopher Fox, Roy Porter, and Robert Wokler, 31–52. Berkeley: University of California Press.

Wolf, Eric R. 1982. *Europe and the People without History*. Berkeley: University of California Press.

Wyatt-Walter, Andrew. 1996. "Adam Smith and the Liberal Tradition in International Relations." *Review of International Studies* 22 (1): 5–28.

Žižek, Slavoj. 2009. *First as Tragedy, Then as Farce*. London: Verso Books.

Index

Abufarha, Nasser, 76
Abu-Lughod, Janet, 100, 103, 158
Africa/African: Africa and IPE, 75; African agency, 89–90; contact/relations with Europe, 44, 68, 86–90, 101, 106, 110, 148–49; exploitation, 10
agency, Eastern, 2, 12, 145–46, 148–49; human, 143; and International Political Economy (IPE), 55, 90, 107, 112; moral, 149, 154n11, 154n2, 155n4; pioneering, 73–75, 92; and rise of capitalism, 145, 147
Almond, Gabriel, 91
Amin, Samir, 99, 154n10
Anievas, Alexander, and Kerem Nişancioğlu, 95, 100, 158n6
anthropology: colonial, 65; of development (modernity), 125–26; Polanyi's economic anthropology, 116, 136; of world, 104
anti-materialism, 40
Aristotle: and the good, 81, 154n2; and inequality, 1, 40
Ashley, Richard, 156n10
Asia: East and South Asia, 147–48; encounter with Europe, 11, 44, 68, 98, 101, 108
autonomy: of communities, 117, 119, 123, 130–32, 134, 137; cultural and

political, 129; exercise of, 133–35; individual, 4, 82; local, 138–39; of units, 83

barbarian/barbarism, 14–15, 74; modern, 29, 73; non-European, 88; and society, 21, 30; and suicide bombers, 78
Barkawi, Tarak, and Mark Laffey, 13
Bell, Duncan, 152n6, 158n12
Bernard, Mitchell, 133
Berry, Christopher, 14, 17, 29
Bienefeld, Manfred, 155
Bishop, Jordan, 157n20
Blaney, David L., 3, 30, 151n5, 152n11, 152n4, 154n11; and Naeem Inayatullah, 2, 15, 20, 39, 41, 44, 51–52, 64, 83, 95, 111–12, 117, 137, 145, 150, 152n11, 154n12, 156n11, 156n13, 158n6
Block, Fred, 118, 119, 155
Block, Fred, and Margaret Sommers, 120–22, 129
Boghosian, Bruce, 6, 151n2
Braudel, Fernand, 101–2
Bretton Woods, 119, 155
Broadie, Alexander, 32
Booth, Ken, 8
Booth, William J., 128
Boucoyannis, Deborah, 71, 99
Boyd, Richard, 16

177

Lightning Source UK Ltd.
Milton Keynes UK
UKHW012211210622
404760UK00001B/21